Heideggerian Existential Therapy

Heideggerian Existential Therapy focuses on Martin Heidegger's philosophy in order to provide both a wider accessibility as well as understanding of its relevance to therapeutic practice.

This book unveils in great depth the core tenets of Heidegger's thinking, without presuming any philosophical background. It attends to the manner in which we inevitably undergo disruptions, disturbances, perturbations, breakdowns, and collapses in the course of our lives, and on the way in which they can be addressed and understood from an existential therapeutic perspective. The text covers Heidegger's ideas with illustrations and examples, in order to free them from the confines of philosophy in a way that then enables them to be brought directly into the therapy room. Each chapter takes the reader from an initial philosophical grounding of this approach towards a clear and concrete way of working existentially with clients.

The text is primarily intended for trainee and practising psychotherapists, but will undoubtedly be of considerable relevance and interest to coaches, consultants, and trainers who wish to expand and deepen their skills and approaches in their own fields.

Mo Mandić is an existential therapist and clinical supervisor in private practice, based in London, UK. He also teaches and supervises trainee therapists at the School of Psychotherapy and Psychology, Regent's University London, and New School of Psychotherapy and Counselling.

'This remarkable book by Mo Mandić is a major contribution to existential therapy from a Heideggerian perspective in its difference to other forms of therapy and an important further extension of Heidegger's philosophy into the field of therapy. The book makes understandable the basic ideas of Heidegger's existential analytic of Dasein, which inspired the work of both Binswanger and Boss in the last century, in their relevance for psychotherapy today. For Heidegger scholars, it is an important contribution to research into the relation of Heidegger's thinking and its practical relevance. The author writes in a clear and accessible style which helps the reader to grasp also the more difficult topics in Heidegger's understanding of the human being.'

Alfred Denker, *PhD, Director of the Martin-Heidegger-Archive, Messkirch; co-director of the Archivo-Heidegger, Seville.*

'Martin Heidegger's impact upon the theory and practice of existential therapy is both wide-ranging and — for many therapists — close to inaccessible due to the originality (and complexity) of his radical philosophical arguments. Thankfully, Dr. Mo Mandić's *Heideggerian Existential Therapy* succeeds in teasing out key ideas and concerns in a highly accessible account that, nonetheless, retains a genuine Heideggerian spirit of enquiry. This is a book that calls into question many of the most foundational assumptions regarding both the aims and practice of therapy. Although of particular pertinence to existential therapists, I have no doubt that practitioners and trainees allied to any of the current approaches to psychotherapy and counselling will be both challenged and enlightened by Dr. Mandić's exposition.'

Ernesto Spinelli, *PhD, Professor, author of* Practising Existential Therapy: The Relational World *(2nd ed).*

'Mo Mandić's *Heideggerian Existential Therapy: Philosophical Ideas in Practice* is a welcome and important addition to the growing literature on Heideggerian therapy. However, rather than tread familiar ground, Mandić's book advances our understanding of existential therapy on several fronts. Alongside serving an accessible overview of Heideggerian concepts, *Heideggerian Existential Therapy* also articulates in vivid clarity how these concepts can be situated in the centre of therapeutic practice. Interspersed with rich vignettes from a diverse range of case studies, the book sheds light on key issues such as breakdowns, identity, and dreaming. Destined to be a formative work within the genre, *Heideggerian Existential Therapy* is a must read for those interested and working within the existential tradition of therapy.'

Dylan Trigg, *PhD, FWF Senior Researcher at the University of Vienna, Department of Philosophy.*

Heideggerian Existential Therapy

Philosophical Ideas in Practice

Mo Mandić

LONDON AND NEW YORK

Designed cover image: © Getty Images

First published 2024

by Routledge
4 Park Square, Milton Park, Abingdon, Oxon OX14 4RN

and by Routledge
605 Third Avenue, New York, NY 10158

Routledge is an imprint of the Taylor & Francis Group, an informa business

© 2024 Mo Mandić

British Library Cataloguing-in-Publication Data
A catalogue record for this book is available from the British Library

Library of Congress Cataloging-in-Publication Data
Names: Mandić, Mo, 1959- author.
Title: Heideggerian existential therapy: philosophical ideas in practice/ Mo Mandić.
Description: Abingdon, Oxon ; New York, NY : Routledge, 2024. | Includes bibliographical references and index. |
Identifiers: LCCN 2023025451 (print) | LCCN 2023025452 (ebook) | ISBN 9781032378275 (hardback) | ISBN 9781032378251 (paperback) | ISBN 9781003342137 (ebook)
Subjects: LCSH: Existential psychotherapy. | Heidegger, Martin, 1889-1976. | Existentialism–Psychological aspects.
Classification: LCC RC489.E93 M36 2024 (print) | LCC RC489.E93 (ebook) | DDC 616.89/14–dc23/eng/20230817
LC record available at https://lccn.loc.gov/2023025451
LC ebook record available at https://lccn.loc.gov/2023025452

ISBN: 9781032378275 (hbk)
ISBN: 9781032378251 (pbk)
ISBN: 9781003342137 (ebk)

DOI: 10.4324/9781003342137

Typeset in Times New Roman
by Deanta Global Publishing Services, Chennai, India

In Memory of my Parents

Miroslav Mandić (1930–2021)
and
Radmila Mandić née Grujić (1938–2020)

For Alexander and Mila

Contents

PART III

Dasein's Challenges   **105**

Acknowledgements

This book has been gestating for a few years over the course of teaching and supervising Masters and Doctoral level students both in the UK and in Serbia. Whilst there have been a number of occasions where I faced the challenge of trying to convey, as concisely as possible, Heidegger's relevance to therapy, this book has offered the space to do something different. However, I have been able to pursue this primarily through numerous discussions and conversations with many students over the years who inspired me to explore those further regions of my thinking that then opened new paths for me. For this, I am deeply grateful to them all.

Two colleagues have made a significant impact on me in my understanding of both Existential therapy and Heidegger's thinking. Professor Ernesto Spinelli's contributions have tended to continually jolt me out of my accustomed way of seeing things, bringing a renewed sense of openness towards the question of human existence. I have also had the good fortune to engage in many conversations with Dr Alfred Denker, who has been especially generous in clarifying aspects of Heidegger's ideas for me, and for being a source of support in my attempts to address a Heideggerian approach to therapy. To both, I owe a considerable debt of gratitude. I am also indebted to Grace McDonnell, Sarah Hafeez, and Jennifer Hicks at Routledge for their professionalism and support throughout this project, and to Emily Boyd for her invaluable help in bringing the work to a more presentable standard.

On a personal note, I would like to express my deepest appreciation to my family for their presence and support, as well as to two friends who deserve special mention. Denise Ielitro has been an inspiration to me in more ways than I can mention here. Nevertheless, I hope that two words will somehow capture my sentiments: *Grazie mille*. My sincere thanks also go to Antoinette Castro, an original and creative artist who works exclusively in the medium of photography and who has an extraordinarily sharp eye for the truth that is so welcome in our lively conversations and, sometimes, disagreements.

Part I

Introduction

I.1 The Approach Taken in this Book

My aim in this book is to provide a detailed account of Heidegger's characterisation of the human being, in order to show how this can both inform and also establish a certain basis for therapeutic practice. Throughout, I take a phenomenological path in explicating and bringing to the fore those aspects of Heidegger's philosophy that then bear relevance to such an approach. Alongside this, a broader aim will be to convey the way that Heidegger develops his account that is fundamentally hermeneutic in character. In this regard, his method involves the initial presentation of Dasein in its everydayness, then revealed in its existential character, with a final explication of the temporal ground of its being.

I also follow Heidegger in terms of reintroducing his ideas and terms at frequent points throughout the book, both to recapitulate but also to clarify and broaden our understanding of the way in which various terms inextricably interrelate and connect to one another. The challenge that his work presents is to appreciate the complexity of both what he is articulating as well as the process that is at work in bringing this to greater levels of understanding. The added challenge that his work poses to his readers is the language that is both familiar at times, but also used by Heidegger in radically different ways.

Throughout this book, I draw on numerous passages and terms from Heidegger's key text, *Being and Time*. In doing so, I use the abbreviation 'BT', followed by the page number in the English edition of that work, to direct the reader to specific references.

DOI: 10.4324/9781003342137-1

Chapter 1

The World of Therapy

When we stop to reflect on the very existence of psychotherapy, and its beginnings since the start of the 20th century, more interesting philosophical questions emerge. Various attempts have been made to define or characterise psychotherapy, including studies that trace its history and evolution (Zeig [1987] and Foschi and Innamorati [2023], for example), with yet others focusing on the numerous theories of personality articulated by leading proponents of psychotherapy. However, very little attention has been given to the underlying assumptions that are foundational to it. The world of psychotherapy has, on the one hand, tacitly embraced these assumptions upon which nearly every form of psychotherapy rests, but on the other hand, taken it that any attempt to question them more radically is baseless. Some, such as Purton (2014), Erwin (1997), and Hersch (2003), admittedly take a more philosophical orientation in their critiques of therapeutic approaches, but ultimately fail to address the fundamental questions that remain at a deeper level. Others, such as Furedi (2004) and Morrall (2008), have pursued more sociologically oriented studies about the role of psychotherapy in society, whilst Aubry and Travis (2015) offer perspectives on the contributions made by therapeutic practices. These all have their place, and provoke further food for thought, but it seems that none have brought themselves to address the most basic question of all: what is it that makes being human possible or intelligible in the first place? This will be the key issue that is addressed in a Heideggerian approach to therapy.

Notwithstanding the fact that Freud's early development of psychoanalytic theory was an attempt to ground it scientifically, the predominant purpose or meaning of psychotherapy since then has been motivated by a certain intention to provide care and attention to those who sought help or support for what was considered to be some form of illness, mental unease or suffering. But from the very beginning, as various other disciplines had emerged towards the end of the 19th century, including psychology, the very question of what it is to be human was left unaddressed, or rather, assumed to have been settled, based on the inherited understanding that was handed down to us from the Enlightenment period and onwards. The essence of the human being as something stable, enduring and unchanging has persisted throughout the ages and down to our time, with no attempt made to grasp the deeper philosophical traps that this carried with it.

DOI: 10.4324/9781003342137-2

Whilst we can identify similar practices that have developed in the historical past since the time of the ancient Greeks, and even before (see Foschi and Innamorati, 2023:7), psychotherapy presents itself as a response to the modern age and our human condition, as we have come to understand it. Its very existence tells us something important about who we are, and who we have become. Having broadly presented itself as an attempt to further understand ourselves, whether in terms of our suffering, unease, and general difficulties in the course of living our lives, psychotherapy has also inevitably brought with it certain presuppositions. This is perhaps only to be expected, since every practice and approach to understanding what it is to be human has assumed certain foundational principles upon which it rests. The concern, in my view, however, is that many therapeutic schools also implicitly assume that they have emerged out of a presuppositionless foundation, or have reached the ultimate ground for the understanding of our way of being. In other words, they harbour a certain conviction that the essence of what it is to be human has been captured and answered completely and adequately through established theories. The rigidity and resistance to self-reflection has brought them to maintain a certain defensiveness rather than porosity to possible change and revision. It is the assumptions accompanying such theories that are therefore simply hidden from view, but need, I believe, to be exposed and challenged.

Psychotherapy addresses an individual human life. In such addressing and attempting to alleviate troubling concerns and various forms of unease and suffering, its broader aim is to grasp the particular way in which we live our lives. The issue rests on the way that we relate to ourselves, and how certain important distinctions inform and shape our lives. For example, many of us pursue lives that are meaningful and rewarding in some way, be that expressed in the form of professional vocations or familial settings, or more artistic endeavours. In such cases, we experience times in which we undergo disturbing disruptions and the loss of meaning, given that those meaningful ways of living can be vulnerable to collapse or deep disorientation. Psychotherapy, in its practical form, is a space of engagement that purports to help us to come to know and understand ourselves, but from our own basis, or ground, rather than from some source that is external to us. The use and application of various theoretical concepts and systems of thought in the attempt to capture the underlying cause or motivation for issues that reflect such confusion, unease, discomfort, or suffering has been a somewhat misguided project. This is, in large measure, due to an epistemological, knowledge-based focus on the therapeutic experience, with a nod to explanation rather than interpretation and understanding.

Whilst the aim of psychotherapy, as I see it, has been to address many of the challenges and difficulties that confront us both in everyday experience and in the more significant and overwhelming events that take place at certain times in our lives, distinctions between 'health' and 'illness', 'wellness' and 'sickness', or 'flourishing' and 'struggle' have all, either implicitly or explicitly, served to some degree as the distorting lens through which psychotherapy has been understood by society in general. This has, to varying degrees, contributed to a greatly narrowed understanding of its approach, purpose, and intention.

From a philosophical perspective, we live in the age of Modernity. Although this has also become a term of use in its relatively more recent cultural meaning, namely, as Modernism, the philosophical sense of the term has a more profound understanding of the birth of a new era of change that came with the contributions of the 17ᵗʰ century French philosopher and mathematician, René Descartes. The legacy of his thinking has left us with a wholly new, reconfigured way of conceiving of ourselves, namely, as the autonomous, detached, rational individual who is separate from the natural world. That attempt to lay down the foundations for what was taken to be indisputably certain has ushered in a radically different way of approaching the human being that prevails to the present day.

Traditionally, Western philosophers have placed the human being at the centre of any enquiry about what exists, on what basis we can claim to know this, and how we are to live in the light of it. Since Socrates and Plato, this has led to a concern over what is essential to the way we are, rather than recognising those aspects of ourselves that are distinctively and uniquely human. For example, Socrates was in constant search of the essence of justice, piety, truth, virtue, and knowledge, amongst other things, whilst Plato spoke of the Forms, those perfect, timeless ideas or essences, that contrasted themselves to their imperfect, concrete, actual, and flawed versions or copies that were to be found in the visual, experiential realm of the human being. The chair that I now see, for example, is an imperfect, time-based approximation of the object that corresponds to the Idea or Form of 'chairness', which is characterised by its perfect, eternal, enduring, and static wholeness. In other words, chairness captures the essence of that very thing that appears to us as a chair. This dualistic picture of the world has been very powerful as an idea that has endured in one form or another down to the present time, and which we have come to call 'metaphysics'.

Martin Heidegger's thinking is a head-on confrontation with Descartes, whose own contributions will be explored extensively in what follows. This is crucially relevant, since the distinctively different approaches between Descartes and Heidegger reflect the different position that a Heideggerian therapist takes to traditional psychotherapy. Descartes' thought has the support of a long tradition of thinking that was already prevalent in Greek philosophy, namely, that we are rational creatures, and that we can therefore rely on reason to identify what was certain and indubitable about us. His overarching aim was to identify the very foundations, or bedrock, of our nature. In other words, he took what is known as a 'foundationalist' approach to enquiry. Moreover, any such approach is, for Heidegger, metaphysical, as opposed to his own line of enquiry, which is ontological.

To summarise, then, this book focuses on the philosopher Martin Heidegger's contributions to the fundamental question of human existence. The overarching reason for this is that his approach offers both a radical challenge to our existing way of thinking about this question, but also to appreciate that thinking itself is in need of serious attention in the world of psychotherapy. True thinking follows its own path, which can be precarious, but this nevertheless is what is central to, and unique about, being human. From a therapeutic perspective, some publications and studies have made valuable contributions in introducing Heidegger to the British School of Existential therapy, as can be found in the work of, among others, Hans Cohn and Emmy van Deurzen. They have opened a path for me to engage in my own reflection and consider further Heidegger's approach to the human being and its impact on therapy. This book pursues this possibility by providing a more elaborately detailed presentation of Heidegger's ideas, and then applying them more practically and concretely to therapy as such. As will also become apparent, I draw mainly from Heidegger's significant work, *Being and Time*.

In order to offer a very concise introduction to a Heideggerian therapeutic approach, I present two invented scenarios of clients who might come to therapy for the reasons described in each case. Both clients introduce issues that I attempt to briefly address using traditional therapeutic approaches, and then contrast with more existential considerations that reflect a different therapeutic focus and attitude.

1.1 Two Client Examples

1.1.1 Svetlana

A professional in her mid-30s, Svetlana finds it very difficult to live her life on her own terms. She left her parents' family home at the age of 18 to pursue studies at University. After a year, she settled into a relatively stable romantic relationship with a fellow student. However, she always felt suspicious of his whereabouts when they were apart. As their studies approached an end, they became estranged from each other, and eventually decided to separate. Svetlana said that she found this heart-breaking, and for a while fell into a depression and withdrawal from everyday life. She moved back into her family home after leaving University, but after a large corporate organisation made a lucrative new job offer, she moved to the city and into a flat share arrangement with several other people.

Throughout this time, Svetlana felt a constant obligation to call and visit her parents on a very regular basis. This was mostly because they always criticised her for not being a good daughter, and for neglecting them whilst selfishly pursuing her own interests. In particular, they ignored her achievements and successes, focusing more on where and how she had failed in her life. She had experienced enormous pressure from them to pursue studies as a medical doctor but failed her exams in order to qualify for admission. Her parents also compared her to their friends' children, who they considered to be more successful, and more agreeable in their attitude towards their own parents. Whatever Svetlana did was dismissed as not good enough, which ate into her as a constant guilt, a sense of self-blame, and 'badness'. She was now at the point in her life where both parents made acerbic comments about her not being married and giving them grandchildren. This all came to a point where she felt deeply hurt and alone, as well as very uncertain about the course of her own life. Not feeling that she had the wherewithal to deal with this herself, she came to therapy.

How might we approach our work with Svetlana, from a therapeutic point of view? At least some therapeutic orientations generally take it that the client can be understood as a consciousness encased in a body, and that we need to conduct an archaeological depth-based study of its mental contents. Any feelings of anxiety that develop as a result would simply reflect the fact that consciousness is at work in its attempt to block any such contents being brought to the surface. Rather than staying simply with what presents itself, we might be more inclined towards identifying a causal origin that lies at the heart of the client. That is, instead of staying with life experience, we are tempted towards abstraction, whether this be theoretical or philosophical. In other words, the aim is to gain some kind of knowledge of Svetlana's issue, rather than an understanding of how Svetlana is making sense of her existence. Further, it is not the therapist's knowledge and appropriate application of theory that is in need here, but rather the client's own further understanding through the possible insights, reflections, and illuminations that emerge and develop in a broader manner. As well as this, language, in the form of words and dialogues, both conceal and reveal something deeper when given space for exploration. Most approaches to therapy take it that words and terms are relatively fixed through the definitions that we attribute to them. For example, we take it that we know what we mean by anxiety, fear, or shame if we subscribe to certain theoretical approaches that already map out for us exactly how to understand these terms, namely, as concepts. In contrast, an existential approach that draws on Heidegger's work never takes our understanding as fixed, but always provisional and open to deeper meanings.

Certain approaches might identify Svetlana's overall pattern of being in relationships, and possibly consider them in terms of 'anxious attachments', for example. But this relies on an understanding of being with others in the first place, and also puts into question whether this approach is moving away from the lived sense of Svetlana's experience and placing her in a category that differentiates her from, say, a secure attachment. In doing so, we place a label on Svetlana and effectively relate to her as an object, rather than a being that is uniquely different to any possible object that we encounter in the world.

1.1.2 Gaston

Gaston is a married man with two children, and now in his mid-40s, has started to have a sense of being off-kilter in his daily existence. He describes himself as feeling worn down by duties and responsibilities, which pull him around in the areas of work, family, and friendships. He expresses it as a deep disorientation, as if 'falling through the cracks' of life, and not managing to get back on track. Somehow, he has lost a certain zest and energy, and can't understand what has changed so much for him to now be experiencing a form of depression. His wife is understanding, but finds him distant when they try to talk about what he is going through at the moment.

Working with Gaston, a common therapeutic approach might be to engage with him on an unconscious level, based on the idea that there are deeper unresolved motives for his current behaviour. This approach detaches him from the world, and focuses exclusively on the workings of his mind, thereby treating it much like a machine. In this approach, an assumption is that Gaston is becoming less rational and ordered, and that this is contributing to his sense of falling apart. Certain as yet unaccountable motivations lie deeply repressed within him, but these need close attention in order that they can eventually be released by recognising the various defence mechanisms that are at play. A Heideggerian approach, in contrast, rejects the introduction of theoretical abstractions such as the unconscious, and even the mind, as such. This is because we never encounter ourselves, in the first instance, as abstractions, but as concrete, involved beings, who find themselves in situations and contexts.

Another approach might hold Gaston as an individual who has a weak sense of himself, because his internal 'logic' does not provide him with a sufficient sense of autonomy. Certain ways of working therapeutically can therefore act as reinforcements to his sense of self-assertiveness. A Heideggerian approach takes it that we are not so much 'logical' or dictated by reason and rationality, but beings who have a pre-cognitive grasp of how living in a certain way makes sense to us. As well as this, we are not detached and autonomous beings who are wholly separate, experientially speaking, but rather, wholly enmeshed in a world with others before we even contemplate this. We might become more transparent, open, and honest with ourselves, though this is only possible on the basis that we are first and foremost always situated beings who are with others at a very elementary level. Another aspect of such an approach is that the general mood or atmosphere in which Gaston lives is left out of this account. This is important since he encounters everything through this mood, and not the other way around.

We might consider the claim that he is trying to childishly rebel from his circumstances, but in an indirect way, so that things somehow change, or that he changes himself through this way of behaving. Typically, therapy would encourage Gaston to express his feelings, and to come to possibly see the destructive nature of his attitude. He might talk about feeling trapped, in which case certain therapeutic interventions might encourage him to see how he can free himself more from certain unwanted roles and duties that weigh him down. A Heideggerian approach might well encourage similar exploration, though his feelings might be understood more as attempts to present himself more truthfully to himself, which is, roughly, a Heideggerian call to being 'authentic'. Rather than remaining fixated only on his everyday existence, Gaston might well touch on his life as having certain boundaries and limits, existentially speaking. Here a Heideggerian approach takes in the impact of these limits, and how Gaston might be inadvertently expressing his care and concern over his own existence in the light of them.

On some approaches, Gaston might undergo some kind of personality assessment, whether this be a Borderline Personality Disorder, or some kind of Antisocial attitude. This is a gross generalisation of Gaston and is based on a more scientific understanding of him. A scientific approach collects a number of instances where a certain kind of behaviour manifests, and then forms a hypothesis that attempts to capture this kind of behaviour through a general law or universal principle. In contrast, a Heideggerian understanding of the human being takes it that his existence matters to him, and that this is being reflected in the way that he experiences his world. Even if we can point to strong similarities between Gaston and others who might undergo difficulties of this kind too, we cannot bring him under a diagnostic classification. This is because he is ultimately responding to the issue of his existence that matters to him. Approaching Gaston with this in mind individualises him as unique, rather than being categorised as an instance of a type.

In considering that Gaston is facing certain difficulties, the issue is somehow 'within' him, and a traditional therapeutic approach might well insist on a need for different behaviours. However, a Heideggerian approach recognises that Gaston lives in a world, or a context, that involves his following norms and certain practices. These typically ground him, and provide him with a sense of comfort and security. Now that world has become disrupted in some way. It may be that the meaning that sustained that world for him has now fallen away, and can no longer support him. He therefore feels ungrounded and disoriented. A traditional therapeutic approach also maintains a strong focus on Gaston and his feelings, which seems appropriate, but does not take in the fact that his *world* is the core issue. Were his world showing up differently, he would have a different experience, and be likely living in a different overall mood, as briefly touched on earlier.

Lastly, a Heideggerian therapist recognises that Gaston can be supported to develop deeper explorations through words and narratives, eventually coming to a different understanding that is more existential than pragmatic. A traditional approach might be inclined to remain focused on applying theoretical concepts to Gaston's experience in order to consider that progress is being made.

What are the broader implications for an existential approach from a Heideggerian perspective? We can miss certain key features of being human if we take a more traditional approach as therapists. We firstly need to reconsider our grasp of the very way that we are in order to be sensitive to those issues that clients are experiencing. In fact, as therapists, we commonly hear clients talk about issues that we ourselves have lived through or may even be currently experiencing in some lesser or greater measure. This should not strike us as so unusual, since this reflects the fact that certain fundamental features of what it is to be our kind of being are being presented to us in the therapeutic relationship.

Chapter 2

Why Heidegger?

2.1 Who is Heidegger?

Martin Heidegger (1889–1976) was born in Messkirch, a small village situated in the Baden region of South Western Germany. His early family life was a comfortable one, though by no means financially secure. As he came of age, Heidegger was destined for initiation into the priesthood and enrolment in theological studies, but this was abandoned in favour of philosophy. His studies were most influenced early on in his reading of the philosopher Franz Brentano's work, more specifically, his studies on being. Heidegger's contributions as a 20th century thinker have made an enormous impact not only in the field of philosophy but more widely in other disciplines and practices, ranging from management and business, nursing, architecture and the arts, cultural studies, and artificial intelligence. His interest in the world of psychotherapy gained particular prominence in his friendship and extended collaborations over several decades with the Swiss psychiatrist and psychotherapist, Medard Boss. Prior to this, Heidegger had also engaged in fruitful exchanges with another Swiss psychiatrist, Ludwig Binswanger, though this later became more estranged. As is gathered from Heidegger's later comments during his close collaborations with Boss, he felt that some aspects of his ideas had been misunderstood by Binswanger.

A particularly important element of Heidegger's life is marked by his involvement in the German National Socialist movement in the 1930s, and this has been the subject of extensive commentary and criticism to this day. Recent publications of Heidegger's *Black Notebooks*, which commentators have criticised and condemned for including certain anti-Semitic comments, has continued the complex debate that relates to this time in his life. I consider his involvement in fascism to be undeniable, and have no wish nor inclination to exonerate him of such appalling behaviour. At the same time, most commentaries on this aspect of Heidegger's past have overlooked the complex nature and intention of his involvement. Rather than bringing a more scholarly awareness and attention to Heidegger's activity at this time, the tendency has been to engage in outright dismissal based on various misinterpretations or prematurely reductive conclusions originating from inadequate research. However, I consider that his philosophy prior to the advent of Nazism

DOI: 10.4324/9781003342137-3

stands apart from such an ideology, and so can be assessed and understood straight-forwardly on its own terms. I do acknowledge that a number of commentators, and a significant number of therapists too, will disagree with me on this matter, but, as I hope to show, *Being and Time* is a work that offers much in terms of its relevance to an existential way of approaching therapeutic work. In this sense, it deserves to be judged on its own merits, and considered for the degree to which it succeeds in offering a true characterisation of human beings.

Heidegger's project is aimed at extricating ourselves from a longstanding histor-ical misunderstanding of ourselves, and thereby offering an alternative approach. He is not interested in providing a definitive essence of being human, since this is exactly what he claims has been attempted over the course of the past millennia. Heidegger's approach, at the same time, is also challenging because we face the difficulty of deciphering his thoughts at certain points in his work. Once we begin to understand this approach and attitude to enquiry, we can then assess and contrast it to more traditional, i.e., metaphysical, attempts to understand ourselves. In his case, Heidegger adopts a phenomenological as opposed to metaphysical form of enquiry. He also maintains a distinction between the ontic and ontological, which is crucially important to his project. This means that he is engaged in the deeper question about being, which leads him to ask not about what kind of being we are (which is an ontic approach), but who we are (which is ontological). All of these terms will be clarified a little later on.

Reading Heidegger's *Being and Time* (1927/1962) offers us a radical perspective on questions that relate directly to human existence. As he develops his account, the approach that he takes – both phenomenological and hermeneutic – engages with a vast number of topics and issues, including deeper reflections on death, on the central importance of moods for an understanding of ourselves, as well as dif-ferent possible ways in which we can live based on the distinction between living in everydayness and embracing our existence as an authentic whole. All these terms are given a specific meaning by Heidegger, and the aim will be to expand on this in order to convey their importance in the context of his overall work. His ideas have presented a significant and profound challenge to the philosophical tradition, which has followed a path that Heidegger claims are based on erroneous assumptions, or at least assumptions that are in need of questioning. It would be no understatement to say that Heidegger's work has left a substantial and indelible mark on our way of seeing the world and ourselves from the 20th century and up to the present day.

One main reason that Heidegger's work is important to therapists is the original-ity of his analyses and reflections on the age in which we find ourselves. However, he is not so much attempting any diagnosis, or assessment on a symptomatic level, but a thinking that goes deeper and beyond this. In fact, Heidegger's approach to thinking – initially explicitly phenomenological but later more poetic – itself contrasts with our own accustomed way of engaging in enquiry. We might com-monly search for a definition, for example, and then use this as a ground or basis for undertaking investigations that proceed in a predictable way. Or we might take the very issue that we already grasp as a thing, or entity of some kind, and then proceed on that basis to relate to it in our enquiry. One example of this is the notion of empathy, which has become a term of common currency in some therapeutic approaches. In fact, I devote some attention to empathy later, in order to illustrate a more Heideggerian perspective on this.

2.2 Heidegger's Project

2.2.1 The Project of Being

As mentioned, the immediate challenge that we face in reading and understanding Heidegger is in grappling with the unfamiliar terms that he employs, and the language that he introduces into his work. In *Being and Time*, and elsewhere, we encounter various neologisms in numerous passages and in his overall thinking, and this makes the task of comprehending him ever more difficult. However, if we take a step back and consider the aim of his project, we begin to appreciate more why he takes this approach. Given that we are so deeply immersed in a Modern Cartesian paradigm, which means that we always already understand the world, others, things, and ourselves in terms of certain basic philosophical principles, we are effectively immersed in a dualism, or dualistic metaphysics, that has not sufficiently deeply questioned its own presuppositions because they are seamlessly woven into our everyday life and are all too obvious to us. But, for Heidegger, one of the issues is that we have a fundamentally mistaken use and understanding of language such that this prevents us from engaging at deeper levels of questioning. In short, we take language as having a purely ontic character. Again, I will clarify Heidegger's terms more fully later on, as we proceed to explicate his account.

The key point about Heidegger's project is that he is against the idea that we can provide a fundamentally theoretical account of human beings that has at its core a story about our theoretical capacities and behaviours. Such an attempt would assume an overarching, abstract, atemporal, and explanatory account of the way that we are. We can, and do, provide a theoretical account of nature and objects, Heidegger notes, but this is not something that we can do when it comes to ourselves, because, in part, we are practical beings. This also bears a major impact on any approach that we take in the various disciplines in the human sciences, including psychology, anthropology, sociology, and, of course, psychotherapy, since they are all preoccupied with the central question of what it is to be human.

If there is any one absolutely central idea that preoccupied Heidegger, it is being. When Heidegger asks, what is the meaning of being, or what does it mean to 'be', and to 'be' as anything at all, he takes this to be the most pressing question of philosophy, one that, in fact, consumed him for the entirety of his life. He points out that, for centuries, various thinkers assumed that they were pursuing this question, namely, what it means to be, but had, in fact, overlooked the fact that they had actually been asking, what is being, which is not the same. There is, he emphasises, a very great difference between our asking about being, on the one hand, and the meaning of being, on the other. It is not simply being, but the meaning or sense of being that he is particularly interested in, and the fact that it is intelligible in the first place.

But let's take a step back. When we use the word, being, we mean that something just is, its being is something that we can claim with certainty. It could just as easily not be the thing that it is, or anything at all, for that matter, in which case, being, as a relevant term here, immediately falls out of the picture. Having grasped what it is that we are talking about here – being – the question then is, how do we begin to explore this so that we can gain a sense of it? Heidegger is at pains to point out that there are mistaken ways of thinking about being, and so we should exercise vigilance. This is not something that we alone might fall into, since, according to Heidegger, past Western philosophers have themselves succumbed to such errors. The most egregious error, he thinks, is that being has been taken to be *a* being, something thing-like, that we can then proceed to analyse. This is really an example of Heidegger wanting us to appreciate how important it is to think properly, since we can become accustomed to ways of thinking that then inevitably miss the phenomenon itself. For example, we might take being to be a universal concept, so that there are also instances of being that fall under this, just as we take the general concept of animal to cover specific cases, such as a cat or dog. In fact, his real concern is that we pose the right kind of question that will then enable us to eventually arrive at the kind of answer that will be relevant to our enquiry.

When we ask about being in terms of what it is, this already distances us from its meaning and significance, and frames it in essentialist terms, as was the case with Socrates and Plato. Rather, when we ask what we mean by being, we bypass or go beyond the entity, and address that on the basis of which the entity manifests in the world (the pen, fork, table, etc.). These two are distinct, though they are one in the sense that both the pen and the being of the pen are an inseparable unity. The pen is both *a* being, an entity, we can say, and it 'is', in its very being. As already stressed, if there were no being, it would not be at all. There would simply be nothing. We could not speak of its being. So, the question addresses being, rather than anything that 'has' being, which is an entity, or a being.

2.2.2 Modes of Being

Given that the question of being itself has now been introduced, Heidegger identifies three modes or types of being:

- presence-at-hand
- ready-to-hand
- existence.

These modes of being are introduced in *Being and Time*, though Heidegger's later work introduces yet more possible modes of being. However, for the purposes of providing an account of being that significantly informs a therapeutic approach, I will cover the three mentioned.

2.2.2.1 Present-at-hand

This is the mode of being that has preoccupied Western civilisation. In everyday terms, the present-at-hand is the way that we identify something as the object that it is, and that it is isolable from other objects. This traditional understanding has taken it that this is the only way of being, in other words, that it is being itself. In our Western tradition, we have attended to entities in a detached, contemplative, or scientific way. This has extended to treating everything – including ourselves – as present-at-hand. This understanding of being goes back to Aristotle, Plato, and Socrates, and culminates most clearly in Aristotle, who thought that being is fundamentally substance. For Aristotle, a substance is a self-sufficient, self-enclosed entity, and that various properties can be attributed to it. A table, for example, is a substance, and as a substance, possesses various properties that can be ascribed to it, such as being brown in colour, 25kg in weight, of a certain dimension and size, and so on. The distinctive way in which something is present-at-hand is that it can be identified as separate from other things, so that we can focus on it, study it, or scrutinise it intently. That is, the way in which we relate to things in this mode is atomistic, since it treats them as stand-alone objects.

2.2.2.2 Ready-to-hand

In contrast to the present-at-hand mode of being, the ready-to-hand mode of being is to treat things as available and manipulable for use. For example, the hammer is available for our use in order to hammer nails into wood, and this is done in the context of some overall project, such as building a house for shelter. Hammering, therefore, is carried out ultimately for the sake of this, but in its interim steps is a hammering that aims towards the completion of smaller, manageable tasks that then extend towards the overarching project of building the house. From hammering nails in wood, to building a partition wall, to plastering the walls to standards of smoothness, to painting over the walls, installing various bathroom and kitchen fixtures, arranging items of furniture, and ultimately having one's possessions placed in each room, these are all interlaced into an 'equipmental totality' or whole, in contrast to the isolable objects that are present-at-hand. In other words, the ready-to-hand reflects a mode of being that is holistic, in contrast to the present-at-hand mode of being.

2.2.2.3 Existence

This is our way of being, which Heidegger calls 'Dasein', a term that is both central to *Being and Time*, as it is too in this book. Heidegger's intention here is only to introduce a term that identifies the formal aspect of a certain kind of entity, rather than a classificatory term that reflects its place in the natural world, or its differentiation from other things that populate that world. In this respect, any entity that is, structurally speaking, Dasein falls under this ascription, though it certainly characterises our way of being. As the account of Dasein unfolds, it becomes clear that Heidegger is intending this term to mean that non-humans, such as plants and animals, are not Dasein.

Existence, as will be explored later on, is characterised by giving ourselves an essence, or meaning, in the ways that we live our lives. Living a human life is, in effect, our own way of responding to the fact that our being is an 'issue' for us, as Heidegger puts it (BT67). But it is not a static affair, since we lead a life that runs from the moment that we are born to our death. We contend with much in our lives, as we constantly weigh up, choose, and decide among various possibilities on how we are to live. In this sense, plants, animals, and persons all live, but only persons exist, because human living involves having to consider what is at stake for us, and the stand that we take on who we are.

Chapter 3

The Question of Human Existence

The question of what it is to be human is central to any therapeutic approach, since its ontology, or the domain that pertains to being, is the basis for the particular methodological approach that any therapy embraces. However, the ways in which we use specific terms to refer to ourselves has come with its own tacit assumptions that are rarely opened to further consideration or questioning. In the way that we tend to use them, terms are static markers that all come with their own background cultural presuppositions that originate from the historical epoch in which they were introduced. For convenience, we can list a selection of such terms, which include the following:

- person
- individual
- consciousness or 'conscious being'
- subject
- soul
- human being
- *homo sapiens*
- a creature of God
- monad
- cybernetic system
- biological organism

Whilst many of these terms are commonplace today, they impose both limitations and misunderstandings of our kind of being. Having said this, I will freely make use of some of them where appropriate at various points, and do so in a way that is interchangeable with the term, Dasein. This is done purely for reasons of convenience and brevity, rather than always trying consistently to maintain a fidelity to Heidegger's terminology. Where a person or human being is mentioned, we understand this to be a reference to ourselves as an autonomous entity, such as we are insofar as we live our own lives, but at the same time, we should bear in mind that this leaves out of the account the fact that this is not how we fundamentally find ourselves in our existence. As will hopefully become apparent in due course,

DOI: 10.4324/9781003342137-4

this way of speaking will make increasing sense as the account of Dasein is laid out in greater detail. It is only hoped that, for those readers who find this challenging and daunting, some comfort can be derived from the fact that this is a familiar experience when first trying to grasp Heidegger's work. In fact, it would be surprising to assume that anyone stepping into an unfamiliar context in which newly coined terms, as well as new meanings given to old terms, immediately settles into an unproblematic understanding of the radical nature of what Heidegger is proposing in his account. Dasein itself, when analysed in terms of the meanings of 'Da' and 'sein', already reveals much that sets it apart from any of the terms that we have become accustomed to using both in everyday life as well as in the domain of therapy.

Chapter 4

Human Existence and Existential Therapy

Since Heidegger's focus in the second part of his significant work, *Being and Time*, is exclusively existential, I take this contribution to constitute an existential orientation to therapy. However, the first part that precedes it, or Division I, as he refers to it, demands attention and a certain level of understanding in order to then appreciate what follows. In particular, Heidegger's more radical approach has seldom, if ever, really been brought out more explicitly and in greater detail in its attempt to offer a therapeutic approach grounded in human Dasein. This will be the aim in what follows.

We rarely find ourselves asking about our particularly human way of existing. For one, we assume and take it for granted that we already know how to answer such a question. But we are easily misled, and there are several reasons for this. For one, we already assume that we are objects amongst other objects in the world. Second, our language transfixes itself into a certain paradigm that reflects this. Third, we take the wrong approach in exploring our kind of being (Richardson, 2012: 59–62). As mentioned previously, we tend to grab for theoretical knowledge (Richardson, 2012: 64), but, amongst other things, theory ignores the 'background' or context in which our existence makes sense. The background understanding is, moreover, historical, and not, as a theoretical approach presupposes, a knowledge-based understanding that is atemporal in character.

As it stands today, existential therapy has proliferated across the world as a distinctive approach of its own, as is clear from numerous publications that testify to this (see van Deurzen et al. 2019 for an extensive account). Moreover, as has also been widely acknowledged, the very question of what it is that characterises and distinguishes an existential therapeutic approach has itself been a topic that has invited considerable discussion and interpretation. Whilst the various perspectives and contributions offer much food for thought and are all welcome challenges on how we are to understand the existential, it seems that a tension exists between the radically different philosophical assumptions that different thinkers and major contributors have embraced, and the way in which these various thinkers' ideas have become somehow integrated or unified into a common language, whether this be enunciated through categories, themes, or concepts. For example, freedom, so central an idea found in existentialist literature, has become a term that seems to have adopted a singular meaning in a therapeutic context. In the main, this appears to

DOI: 10.4324/9781003342137-5

be related to a particularly familiar challenge that readers of Heidegger will surely have encountered: that of prising ourselves away from a Cartesian approach to enquiry and thereby endeavouring to bring to the light the phenomenon as it shows itself. This is no easy task, I readily admit, but the implications of not doing so is that existential therapy remains firmly entrenched in a Cartesian framework and its conception of the human being, with all its ramifications.

The attempt to really understand the legacy of a Cartesian way of thinking in the world of therapy is not sufficiently explored, for example, by going back to his writings and seeing how his approach took hold and reconfigured our whole sense of understanding ourselves as human beings. In what follows, I place Descartes under a phenomenological microscope, in order to see how his account suffers from some major oversights that impact on our own understanding of human existence. Highlighting the way in which Descartes provided a misconceived picture of the human might ultimately afford us alternative possibilities in the way that we engage and work with clients.

We should also keep in mind that existential philosophy has generated a rich contribution of ideas that make valuable attempts to address the key questions and concerns of existence. In this sense, Heidegger is only one among a number of other thinkers and philosophers who make worthy contributions and should not be ignored or marginalised. As has been demonstrated over the course of the last century in particular, it is not only philosophy, but the arts – literature, sculpture, theatre, drama, and painting, among others – that have also illuminated our existential condition in ways that demonstrate that no one domain of exploration or approach in the search for truth can be ignored. Works of art, for example, as is particularly the case with great artists like Cezanne, van Gogh, and Matisse, offer us a way of understanding ourselves that no theory or science, or even philosophy, can emulate. The same can be said of poetry as well.

What philosophy, literature, and the arts all have in common is in their pursuit of truth. In order to grasp the fact that this is central to being human, there is a need to recognise that traditional ways of thinking about truth have been correct, in one sense, but also mistaken, in another. Such traditional thinking is presented as 'common-sensical', thereby becoming so ingrained and sedimented into our everyday practices that it might even be considered a form of delusion to challenge this. To be clear on what is at issue here, one main current conception of truth is that it is a correspondence relation between the thinker or speaker's thought or talk, on the one hand, and whatever it is that the thinker or speaker is thinking or speaking *about*, on the other. But, to put it somewhat concisely, nothing in this account takes into account a background against which this is possible in the first place. The reason that it does not do so is because its entire philosophical foundation is committed to making everything explicit and foregrounded rather than acknowledging the fact that this is only possible against that which withdraws and 'hides', so to speak. With this prevailing prejudice that pervades our existing world and its practices, we face the considerable challenge of undertaking a radical existential overhaul in order to put us on a different path.

At the same time, if there is to be any attempt to follow a path that reflects more closely what it is to be human, it will also inevitably mean that a radically different understanding of language is required. This is the most demanding task of all, since it is almost as if we are insisting on something that, practically speaking, cannot be met. As we commonly assume, language articulates what it is that we experience, such that our experience comes first, and language then follows in giving description to it. But, as Heidegger eventually comes to realise, it is, in fact, the other way around, even though this might appear counterintuitive to us. We are already suffused in language such that whatever we happen to experience is already framed by it. In other words, language constitutes the background of experience. One of the reasons that I am presenting a Heideggerian approach to therapy is that it introduces us to a new language that attempts to capture the human with greater phenomenological acuity, but it also jolts us into a different way of thinking that no longer takes a decidedly anthropocentric view on matters. Alice Holzhey-Kunz has already pointed us to this in her own writings on Medard Boss and Heidegger (Holzhey-Kunz, 2014:20), but it is also a concern that other thinkers, such as Maurice Merleau-Ponty, have attempted to address in their own work. If the impact of language on our way of seeing ourselves in relation to the world is in need of further elaboration here, consider the way in which we structure our sentences in subject-predicate terms, such that the 'I', or subject, is the pivotal starting point in the sentence towards which we ascribe or attribute a description, quality, action or qualification. A simple example is 'I am excited by the party'; this might alternatively be cast, following Heidegger, as, 'The party elicits an exciting mood (in me)'. In a related way, we have also overlooked some other aspects of language, such as the 'middle voice', which is a form that is particularly relevant to Heidegger's explication of the term, 'phenomenon' (BT51), but also in his work as a whole. This, in brief, is the way in which a verb can be used in neither a passive nor active way in language. Examples of this are found in the phrases, 'washing myself', and 'getting married'. However, this all becomes an important consideration when working with clients, given the ways in which the use of language usually reflects either an active voice, such as 'I talk to my partner about this', or a passive one, as in 'a conversation took place'.

The various distinctions that Heidegger introduces in his work, when considered in relation to the question of what it means to be human, allow us to move towards a closer phenomenological understanding of who we are in our being, rather than inadvertently falling into a search for our essence. The world of therapy itself, unfortunately, but I think predictably, has on the whole taken it that the latter is its core task, thus entrenching itself in knowledge, rather than attending to the ontology of human existence. Moreover, the practice of psychotherapy has sadly come under the overbearing and stifling influence of various accrediting and regulating bodies, as well as training courses, that reflect what Heidegger refers to as *das Man*, that is, a way of conducting itself according to norms and established, predictable rules for the practice of therapy. Perhaps this is an inevitable consequence of our world today in which ordering and controlling becomes a prevalent and normalised way of understanding our practices.

Chapter 5

Methodological Considerations

5.1 Terminological Distinctions

In pursuing a Heideggerian approach to therapy, a number of different distinctions necessarily come into consideration, as Heidegger himself employs and introduces in the course of his own investigations in *Being and Time*. I will cover these here but intend to revisit and elaborate on their meanings later where appropriate. Some terms have already been previously mentioned, but not sufficiently elaborated as I now attempt in the following sections.

5.1.1 Ontic and Ontological

In order to address being, Heidegger identifies two types of enquiry, or approach, that we can take. One he calls ontic, and the other is ontological. An ontological enquiry is one in which we are investigating the meaning or significance of the phenomenon or entity that we have in view. To enquire about meaning here is to ask about the sense or the intelligibility of something. We can see this reflected in the attention that we devote to understanding such phenomena as history, time, or ourselves, for that matter. They each mean something or other, rather than standing as bare facts. In considering our way of being, which Heidegger calls 'Dasein', meaning itself is a central feature of what is human about us. To undertake an ontological enquiry, then, is to take into account the historical, cultural, or social meaning that makes something the phenomenon that it is.

The 'what is', or what shows up, whether it be a pen, a table, or Dasein itself, is what Heidegger calls an entity. To enquire into the entity itself, and address the question of what it is, is an ontic enquiry. We can say that almost all of our traditional approaches to enquiry about the human being have been ontic in character. We have tended to ask about what the human being is, but not what it is from its historical sense, for example, or from the perspective of its deeper, structural understanding. This leads us to the point that meaning, which the ontological addresses, is related to a central term that Heidegger introduces, which is 'care'. This is a structural term, and will be covered in detail later, but suffice to say that meaning matters to us, in contrast to the way in which chairs don't have care woven into the structure of their being.

DOI: 10.4324/9781003342137-6

There is an aspect of the kind of being that we are, which is that we have a pre-ontological understanding of ourselves in our being. For example, we relate to other entities around us insofar as we understand their being: a chair is for sitting on, and not for eating, and a piece of chewing gum is not for hammering with when I want to assemble a stool. Nor do we park our car in a large tub of ice cream. In other words, we are able to distinguish between ourselves as human beings and non-human entities, but this is not something that we actively maintain in the forefront of our awareness as we go about our affairs and activities. To add a little more technically oriented language to it, we already have a sense of the ontological 'categories' that distinguish between being human and being a thing or entity. Heidegger brings out these ontological categories of being, which have already been discussed, namely, the ready-to-hand, presence-at-hand, and existence.

5.1.2 Being and Entity, or Being and Beings

Even though this was addressed earlier, we should always keep this simple but crucial distinction in our consideration whenever engaging in Heidegger's thinking, since this also bears relevance to our approach to therapy. This distinction is between being, the 'to be', or what it is to be, on the one hand, and on the other hand, entities, beings, things that are. The point of keeping this in mind is that we can easily disregard, ignore, or 'forget' about being, and then just focus on the client before us as an entity, without also recognising that their being is what is central to our therapeutic approach. When we attend to the being of the client, we are then immersed in a wholly different exploration, and way of seeing, that is, understanding the client's way of being. This basic distinction is what Heidegger calls the 'ontological difference', the difference between the *being* of an entity, and *a* being. These, as has been emphasised, are not the same. Keeping the ontological difference in mind means that we don't treat the being of the client as a thing, or an entity, as if it's yet one more property that she or he possesses.

5.1.3 Existentials and Categories

This is a simple distinction between two contexts in which enquiry can take place. If I am conducting a categorical analysis of something, I am attending to it as a substance with properties. We can see how this originates in a certain way with past philosophers – Aristotle and Kant are its foremost proponents – to ascribe features to a human being that are drawn from categories, such as quality, quantity, relation, place, and so on. By contrast, an existential analysis proceeds by referring to the ontological structures of human existence, which is Dasein, or being-there. The existential approach is one that draws on the numerous constitutive features of Dasein, such as its always finding itself oriented to the world in a certain way, as well as being temporal in its way of being-in-the-world. Taking a categorical approach to Dasein, on Heidegger's account, would be a wholly mis-conceived form of enquiry, though it is one that prevails in our current tradition and practices.

5.1.4 Factical and Factual

Similarly, to attend to Dasein in factual terms is to draw on categories, as if it were a substance or mere thing that was under investigation. In other words, it would be tantamount to treating Dasein as having an essence, as would be the case if we attended to a table or chair, and then laying out its various attributes that conform to facts about it as the kind of thing that it is. The factical, by con-trast, conveys Dasein's 'thrownness' – a term that will be covered later – though distinguishes itself by the way in which Dasein makes something out of those aspects of its thrown character. For example, I was born as a man, biologically speaking, which is a fact, but the way in which I interpret and make sense of this fact based on the background culture, that already understands this in a certain way, is my facticity.

5.1.5 Existentiale and Existentiell

An existentiale is that structural feature of Dasein that is constitutive of its being. For example, every Dasein is a mortal being, and 'being-mortal', although Heidegger calls it 'being-towards-death', is an existentiale, as is 'being-with', which is its fun-damental 'withness' without which it could not be Dasein. That is, we are unlike the table, which has no capacity for relating, in the sense of being-with, to any other entity. The existentiell, by contrast, is an ontic or concrete instantiation of the existentiale in question. For example, the existentiale, being-with is expressed concretely by a person, as in the way one associates and socialises with others: this is the existentiell manifestation of that existentiale. However, insofar as Heidegger makes explicit those existentiales as are introduced in *Being and Time*, I provide them as follows:

> Being-in; Being; Being-amid[1]; Concern; Worldhood; De-severance; Directionality; Making room; Being-with; Solicitude; the One (*das Man*); Disposedness (*Befindlichkeit*); Understanding; Possibility; Projection; Meaning; Discourse; Truth; Ending; Totality.

Most of these will be explicated in Part II. This, we should note, does not mean that Heidegger has identified every single existentiale that constitutes Dasein's exist-ence. For one, this would be too onerous, even impossible, as an undertaking, and second, those identified by Heidegger are only those that happen to be immediately relevant to his project that is *Being and Time*.

I have attended to other existentiales in later sections, such as being-towards-death and being-embodied. Some difficulty, however, resides in the fact of decid-ing what is deemed an existentiale and what is not. For example, as Aho (2006) has emphasised, being-embodied might not be rightly considered an existentiale, as is also the case with care, temporality, and spatiality. This perhaps reflects the fact that any attempt to describe or provide an account of human existence as such always requires a continuously extended hermeneutic interpretation that reaches beyond its current horizon of understanding. That being said, the challenge we face is to identify those essential features of Dasein's being that have thus far not been identified, or made explicit, and that are relevant for our understanding in a therapeutic context, though some existentiales also need to be explicitly identified, such as being-in-the-world.

5.2 Methodological Distinctions

5.2.1 Phenomenology

Phenomenology is the study of that which is brought to our awareness. What is brought, then, is the givenness of the phenomenon. To study a phenomenon, for Heidegger, is to undertake a certain kind of investigation in order to disclose its being, rather than to simply focus on what it is. The important element in all this is the givenness by which the phenomenon is presented, rather than it being somehow asserted, willed, or instigated by us. The temptation here is to approach this in traditionally accustomed ways, so we should exercise care when attempting to capture the meaning of the term, phenomenology. As it stands, we identify two elements that are reflected in this word: phenomenon and -ology. First, what do we mean by 'phenomenon'? It is any thing, fact, or occurrence that appears, or 'shows itself in itself'. Phenomena can be the pen, or cup, for example, but can also be gravity, or democracy. In that sense, a phenomenon is an entity, which, again, just means 'what is', or 'that which is'. From an etymological perspective, it is that which shows up in its appearing. The second element of the term reflects that it is also an '-ology', which derives itself from the Greek *logos*. We can simply understand this in terms of being an account, or discourse, which now means that phenomenology is the way in which we talk about the phenomenon. By way of contrast, we can think of the *logos* of science or the *logos* of art, for example, as being discourses, whilst also being very different from each other.

  To recapitulate quickly on what has been stressed already, Heidegger's phenomenological approach to our kind of being cannot be simply pursued as if it were a thing, or object, since such entities have modes of being that are completely different to Dasein. Rather, because our way of being is existence, we have to take into account the way in which the phenomenon can be covered over or hidden, in this mode of being (BT60). And as Heidegger says, '[j]ust because the phenomena are proximally and for the most part *not* given, there is need for phenomenology' (BT60).

  Heidegger employs phenomenological *method* (BT61), which we might associate with a rigid rule-following that directs us towards a conclusion. However, his understanding of 'method' is reflected in the idea of a path or way towards the phenomenon in question. Heidegger also makes clear that phenomenology is description (BT59), and that the two terms are the same.

5.2.2 Hermeneutics

In addition to a phenomenological form of enquiry, Heidegger says that '[o]ur investigation itself will show that the meaning of phenomenological description as a method lies in *interpretation*' (BT61). And further, 'The phenomenology of Dasein is a hermeneutic…where it designates this business of interpreting' (BT62). In other words, the *logos* of a phenomenology of Dasein is already interpretative in character, because the very mode of being of Dasein – existence – is structured in a way that covers over, hides, and conceals the phenomena as they are in themselves. A hermeneutic process of investigation will therefore uncover the phenomenon and bring it to light.

The significance of a hermeneutic approach is also that it rejects a *pre-deter-mined* procedure or systematic method, as we typically find in any scientific form of enquiry. This is because the illumination of the truth of Dasein requires a different approach to those embraced in the human sciences and in our traditional practices. For one, Heidegger says that '[t]he "essence" of this entity [that is, Dasein] lies in its "to be"' (BT67). This is a being-towards (Richardson, 2012:60), which is simply the idea that we are always projecting ourselves forwards towards ends and purposes. This reflects the way that we exist. However, put in this way already misses its existential character. Instead, an approach is required that studies the way that this manifests, and that can't be captured only by straightforward description.

5.2.3 Formal Indication

Both the formal structure and its indicative pointing towards a phenomenon are what Heidegger means by 'formal indication'. In approaching the term in its formal presentation, the content is held in temporary abeyance, in order to gain greater clarity on the formal structure of the term whilst holding in view that it is pointing towards something. Heidegger does disclose something of the process of conducting an enquiry by means of formal indication, but never makes this explicit by way of further elaborating what he is doing. However, formal indication occupies a central place in his hermeneutic approach to enquiry.

Therapists who adopt a certain relation to words and language generally approach clients' narratives and particular reflections with a questioning or probing attitude. In the midst of a therapeutic dialogue, certain words might stand out that are seemingly straightforward and transparent in their meanings, but that warrant closer examination or clarification. If, for example, a client says that she feels resentment towards her employer, the feeling in question is simply a linguist placeholder, a form of marker that invites deeper exploration. In this sense, the therapist takes the word or term as a formal indication, and not as an established concept that is in no further need of investigation and clarification. As well as this, we can take it that the term has a certain formal structure to it that distinguishes it from other emotions, such as resignation, for example, or acceptance. Later, in Part IV, I illustrate the therapeutic application of formal indication by addressing the phenomenon of resentment itself.

For now, however, in order to map out the way in which Heidegger uses formal indication, I will offer an example that illustrates its application. I use the example of 'boredom' here, drawing significantly on the work of Elpidorou and Freeman (2019), but also sourcing from Heidegger's writings on this. Boredom is a formal indication, in its 'provisional' sense, given the way it is usually understood in our everyday experience, namely, that I am bored *by* something. I explore this further, teasing out the phenomenological aspects of the way that this mood grips me. For example, I describe a situation in which I am bored by the long wait for the bus. It seems to never arrive, and in the meantime, I note the sense of heaviness and ennui of my waiting, as if it's taking forever to show up. Part of it has to do with the fact that I have nothing to preoccupy me in the meantime, I have nothing else to do to fill the time taken up by waiting. At this point, the phenomenological description has presented an ontological clue, namely, that this kind of boredom is marked by looking at how we pass time. The struggle that consumes me is a concern with trying to shorten this time, but without any means or success to do so. As I proceed with this formally indicative approach, given its attention to the structure, or form of the phenomenon (boredom), and relate to it simply as a pointing, the structure unveils itself in terms of an 'in-limbo' kind of experience, as Elpidorou and Freeman put it. This is reflected in my undergoing a certain flatness of discontent, which persists endlessly in my experience. The bus hasn't arrived, and as I wait, and the longer that this experience continues, I am disconnected from those projects that await me when I arrive home, for example.

In the formal indication, I now explore the way in which the phenomenon is open to a more elaborate understanding that had not previously been apparent in my first phenomenological description of being bored by something. In the case of my example, I now board the bus, and am on my homeward journey. As I sit in my seat, I have a sense of being bored *with* something. This is the second form of boredom. I have just attended a meeting with some colleagues, it was a pleasant enough affair, and generally went well. This form of boredom, however, provides me with no insight or access to understand how it manifests. So far, then, 'boredom with' is a development that comes from taking boredom as our formal indication, as it keeps pointing towards the form of the phenomenon as a placeholder, and not drawn into offering content. Since it is not immediately clear how this boredom manifests itself, engaging in further phenomenological description and interpretation allows something more to become apparent to me that had previously not been accessible. I have begun to bring the phenomenon 'towards' me, or to 'existentialise' it such that it now 'says' something about me. I realise that this second form of boredom comes from *me*, as Dasein, and *not* from the situation.

In other words, it is not the meeting that was boring, but something else. This is not a conspicuous presence of boredom, as in the first case, where I could point to the mere waiting for the bus that was boring. In that first case of boredom, I could distance myself from it, or try to escape it in some way. In this second form, this option isn't available to me, because it is a different kind of boredom. In fact, this distinction has now become apparent to me, in the light of the hermeneutic spiral, or movement, such that I am now at a different depth of understanding of the phenomenon. This second way of being bored comes to me in the light of now realising how I have spent my time. Moreover, I realise that I have just gone along with what everyone else was doing in attending the meeting, and that I was doing the same. I didn't reflect in advance how I wanted to spend my evening, and so my relationship to time, in this case, was inauthentic. Rather than immersing myself in something that was absorbing and meaningful, which would have embraced all three tenses of temporality – past, present, and future – I trapped myself in a not-so-meaningful present.

The formal indication has brought a deeper understanding of the phenomenon that has relied on a hermeneutic process of investigation, in moving from a third-personal situation to a first-person stance. The first and second forms of boredom now allow me to stay with the formal sense of boredom as a linguistic 'pointing to' something, such that a third form of boredom now emerges. It is even more remote from our everyday sense of the term, but we see that undertaking this whole process of investigation is what has enabled or facilitated the uncovering of this form of boredom. We might call this an 'ontological boredom'. Imagine that I am now walking home, and I have a sense of nothing absorbing me, a certain emptiness that overwhelms me. There are things that I could do, but none of them are within my reach. They are all beyond or away from me, which amplifies my boredom. I lose a sense of myself, such that even my experience of the passing of time is absent. This form of boredom reflects being somehow 'detached' from the world, as if I am its spectator. In other words, I have a very disorienting sense of not being in or of this world. As well as this, I become all too aware of a world per se, given that I experience its absence through this sense of boredom. This existential development has now brought us to a full disclosure of the phenomenon of boredom through formal indication.

5.3 Therapeutic Distinctions

What is so important about our pursuing this Heideggerian project and not one that commonly subscribes to embracing an established theoretical approach to therapy? As is common practice, clients' presenting issues tend to be addressed by drawing on relevant theoretical accounts that offer the therapist a direction and understanding on how to proceed in their approaches. The sheer explanatory power of theory, rather than any more explicitly philosophical orientation, has been the overriding orientation of therapeutic practice. However, whilst theory offers something compelling and satisfying, this overlooks the fact that all practical and theoretical orientations are founded upon certain philosophical underpinnings that a therapist takes in their very way of engaging with the client or patient.

In summary, the distinction between being (itself) and *the*, or *a* human being, or the ontological difference between being and the being, or entity, has been emphasised as the basis of a Heideggerian approach. As a therapist, when I address the *being* of the person, I am attending to the person as *a being*, but their being means something different. In this sense, I am attuned to the person from both an ontic and ontological perspective. The person is an entity, but their being (itself) is not. In being attentive to this distinction, I am engaging with them not as a thing that is yet one more item that fills the world with various other identifiable things that occupy space, but as something uniquely its own in its being. The client *is*, we might say, rather than nothing at all. This very way of putting it strikes me with the realisation that the issue that the client might be bringing to therapy is not necessarily some kind of disruption or deeply felt sense of unease in their lives, although this might certainly be true, but being itself, or how to reckon with and settle the issue of their own being.

As will become apparent as I proceed, clients' lives are affected in some way by the circumstances in which they live, and this threads back to the relevance of existentiales, as well as those existentiales that are relevant to the client's circumstances. Lest we lose sight of this fact, a life is lived, temporally speaking, and so can't be deciphered or understood by approaches that apply measures or calculations to 'calibrate' or 'adjust' the person in some way. This misplaces us by positioning the human being according to a certain scientific framework, such that it misses and disregards the fact that we dwell. We are *living* beings, and life can't be measured or quantified. Perhaps the most striking feature of our existing is that we are temporal, and that we 'historise'. This will hopefully become clearer as the account of Dasein proceeds.

Note

1 Along with Braver, I prefer to use this translation of the German, *Sein bei*, rather than Macquarrie and Robinson's 'being-alongside' (Heidegger, 1927/1962).

Part II

Dasein

II.1 Introduction

In *Being and Time*, Heidegger pursues the project of being. In the course of doing so, he claims that we are the kind of being that has a pre-ontological understanding of what it is to be, such that an analysis of our kind of being will bring us towards an understanding of being itself. In undertaking this enquiry, he conducts an analysis of Dasein that starts from its existence in everydayness. It is in everyday existence that Dasein essentially finds itself in its most basic and immediate way of being, which is an accessible point from which to start the analysis. In the course of the enquiry, Heidegger elaborates what it is to be Dasein, which is being-in-the-world. This, in turn, is subjected to phenomenological 'interrogation', as he puts it, by recognising being-in-the-world as a unitary phenomenon, but, at the same time, taking a closer look at its constitutive elements, being-in, worldhood, and the 'who' of its world. As the analysis takes its course, a more detailed and richer account of Dasein is provided, all the while being conducted from the perspective of Dasein in its everydayness. This part of Heidegger's analysis of Dasein constitutes what has been assigned by him as Division I of *Being and Time*.

Given that Heidegger's phenomenological exposition in terms of everydayness has offered an incomplete account of Dasein in its existence, he moves the line of enquiry in a decidedly existential direction, which constitutes Division II of *Being and Time*. In so doing, he performs a significant hermeneutic turn, or movement, such that he addresses those aspects or features of Dasein in its being that had either already been mentioned in the preceding analysis in Division I or were radically new phenomena. Heidegger is now able in this section of his analysis to introduce those aspects of Dasein that it had previously not been possible to articulate. In short, we can say that Division I had provided an account of Dasein in its inauthentic way of being, whilst Division II extended this to an exposition of Dasein in its authenticity.

Division II addresses Dasein as a whole, rather than in terms portrayed in Division I, namely, as existing in a 'partial' and incomplete way, i.e., not grasping itself as a whole. When Dasein is seen as a whole, it takes into view its birth and death, not as events, but in terms of existing authentically in the light of both its

DOI: 10.4324/9781003342137-7

finitude and its thrownness. The distinction between Dasein in its everydayness and in its authentic existence is essentially grasped in terms of its temporality. Heidegger's challenge is to bring us to see that Dasein's temporality is nothing like our traditional concept of time, just as Division I of *Being and Time* enabled us to see that our traditional conception of the world as an aggregate of things in a holding container is wholly at odds with an understanding of the human world.

Chapter 6

Dasein

The attempt to articulate this central term in *Being and Time* prompts the question, why is it important for existential therapists to consider their approach in terms of an understanding of the being of Dasein? As well as this, a difficulty or challenge emerges in our very attempts to engage in Heidegger's ideas, which is based on the dominance of Cartesianism in both psychotherapy and also in everyday common-sense thinking and reasoning. We are all also vulnerable to the real possibility of either simplifying or mischaracterising his ideas, but also of failing to find a way of presenting them in an accessible form for therapists in their own approach as practitioners. Such concerns apply throughout as we proceed to explicate Heidegger's ideas over the course of this and other parts of the book.

Heidegger offers an account of being-in-the-world and Dasein in a way that makes explicit what is already familiar and implicit in our coping and dealing with situations and circumstances in everyday life, namely our pre-ontological understanding of being. I go about my affairs, move from one place to another, tackle certain jobs at hand, and make use of certain things that are relevant to me at particular moments, along with various forms of contact in my liaising with colleagues, friends, and family, all in a transparent and seamless way. I do so without reflecting on what it is that I'm doing, or how I am faring, whilst being involved in these activities. In other words, I always already express a kind of 'know-how' as I go about my world, from the way in which I join a queue in order to check-out various items when in my local supermarket, to the manner in which I travel to work on public transport on certain days. These are all relatively mundane matters, and Heidegger characterises them more generally in terms of the 'average everydayness' of Dasein.

To set out a clear picture of Dasein in its customary way of being, Heidegger devotes the first part of *Being and Time* to initially map out in some detail the structural elements of being-in-the-world, namely, being-in, world, and Dasein's 'who' that is in the world. As he brings out these elements of being-in-the-world, Heidegger coins new terms so that he can name exactly that which is so obvious to us and yet obscured from our awareness because we hardly ever notice it. Previous attempts to name the phenomena in question have been overlooked, or ignored, and so this makes it challenging to capture and articulate them clearly in words. Part of

DOI: 10.4324/9781003342137-8

the issue is also that our language, as it is structured, already limits and constrains what we can express and say in our speech. This is because language reflects the fact that we are immersed in a certain metaphysical understanding of our world that is exclusively ontic: we report on entities and things in their stand-alone, static character, but we fail to talk of their being because of the limits of language. In order to reach or go beyond such limits, Heidegger coins new terms, but his challenge is nevertheless to do this *within* these constraints of our traditional language, and this is a daunting, if not ultimately doomed, task. As well as this, Heidegger's terms attempt to capture those aspects of our existence from which we distance ourselves, because they are significantly unsettling for us. One clear example of this is in his treatment of death, which ontically is farthest from us as an event, metaphysically speaking, but is closest to us in its real and present possibility as being-toward-death, existentially speaking. In order to bring these phenomena to light, Heidegger undertakes a phenomenological approach to analysis. However, as regards the issue of language that has been brought out here, this remained a central concern for Heidegger throughout his life, and is particularly strongly conveyed in his later work.

6.1 The Modern Understanding of Being Human

As has been previously discussed, psychotherapy in the Western world is founded upon a particular kind of understanding of what it is to be human, and one that is applied universally. This is the seemingly solid foundation that serves the basis for almost all the therapeutic approaches that we encounter, whether it be the Cognitive-Behavioural, Psychodynamic, Systems-Oriented, Transpersonal, or Gestalt orientations. None escape this foundation, as this is based on our Modern understanding of what we essentially are as human beings.

The challenge that we face is in grasping our understanding of this foundation. In attempting to answer this, let me set out in some detail the background and contribution of a seminally important 17th century French thinker who reconfigured our whole understanding of what it is to be human: René Descartes (1596–1650). I will then briefly mention the impact of the work of Edmund Husserl (1859–1938), universally recognised as the founder of phenomenology, since his philosophical approach impacted significantly on Heidegger's thinking. The aim will then be to assess the way in which Heidegger's account offers a much more compelling picture of what it is to be human, or what is distinctive about our kind of being.

6.1.1 Descartes

It is the long arc of Descartes' legacy over the more recent centuries that underpins and frames the many therapeutic approaches that we encounter today. Descartes was a French philosopher, scientist, and mathematician who also made significant contributions to geometry and, in particular, method itself. Rather than seeing it as a 'way towards', Descartes developed a more rigid, procedural understanding of method, much like that found in his own areas of interest and expertise:

science and mathematics. As it turns out, method itself is of great relevance in a therapeutic context too, which will hopefully become more evident when we consider the differences between Descartes and Heidegger as we proceed.

Consider the period in which Descartes was alive and working on his intellectual projects. It was the 1600s, and the Scientific Revolution was going on. His elder contemporary, Galileo Galilei (1564–1642), a Florentine scientist, astronomer, and general polymath, was immersed in experimental method and its path to knowledge. Very crudely, for Galileo, there were two 'books' available at the time. One was the Christian Bible, written in metaphor and symbol, which provided the knowledge to achieve salvation of souls. The other book was the physical universe, which was written in mathematical 'language', and was composed of circles, squares, triangles, numbers, and so forth. In order to understand the universe, and nature itself, according to Galileo, a mathematician's stance is required, because nature is 'written' in mathematical characters. That is, reality is a mathematical structure: what is real is mathematical. To grasp that reality, we therefore take an approach to nature that is mathematical in its method.

In the course of his findings, Galileo met with strong condemnation from the Church, due to his Copernican theory of planetary motion, since it was in complete opposition to prevailing Church doctrine. The overall project of science (and mathematics) then encountered a problem, as it could not proceed, in view of the Church's censure. Descartes, aware of this, became more circumspect as a result, since he was similarly subject to the pressures and prohibitions of the highly centralised French state of his time. Aware of Galileo's house arrest by the authorities, he took a step back, and instead of pursuing certain lines of thought that were in agreement with the Florentine, decided to publish his renowned work, *Meditations on First Philosophy* (1641). It is at this point that we start to see the increasing relevance of Descartes' ideas to our own projects and approaches as therapists.

In this work, Descartes went back to first principles. The reason for this was that he wanted to create a basis for human knowledge, and to set out a foundation in a way that creates no conflict between the two books mentioned. He agreed with Galileo, and wanted to set philosophy on a straight path, so that the Church could leave untouched Descartes' reflections on the non-theological world, that is, nature.

Meditations is composed of six sections, which he also called 'meditations'. These stand as separate paths of thinking, but they each build on, and develop from, one section to the next. I will confine myself only to the first three meditations since they will be sufficient for our purposes here. In the 'First Meditation', Descartes says that he will apply himself to a methodical scrutiny of all his formerly taken for granted beliefs and opinions. Where he finds the slightest grounds for doubt in such a belief or opinion, he will dismiss it or simply put it to one side. As he proceeds, he tries to identify the foundation for all of his former beliefs and opinions, rather than simply going through them, one by one. Next, he asks whether everything that he has learnt through the senses is a knowledge that is secure and immune to doubt. For example, consider the straight stick that has been placed in water: the part of the stick that is under the water surface appears bent to us. However, once taken out of the water, the stick has resumed its straightness. The question now arises over the reliability of our senses, and its relationship to our beliefs. But, at this point, we might insist that we can make a distinction between optical illusions and sensory experiences from which we derive knowledge, as with the stick example. Descartes then goes on to consider another example relating to the senses, that of being awake and of being asleep. This is a deeper argument about knowledge based on the senses: how do I know, at any particular moment, that I am not dreaming? He observes that sometimes when we are dreaming we are convinced of the reality of what we are experiencing in our dreams, but then wake up and realise that it was just a dream. So, we are now left with the feeling that it does seem correct that we can be quite radically deceived by our senses.

Thus far, then, Descartes has managed to introduce the idea of the very possibility of our being deceived in some way or other, which undermines our conviction that our beliefs can all be true and infallible. In employing his method of doubt, he is looking for its counterpart, certainty, something infallible and not susceptible to doubt. In certainty, we arrive at a foundation for our knowledge, or epistemological certainty. In the example of dreams, we do experience ourselves as immersed in a three-dimensional world. But what if some all-powerful demon is all-bent on deceiving us and somehow placing those images in our minds? This is, according to the argument presented by Descartes, rationally conceivable. So there are rational grounds for doubt when it comes to our sensory experience as a whole, and not just specific experiences in which this is the case. That brings us to the end of the 'First Meditation'.

In the 'Second Meditation', Descartes says that, after all these considerations, he has found one thing that is immune to any possible or conceivable rational doubt: I am, I exist. This is the starting point of what is commonly referred to as Modern philosophy. Descartes' central claim is that, if I put forward any proposition, such as a thought, belief, opinion, or assertion, even if I am being deceived by anybody or anything, I must exist in the first instance in order that I *can* then be deceived. As well as this, I must exist in order to be doubting anything. Thinking is the core thing that Descartes discovers is indubitable and that gives him the knowledge-foundation that he exists. Put back into Descartes' language, as long as I think, I am certain that I exist. If I am thinking, I must exist, so I am certain that I am a thinking thing. A thinking thing, as Descartes expresses it, is otherwise expressed in a term that is familiar to us, namely, 'consciousness'. At this point, having arrived at our being a consciousness, Descartes' approach has not managed to provide any account of the body. All that he is saying thus far is that I may well be a body as well as consciousness, but I am not certain of that. All that I am certain of is that I exist as a consciousness.

In summary then, Descartes' First Meditation introduced doubt as a method or approach that attempts to break down those beliefs and assumptions that he held to be true. He is on the quest for an epistemological foundation, or what we can claim to know with certainty. In the Second Meditation, having doubted everything that he can reasonably doubt, one thing that escapes doubting can be stated with two claims: first, 'I am, I exist', of that I am certain as long as I think; and second, which follows on from this, I am certain that I am a thinking thing (that is, a consciousness). The 'Third Meditation' then takes it as its task to build up from the certainty of (internal) consciousness to establishing the existence of the external world.

At this point, whilst we have arrived at both the beginnings of Modern philosophy, this has also illuminated one of its main problems. The problem starts with the fact that Descartes does not want to remain at this point of only being a consciousness. He needs to find a way to bridge consciousness with the external world. But why is this a problem? Let me put it this way. If I describe any of the various experiences that I have, which are simply certain modifications of my consciousness, then as long as I stay at the level of experience, or consciousness, my claims and utterances can be said to be certain, or indubitable. The problem then arises in my assuming that my experience is an experience of something *outside* consciousness. If I make this unwarranted leap, I move from an *internal* realm to an *external* one, and this invites the possibility of error. The problem of establishing the existence of an external world remains.

Philosophers who have followed Descartes made various interesting attempts to overcome this. One such attempt was made by Edmund Husserl, the founder of phenomenology, who took up the epistemological project bequeathed by Descartes, and identified consciousness itself as the foundation and basis for philosophy as a rigorous science, as he put it. Since consciousness provides certainty, that is where we should place all our attention. The external world, for him, can simply be bracketed away through what he calls the phenomenological *epoché*. As already laid out, however, this evidently poses its own problems, and will become clear when we come to look more closely at Heidegger's approach. Other important philosophers worth mentioning here, but only in passing, include the French-Lithuanian thinker, Emmanuel Lévinas, who focused in more closely on the latter part of Descartes' Third Meditation, offering his own interesting responses to Descartes. As well as Lévinas, we also see Sartre make much of particular sections of the Fourth Meditation, in which Descartes writes about our kind of being as lying 'between God and nothingness' (Descartes, 2003:45). From this view, then, understanding Descartes' position clarifies the later existentialists' contributions in responding to the question of being human.

The legacy of Descartes' thinking and philosophy is that we relate to ourselves as detached Cartesian contemplators, or thinking things, without a world. This leads us to say that there is an *external* world, which is contrasted with an internal, private world, and usually referred to in terms of subjectivity. It is important to see how Descartes' thinking carved into our fundamental outlook a whole way of seeing things in terms of 'inner' and 'outer', and in a way that was not prevalent before him.

In this account of Descartes, I have endeavoured to bring out the way in which his approach was his own response to the issue of being human. Tracking his process of thinking in greater detail offers us the chance to see how it both misses important features of human existence, and relatedly, how current ways of thinking follow similar lines of enquiry. It also contrasts with an existential approach that, in effect, takes it upon itself to pursue an experience-near path with respect to our kind of being.

6.1.1.1 Heidegger's Critique of Descartes

Heidegger made numerous references to Descartes in his lectures and writings at various points in his life. On the one hand, this reflected a mark of his respect for Descartes' contributions, whilst, on the other, offered Heidegger an opportunity to engage in what he called an *Auseinandersetzung*, or productive and creative setting himself against such thinking as a way of further developing and clarifying his own position. In my attempts here to set out his critique of Descartes in what follows, I hope to thereby bring out more clearly what made Heidegger's argument so distinctive and original.

In my presentation of Descartes' meditations, or reflections that constitute his overall epistemological project of establishing the true foundations of knowledge, I have tried to convey the way in which he was deeply attentive to the logical steps of thinking through to his own conclusions. However, in Heideggerian terms, we can critique and point to the way in which Descartes happened to ignore his own way of being human, even before he engaged in reflection. I will run through a number of assumptions that he makes that at the very least call into serious question the picture that his project presents.

First, as a human being, one can say that he was already immersed in a particular kind of mood or attunement towards issues that mattered to him. It is, in other words, a project that absorbed him. There is a particular kind of atmosphere that Descartes entered into in his meditative thinking, though he did not really acknowledge this, other than saying at the outset that he had secluded himself away in a warm room, by a hot stove, and away from others. Acknowledging this mood was already an added essential feature of being human that Descartes ignored, or else somehow avoided or extricated from his approach. In some unacknowledged way, he assumed that he could simply question his beliefs and that, in doing so, this somehow addressed what is fundamental about being human. He treated himself, following Braver (2014:15), as a thinking thing from the very outset, so it is unsurprising that this is what he finally 'discovered'.

Descartes made the fundamental assumption, and one that has become so ingrained in our common-sense thinking, of dualism that characterises human existence. We are a mind, or thinking thing, and a body. The mind is internal to us, or subjective, whilst the body is external, or objective. As well as this, it is a dualism that claims that there are two fundamental kinds of 'stuff' (to call it 'substance' is to already commit to a physicalist or materialist account): a mental stuff and a material stuff. One cannot be reduced to the other: whatever is mental cannot be expressed in language that is steeped in materialism. In therapy, we commonly find ourselves exploring those aspects of the client's experience in inviting them to articulate what is going on 'inside' them, whether this be a feeling, belief, or even value. This is set against an external world of others and the relevant situations and environments that bear on their reflections. This, however, sets up a particular difficulty, as it invokes a separation that cannot then be brought back again into a unitary whole, which is how we commonly and originally understand the human being. Similarly put, this separation between the objective and subjective has been driven so far apart that this prejudice persists without any opportunity to really address it. An added difficulty that we find in dualism is the inability to claim with accuracy or certainty that one's mental experience matches or represents the external world, since there is no 'third' element at play to act as guarantor for this. Descartes invokes the idea of God to do this, but this brings in yet another assumption that is open to challenges.

The consequences of this dualism are clearly in view when it comes to the world of therapy. When we take the external world to be stable, enduring, and objective, we endow it with a sense of reliability and measurability. On this account, then, it can be quantified and rendered into facts and theories that escape temporal and other variations. The external world is therefore knowable, through science and mathematics. By contrast, minds cannot be measured in similar ways, since they fall within the subjective sphere, even though various scales of measurement have been introduced over the past decades and up to the present, purporting to assess the degrees and intensities of certain emotions, thoughts, and feelings. This is a long way from any exploration of the being of clients. In setting into place the objective-subjective distinction, then, the objective is underwritten by the role of science to address the natural world and provide facts and certainties, whilst the subjective is understood as fallible, open to different perspectives, and susceptible to certain limitations. The Cartesian approach, therefore, assigns a certain importance to the scientific approach, whilst the subjective, which can be said to fall within the domain of ordinary everyday life, is vulnerable to unreliable and untenable expressions of views, opinions, preferences, choices, beliefs, and values. As such, it is wholly anathema to objectivity, which reaps knowledge and certainty. The outcome of all this is to place relatively little importance on such things as feelings and values, since they do not reflect the power and authority of the external world. In therapeutic terms, the tendency of some approaches is reflected in an attempt to bring the client towards a way of conforming to the world rather than staying with the truth of the client's way of being-in-the-world.

Various terms and expressions in our language have also perpetuated the problem. Cartesian thought itself has led to talk of belief, value, choice, and feeling, without really grasping the import of this. Of course, each of these terms express something about our human way of engaging with the world and ourselves, but this assumes that it is in possession of the correct foundational starting point for an understanding of our kind of being. A more fundamental understanding that motivates and underlies all these expressions is the basic sense of a mattering that grips and pulls me, such that I already care in a certain way, rather than the customary way of thinking reflected in our *placing* value on something or other. In other words, something claims me, rather than my cultivating a stance in which I claim or pronounce value upon something or other. We only need to think of the importance that our families have for us, in that they deeply matter, in a way that simply placing a value on them by making certain pronouncements on this misses the point. In this way, certain therapeutic approaches and practices, such as Improving Access to Psychological Therapies (IAPT), Cognitive-Behavioural Therapy (CBT), and other evidence-based therapies are surely egregious examples of the way that quantitative measures are applied to values and beliefs rather than attending to the client's being. Typically, proponents of these approaches conduct assessments of relevant feelings or dispositions that run along a range from low to high degrees of severity in order to then determine the client's 'improvement', in getting 'better', or 'healthier', and present evidence for behaviours that reflect a certain assumption of normality. This, of course, also bears on such therapists' own understanding of themselves as competent and skilled practitioners in their field. Both therapist and client are caught in a Cartesian framework that perpetuates the very problems that a Heideggerian approach to therapy is attempting to address. For one thing, values and choices can be alternatively approached both phenomenologically and existentially, and not scientifically or theoretically. From a Heideggerian perspective, a key difference in approach is based on the importance of a constitutive aspect of Dasein, namely, disposedness, which I will address in greater detail shortly. This reflects the way in which the world and its situations already show up for us in a certain way, rather than our being the architects and foundational creators of our world.

As a final set of comments, Descartes takes his own approach to be fundamental, when, in fact, it is derivative of something more primordial, namely, our way of being, which he leaves untouched. That is, he takes us to be more object-like, such that we can be treated like things that can be placed under examination. This conveys a scientific or theoretical attitude, which then inevitably excludes various significant ways in which we are human. We can even see how this is reflected in the language that Descartes employs in the course of his enquiry in the *Meditations*. From the very first paragraph of his overall account, Descartes refers to the 'I' when speaking of himself. He takes it that this captures the way that we are in our core being, but his approach treats this 'I' as ontic and present-at-hand. Heidegger, as we will see, rejects this view by taking a radically different approach.

6.1.2 Husserl

Drawing on our previous consideration of Descartes, we can now assess the impact that his project made on Husserl, since he developed his phenomenology straight out of the Cartesian approach. In fact, by the time we arrive at the Third Meditation in his *Meditations*, we have been introduced to the basic principle of Husserl's phenomenology. I can experience myself being in a room, just like Descartes, with chairs, a table, a warm fire, a dimmed light source, and so on, but this is just an experience in my consciousness, that is, my sensory perception of things. If I am seeing a patch of red, for example, and this red is the red of the sofa that I am sitting on, I take that experience of red to be a certain alteration or effect or modification in my consciousness. But if I am to remain true to a rigour of certitude, I am not going to make the additional assumptive leap that there is a *real* object – the sofa – that I am experiencing, because that might just be false, or liable to errors of various kinds. In Descartes' language, a malevolent demon or force might be putting that experience into my consciousness. So, I must simply stay with the contents of consciousness and 'bracket away' any idea of a world. In so doing, I make concerted efforts to describe these contents, without adding anything that is extraneous to them. In other words, Husserlian phenomenology takes itself to be describing the structure of a certain experience in consciousness, without making any presupposition about the experience being an experience of something *beyond* consciousness. The principle here is that we are in a position of absolute *certainty* whilst in this mode of providing a phenomenological description of our experience in consciousness.

Heidegger, to put it bluntly, says that this is not a way to do phenomenology. For one, it distorts our everyday sense of living in the world. That is, we are already absorbed in a context, or situation, or horizon, and to pull ourselves out or away from this is to wholly mischaracterise our way of being. Second, Husserl conducts his phenomenology within a Modern conception of being human, namely, that of being a consciousness, or mind, whose contents can be described and articulated without succumbing to any presuppositions. Whilst Heidegger agreed with Husserl that a different philosophical approach was required in order to attend 'to the matters themselves', he also radically disagreed with Husserl's Cartesian epistemological project. This is because it already assumed, as Descartes did, a dualism that ignored any attempt to address a fundamental ontology of being.

Another important element to Heidegger's approach is his starting point in addressing the question of being. He identifies the kind of being who already has an understanding of being, albeit that this understanding is vague and 'dim' for us, which is Dasein. Human beings fall into this kind of being. But what he means by Dasein is really very general and also concrete. It is general because Heidegger is not necessarily excluding the possibility that other beings, such as chimpanzees and dolphins, could also be Dasein. That is because of the form of the question being asked by Heidegger, about the *being* of Dasein. All he wants to do is to take that particular way of being and interrogate it. That, as has already been said, will further his overarching project, namely the meaning or intelligibility of being itself. Dasein is also concrete because interrogating Dasein is wholly at odds with an abstract approach to the issue of being. Heidegger, as we are already aware, pursues the question of the *being* of Dasein instead of simply addressing the question, what *is* Dasein. To determine what a human being is, rather than what it *means* to be human, is to walk the well-trodden path of traditional, or what is called, 'metaphysical' thinking.

Heidegger recognises that there are different modes of being, not just one, whether this be the mode of being of Dasein, or the mode of being that is substance.

But what is important for us to remember is that Dasein's mode of being is more basic, since it already has an understanding of being, and so can apprehend such other modes of being. So, things themselves have different modes of being, in being the kinds of things they are, but the Western tradition has lost sight of this in favour of the idea that there are simply different kinds of things. Once identified in this way, the established way of identifying and naming their features and properties fills out the account in a way that then erases their being. The idea that there are different kinds of things has been the traditional approach that has dominated our understanding up to the present day. Once this has taken hold, we have then addressed the issue of what each thing is, and what it has in common with all other things. One outcome of this has been to see everything in terms of substance, and in our Modern understanding, two different kinds of substance or 'stuff', namely, thinking stuff and material stuff.

In summary, we can see that Husserl, as Richardson notes (2012:69), is holding to the idea of the human being, or self, in three ways, or senses:

1   a thinking thing
2   a theorising, conscious subject; and
3   a substance.

Being a thinking thing points to the fact that we have a theoretical relation to the world, that this relation is one of knowing, and that this knowing is couched in terms of a cognitive understanding that includes talk about beliefs and values.

6.2 Dasein as a Heideggerian Understanding of Being Human

In the widest possible sense, psychotherapy is a particular set of practices that facilitate a form of engagement with a person, or client, who expresses the wish to address certain issues, questions, feelings, and beliefs that are of concern to them. It distinguishes itself in its approach from other practices, such as coaching, mentoring, and befriending, primarily through the form of care that it offers through specific kinds of dialogue, and in the depth of enquiry that it pursues.

For many in the field of psychotherapy, whether as training or practising therapists, the crucial and fundamental question becomes: what is it to be a person at all? We, all of us, already carry deep assumptions about who and how we essentially are, at a very basic level. This understandably offers us all a very clear and reassuring ground on which we can stand. One such assumption is that we have an absolute and unassailable picture of what a person is, in its most basic sense. In pressing forward and beyond the accustomed and assumption-led way in which we talk about the human being, a space can be opened to explore and probe yet further into the fundamental question of our way of being. With this, the challenge here is to both reassess and dismantle various terms that we use in everyday language that reflect certain deep limitations in the ways in which we talk about ourselves. In doing so, however, we need to also acquaint ourselves with some basic terms that Heidegger introduces in his account of being human. These will now be addressed.

6.2.1 Being-in-the-World

Dasein's being-in-the-world is a term that intimates its totality, or unitary whole, rather than a composition of parts. To be a human being is to be in the world, which is to say that the world is constitutive of being human. To convey this as unitary, or whole, Heidegger employs hyphenated phrasing: being-in-the-world. This gets us away from our accustomed way of thinking of the human being as a distinct, separate entity that is detached from the world. Contrastingly, previous accounts of our kind of being take us to be composed of parts, as has been put forward by the whole tradition of thinkers from Plato onwards, down to the present day. But most importantly, the tradition's understanding of 'world', in Heidegger's sense, has either been neglected or omitted in its thinking.

As well as being whole, we should also keep in mind that it makes no sense to ever speak in terms of *not* being-in-the-world, for Dasein; it is our inescapable condition. As Dasein, I am always already a situated being, immersed and absorbed in a setting, prior to any reflection or thinking about this. The question then becomes one of gaining a clearer understanding of those aspects of being-in-the-world that constitute it, so to speak. Following Heidegger, we need to extend our analysis – one that is ontological – in order to appreciate the meaning of being-in-the-world. To do this, we can attend more closely to these aspects, namely, being-in, world, and the who, whose mode of being is existence, and which reflects being-in-the-world.

6.2.2 Being-there

In our current age, we have taken to a certain understanding of ourselves that is seemingly so obvious and straightforward that it excludes any other possibilities. As has been previously elaborated, reference to the 'person', for example, is to, in the first instance, think of ourselves already as body and mind, something inside or internal, and an autonomous being that thinks, feels, desires, believes, reasons, and acts. Such an account insists on the fundamental starting point that we are individuals, independent and separate from each other, and from objects, things, and the world itself. This is what Haugeland means when he refers to the person as a 'count noun' (2013:9).

Martin Heidegger offered a radically different way of describing human existence. In this, he employed a whole new set of linguistic terms and ideas. This was necessary to challenge, or pull us out and away from, the traditional ways of understanding ourselves. One such term, which replaces others such as 'person', 'individual', and 'subject', is *Dasein*, which he, at times, presented in other writings in hyphenated form. It is a German term, meaning 'existence', but Heidegger gives it a rather different meaning in his description of our kind of being. Because it is left untranslated for English readers, it suggests something rather unwieldy and unfamiliar, but it is, in fact, intended to convey something very simple and straightforward.

There is no essence of the human being, as we claim when we refer to a consciousness, spirit, or soul. When we speak of ourselves in terms of an essence, we are separated from the environment, and can therefore either be taken out of it, or placed within it. This is a flawed picture or understanding because it fails to see that we are already 'there', and that the 'there' is what it is to be our kind of being. When I speak of myself as a 'mind', for example, I lose any sense of 'there'. In fact, I configure a world that is an abstraction, and that is parasitic upon something much more fundamental about us. The temptation is to look for something or other that defines us, as given by the earlier examples, but in doing so, being, or what it is to be our kind of being, is effectively lost, or forgotten. In order to emphasise 'being' and 'there' as a unitary phenomenon, we hyphenate this as 'being-there'.

Dasein as introduced is intended to capture the way in which we are always already caught up or immersed in the world, in a context of relations and meaning structures. In this sense, 'world' conveys what we mean when we refer to the therapy world, the world of publishing, the business world, and so on, rather than the oblate spheroid-shaped planet on which we live. With regard to Dasein, however, 'sein' means 'being', which is to point to the most basic fact, or fundamental truth, that something is and is not nothing at all. So, we can talk about the being of the tree, and all we mean by this is that its being is that it simply is, and is what it is when being a tree. Its being is in its being a tree. Here we therefore have both the idea of being, and also *a* being. The very expression, 'being a being' (a being such as a tree), clearly captures the fact that these two terms cannot be separated from one another, in any true sense. Being has to relate to *a* being: being does not just float about in the universe of its own accord. In order for being to be being, then, it is the being *of* a being of some kind or other. Similarly, Dasein is a being, insofar as its being can only announce itself *as* a being. In being, there is something (or a being), rather than nothing at all. In fact, Dasein has the privileged ability to understand, or grasp an entity's being, and distinguish this from its possible or actual absence as a being and, moreover, its being as anything at all.

6.2.3 Da, or There

There is an additional step to this, given the Da- in Dasein. My being is not simply like the being of the tree, the pen, or the table, but the being of a being that is always situated, contextually given, oriented, which is a 'there', or 'Da'. The cup, in its being, cannot be said to be 'Da': there is no sense in which its being also draws in the situation or context in which it finds itself, as is the case with our kind of being. It has no sense of world, or context of significance. Out of this, we note that Dasein is a particular kind of being, and that its being is different to other kinds of being, as with the being of the cup, the stone, or the pen.

The being of the cup has nothing woven into the very fabric of its being a cup that suggests anything about the 'how' and 'where' it finds itself. By contrast, it is in the Da that we also encounter Dasein's being that already matters to it. Since the cup is 'Da-less', or denied any 'Da' that can be attributed to it, it does not strictly have a world, or worldliness, whether this be towards other things around it, or projects that it identifies as important and meaningful, or a self-interpretative role, such as being a therapist or philosopher. Perhaps a really important distinction that can be emphasised here is that, whilst the cup cannot, and does not, relate to me, I can, and do, relate to the cup, because my Dasein always already encounters a world, a Da, or 'there'. Moreover, that which is there, Da, is reflected in care, structurally speaking, and which we might express in terms of a fundamental mattering.

6.2.4 Mineness

The Da, or 'there', but also rendered as 'here' in Dasein, reflects the fact that we are each uniquely in our own moment, place, world, and temporality. We are not, in our very being, substitutable, as if another person could step in, take over, and 'be me'. If we imagine this as a possibility, then 'being' and 'here' will have been prised apart, thereby turning us into objects. Heidegger's writings on technology and our understanding of ourselves in our age has much to offer in this regard. We are beings who relate to the world, but this relationship is who we *are* in our being, and not a case of me, on the one hand, and the world on the other. If we follow that path of thinking, as we have already encountered with Descartes, we take 'here' as internal, and the world as external, which then sets up a whole host of questions, including how the two are mapped on to each other, how and in what circumstances they might 'fail' to do so, and how we then understand such failures. On the last point, accounts that talk of psychosis, hallucination, dissociation, and so on, might be proffered by those inclined towards this way of thinking of the mind.

Heidegger says that Dasein's being is an issue for it (BT67). This is because the being of Dasein is 'in each case mine' (ibid.). Here we understand Dasein as self-relating or standing in its relation to being, or a 'comporting' towards its own being in its self-reflexivity. As Dasein, my existence is my very own, and it is incumbent on me, and no-one else, to take some kind of non-cognitive stance on it, even if I, so to speak, do nothing at all. I still fashion my existence out of this, since my kind of being binds me to having some kind of 'take' on it. Things that are not Dasein, such as a stone, or a piece of wood, or a house, lack this altogether. They have no sense of mineness because they are not able to be in this way. This comes down in part to the fact that they are not self-reflexive.

Perhaps to illustrate this in a more concrete, ontic, and familiar way, this can manifest in everyday life in more explicit and vivid contexts. Consider a situation in which a friend is being mistreated or disrespected by another person. As an onlooker, I feel angry, harbour a sense of indignation, and experience a tension of being both present as witness, but also a little detached and distant in this scenario.

If the situation becomes prolonged, I launch into some kind of accusation or vilification of the other person. As I do so, the focus changes from its being towards my friend to now being on myself. I feel the weight of my own self, or *my mineness* being at stake, and no longer in a position of solely representing my friend. In this case, I must take some kind of stand on *my* being, whatever I happen to do, whether I withdraw or become more involved in disagreement and argument with the other person. In having a sense of 'mineness' in the situation, this now calls on me to either be resolute, or fall into irresoluteness. That is, I face the issue of being either authentic or inauthentic.

Essentially, *what* I am is a human being, something that I have in common with others, but *who* I am is mine in an exclusive sense. In being mine, I can, in turn, own myself, or lose myself, or only seem to own myself, to the degree that I live in a way that reflects either being programmed or conditioned in my overall attitude and approach to life, or resisting this. To use another example, I can become so fixated on myself as a 'with it' person, taking it that I am always in step with the latest fashions, or identify myself wholly with having a successful career, to the extent that I take these as effectively defining who I am. I drift along, being led by these features of how I live, rather than acknowledging that they reflect only one of the many other possibilities that I have adopted for my life. I grasp that they are not necessary features of my being, and not definitive of me.

Fundamentally, then, Dasein is a practical kind of being, immersed in the world through activities of one sort or another. The tradition takes the opposite view as it approaches an understanding of the human being in theoretical terms. To adopt a theoretical understanding is to take a third-personal, detached stance towards ourselves, as if we are able to treat ourselves as objects, or self-subsisting substances. As a practical being, our being, which is existence, matters to us, such that we take a stand on that being. There is a certain way in which we take a stand on our being and the being that we are all the time though the kinds of activities in which we are engaged. I take a stand on being a therapist, for example. In doing so, so many things that I do in my numerous activities will reflect this in one way or another. This is not something I think about as I go about my daily activities, nor can I be said to explicitly identify myself in this way either. That is, no cognitive perspective has been introduced into this. It is simply manifest in everything that I do: how I approach each situation, and how I engage in certain matters for the sake of my clients and the world of therapy as a whole. It means that I sacrifice certain other activities and ways of life in order to take a stand on myself as the kind of being that I am, namely, in being a therapist.

To summarise, then, in rejecting the idea that we are understandable as theoretical entities, our kind of being is one that takes a stand on itself. That is to say, we are characterised by the relation that we have to ourselves. Whilst this says something very fundamental about us, we also exist in relation to others, as well as to entities in general. This does not discount the fact that we do sometimes fall into ways that take a theoretical stance with respect to ourselves. At such times, we can reflect on our own states and understand them as 'inner', or internal, with certain kinds of contents, such as beliefs and opinions. The Heideggerian challenge, however, is that this has traditionally been taken as the only stance that is possible or available for us. For Heidegger, the theoretical stance is only possible on the basis of the practical stance that fundamentally characterises our kind of being.

6.2.5 Possibility

Heidegger emphasises that what constitutes us as human beings, or Dasein, is not captured by a sense of ourselves as essentially fixed, or as actualities. For example, even though I am a therapist, this is simply a role or aspect of myself that I express through my continued activity in weekly encounters with clients, meetings with students, attendances at conferences, conversations and discussions with colleagues, and so on. I am deeply committed to this role, and take it seriously. It is who I am, insofar as it gives me a sense of identity, but it does not define or claim me, in an ultimate sense of who I am. Being a therapist is what shapes my adult existence insofar as it is deeply meaningful to me. But I hold this identity as a possibility rather than as a fixed, essential actuality about me. Were I, for some unforeseen reason, unable or unwilling to continue as a therapy practitioner and teacher, then I would experience a certain breakdown or disruption of my world, given that this has been the identity that has secured a certain meaning for me over time. But, as I break free of my former way of being, that possibility closes off, as other possibilities become available to me.

Some of the difficulties that we encounter or face in our lives are reflected in our ways of investing ourselves deeply in our world insofar as they give us an identity of our own. The potential challenge comes when we appropriate it in a rigidified way or take it to be who we essentially are as our core sense of self. We take ourselves and our world to be immovable and fixed, when we are, in fact, a constant possibility. It is not so much that such a way of relating to ourselves as essential and fixed is wrong or bad, since we experience a solid sense of meaning and understanding of ourselves as we live our lives. But this ultimately mischaracterises the kinds of beings that we are because we fall into a way of *mis*understanding ourselves as actualities. This misunderstanding carries the possibility of disclosing this to us when we face moments of crisis and breakdown.

I will return to the idea of possibility as an existentiale, namely, those aspects or features of Dasein that are essential to its existence.

Chapter 7

Dasein's Way of Being

7.1 Some Terms and Distinctions

7.1.1 Existentiale and Existentiell

Given the distinction between being and beings, or the ontological difference, as we have already encountered, any basic and ineliminable constitutive element of Dasein is, for Heidegger, an *existentiale*. An existentiale is a structural element or feature of Dasein's being. Heidegger identifies various existentiales throughout *Being and Time*, though he doesn't provide an exhaustive list that covers them all in their entirety. This effectively leaves us to reflect on those additional existentiales that we might consider in characterising Dasein, such as being embodied, or being centred, in the sense that Dasein is always actively trying, in one way or another, to 'optimise' or 'ground' its relation to situations. Certain terms introduced by Heidegger complement each other or align themselves in relation to the ontological difference. For example, an existentiale reflects the form of enquiry that is being carried out on Dasein, which is ontological, rather than when Dasein is considered as an entity, which is ontic. To repeat, when considered as an entity, it is the 'what' that is in question rather than the sense in which Dasein is intelligible at all in its being. An ontic enquiry therefore treats the entity under investigation as a 'what it is', whilst an ontological enquiry attends to Dasein in its being, or its 'that it is' (as anything at all).

As basic constituents of Dasein, all the many existentiales are lived in an *existentiell* way, or *existentielly*. For example, the way that I exist existentielly with regard to the existentiale that Heidegger calls *das Man*, commonly translated as the One or the They, is particular to my way of concretely manifesting this existentiale. Such a concrete way of manifesting this is ontic. I might, for instance, rigidly follow the various norms, practices, conventions, and customs in a way that reflects my behaviour of constantly fretting over the possibility that I have neglected or overlooked some expected way that I should act or behave; or I might be so dismissive of such norms and practices that I find ways to break or ignore them, including any social taboos that seem to me to be too constraining and unnecessary. Given that I am an interpretative being, I cannot remain indifferent to these existentiales, since my being is an issue for me, and this means that I have to take some stance or other on it.

DOI: 10.4324/9781003342137-9

From an existential perspective, then, it follows from this that the therapist can discern which of the many possible existentiales might seem most relevant or resonant to the client's situation as they present certain issues that they find disconcerting or disorienting, and then explore phenomenologically how the client has made such existentiales manifest in their own existentiell way of acting and engaging in the world. The purpose of the investigation is purely one of exploration, rather than pathologisation or correction, whatever guise that might take. As already mentioned, the investigation is ontological and ontic, or ontico-ontological, since our only human access to the existentiales is ontic; we can't access the existentiales directly, but only through a hermeneutic analysis. Nor is it epistemological, which would assume a knowing stance towards the client's way of being.

On a more general level, however, a Heideggerian approach to therapy offers a reflection on the way in which we all (given that we are Dasein and exist according to fallen modes of being) pursue ways of living that cover up or cover over what it is to be Dasein. We tend to conceal and obscure ontological aspects of our existence such that we fail to understand what it is to be, and take our everyday existence as what makes us distinctive in our being. This goes to the heart of the distinction that Heidegger makes between inauthentic and authentic ways of existing as Dasein. Inauthentic existence is reflected in a way in which Dasein's existentiales are taken up in the world. For example, the existentiales, being-with and solicitude, can be taken up existentielly in any number of ways. One might pursue a more directive approach in therapy by advising the client on how or what to do in a specific situation that has been troublesome for them. Such a way of being is inauthentic, as it covers over these existentiales by manifesting a way of treating the client as a thing to fix or remedy, much like a car engine, which misses the sense of being-with, for example, that is deeply human and not mechanical. Another therapeutic approach might involve a certain capacity to let the client find a way to be with their predicament, and to determine for themselves ways to take even small steps in reaching a resolution to the presenting issue. In other words, the therapist steps away from leading the client down any path, and instead holds the possibility for the client to take greater responsibility for making their own way, such that it invites or offers possible moments of discernment and disclosure. Such a way of being-with on the part of the therapist is authentic.

7.1.2 Inauthenticity and Authenticity

Inauthenticity and authenticity are Dasein's two modes or ways of being (BT68), says Heidegger, and of being-in-the-world. They each relate to the ways in which I address the issue of my being, that is, the mineness of my existence. In the everyday world, these two terms tend to be used in a moral context, whether we think of someone as good or bad, real or superficial, or genuine or flawed in some way or other. This is not what Heidegger has in mind here, however, because he is careful to avoid setting out an ethics of any kind. These ways of being therefore are not to be understood as being grounded in morality. Moreover, he is emphatic that one way of being is not superior or 'higher' than the other. Rather, these two terms relate to the ways that we have taken up the issue of our being. These ways of being are specific to Dasein, and not to the many entities that are not Dasein, such as animals, plants, or tables. What distinguishes Dasein from other entities is that it determines itself in its relationship to possibility, or potentiality-for-being (an expression covered later on).

Being a therapist can also be reflected in two distinct ways of being: inauthentic and authentic. In the former case, were I to pursue a way of being in sessions that adheres to the general consensus of what it is to work existentially, for example, because reference sources and books lay this out in considerable detail, then this reflects a falling into an inauthentic way of being an existential therapist. However, if I acknowledge that the issue of being a therapist is my very own, and that this calls on me to take a stance on my own way of being a practitioner, then I am authentic. This, to be clear, in no way ignores or invalidates the guiding principles of the accrediting bodies and professional associations of which I am a member. Rather, I address their ethical frameworks and standards of professional practice by taking the responsibility to clarify for myself the stance that I take towards them. The inauthentic-authentic distinction will be developed further as I address other aspects of Dasein's way of being. So, to summarise in brief, being inauthentic reflects how I deal with the situation that presents itself: treating it as a situation that falls into a generality. Being inauthentic is reflected in a certain way of living my life, such that I hold to certain routines and deal with situations as they arise in predictable and generalised ways.

7.1.2.1 Inauthenticity

Being inauthentic relates to drawing, or depending on the dictates of the One, such that one can be said to be One-self, rather than the self that is one's own. The idea of the One will be covered in greater detail later.

In this regard, a question for therapists might be: to what extent do we conform to the school of therapy that informs the way in which we practice, such that we follow the theories laid down by its major proponents, and to what degree are we opening up ways of working with clients that reflect our *own* path of thinking? Moreover, what is our stance in embracing the fact that we do not possess the ultimate answers, shortcuts, formulae, or nuggets of wisdom as therapists? This approach encourages a loosening of any possible hold towards theory, and an acknowledgement that it is our being and its presence, in its care-ing, that is central. In other words, how as therapists are we being inauthentic in the situation, or therapeutic situation, such that we entangle ourselves in questions related to how we *should* work as existential therapists? Such questions open the issue of authenticity rather than undermine the role or identity of being a therapist, but also point to the possibly over-rigid grip on established ideas that themselves are provisional attempts or indicators that characterise our way of being.

7.1.2.2 Authenticity

We commonly think of authenticity as a way of being honest and sincere, open and frank, much like a certain virtue that is reflected in our attitude and behaviour. In contrast, Heidegger means by this term a way of being that responds to the uniqueness of a situation. In doing so, Dasein is resolute. Rather than fleeing from ourselves and existing as a tendency towards falling, being authentic faces up to the situation. In other words, we encounter the uniqueness of the situation, and this calls us to respond in a way that is uniquely appropriate to it. As will be elaborated later, authenticity is a more complex term for Heidegger, given its temporal character.

7.1.3 Thrownness

Heidegger poses to us the challenging issue that what we have taken to be the person, or individual, or subject, is not who and how we fundamentally are, when we attend more closely to our everyday lived experience. When we consider the way in which we are very much unlike objects, one particularly striking aspect of the way we are is as movement, or dynamic, rather than as static. Translating this more directly to Dasein, I always find myself thrown or moved into situations and circumstances. Such moments are not chosen by me in advance, as if I pre-determine my being in a situation of my own choice. Our being thrown (*Geworfen*, literally translated as 'en-thrown'), then, is a core characteristic of what it is to be Dasein. As well as this, Dasein is always a 'thrower', always throwing forwards and beyond the thrown situation. Without this throwing aspect, I would be just like a stone or pebble, thrown into a pond, inert rather than 'there' in some way or other. But as Dasein, I find myself thrown into the moment, and also at the same time, I throw myself forwards and, in effect, beyond this thrown aspect. Such being both thrown and throwing is what constitutes this movement. When we return to the idea of the individual, or the person, or subject, nothing of this characterisation of Dasein so far described can be discerned when using such conventional terms.

Taking this into a therapeutic context, I see my client as Dasein, rather than in the accustomed way of being a person. In fact, in contrast to traditional ways of speaking, their being a 'client' falls away, as we both become immersed in our therapy session. I think of the other as the Dasein with whom I am engaged that exists as a living movement. Simon Critchley puts it aptly in terms of being caught or sucked into a turbulence as it projects itself forwards or beyond its situations and circumstances, only to then also fold back on itself (2002:155). This is, then, not a linear movement, one that goes from being thrown and then throwing, but is rather more like a constant turbulent movement. To put it more plainly, this translates into the client's very experience of living temporally and dynamically. As such, I do not relate to the client as a static object to study, and therefore simply ignore their being Dasein. Were I to do this as a therapist, I might fall into a way of assessing the possible ways in which the client fails or succeeds in living as a 'fully functioning person', as Carl Rogers expressed it (1961:183). Such an approach, however, reflects a failure to embrace and understand the client in their actual way of being, and, moreover, the meaning of their way of being, that is, how they have been and are addressing the issue of their being.

On the most general level, in our thrownness there comes limitation, since we are always thrown into a distinct historical world, namely, *this* world. This means that we are thrown into gender, as well as socio-economic and political paradigms and frameworks, for example, in and through which we live, such that everything becomes intelligible to us. The question is then one of realising that we can try to grasp these limitations in a way that allows us to relate to them either inauthentically or authentically.

7.1.3.1 Facticity

Thrownness is tied to another term that Heidegger introduces, namely that of facticity. This is based on the idea that I am not the origin or source of creation of my existence, or the world. In fact, on BT330, Heidegger mentions, with my own slight modification, that 'I *never* have the power over my ownmost being from the ground up'[1]. Incidentally, this is the very thing that Descartes thinks *is* possible for us to achieve, as he tries to demonstrate in the *Meditations*. From the moment that I am born, I have no say or ability to choose or decide which things and entities will show up in the openness that is the world. Rivers, buildings, as well as our families and relations, are already there, so to speak, and address us in a way that elicits a response from us. We interpret them in certain ways. For example, as I come to familiarise myself with my world, I eventually grasp the kind of entity that is before me as a tree, or the entity that is in motion as a car. That is, facticity always requires a response that involves an interpretative 'as' on our part in order to render it intelligible.

To put it bluntly, it all 'starts from' facticity. Facticity, or that which is given, also includes the finitude of Dasein: it is not something from which we can escape or avoid. In fact, inauthentic Dasein attempts to find ways to deal with this, whether through denial, distortion, or metaphysical lines of thought, for example, all of which reflect a resistance to an acceptance of its facticity. Facticity is what determines the being of Dasein, because it is thrown into a particular historical world, language, and way of life that relates to that world and not to another epoch. Dasein is always thrown 'away' from itself at the very outset of its existence, since it becomes acculturated into moral, social, and cultural norms and expectations as it engages with the world. Being away from itself means that it holds tenaciously to a compliant way of living, by absorbing those ways of acting and behaving that conform to the norms and practices in which it exists. This is an inauthentic way of being, because Dasein is not itself; it is a 'someone'. If Dasein is thrown away from itself, it has the possibility to 'get back' to itself, which he identifies as an authentic way of being. The second part (Division II) of Heidegger's *Being and Time* explicates the way in which this can happen. In getting back to itself, it throws off the tendency to interpret its own being from the being of entities that are *not*

Dasein. That is, it is no longer immersed in a ready-to-hand or present-at-hand way of relating to itself, but, rather, takes hold of itself in its own mode of being, which is existence.

7.1.3.2 Falling

This is a term that Heidegger uses to convey a form of inauthenticity that is reflected in the usual, everyday way in which we exist. We 'fall into' accustomed ways, norms, habits, stances when in situations and with other people, such that our actions, behaviours, and attitudes are in alignment with the general ways in which a culture and its practices prevail. We already fall into a queue at the supermarket checkout, for example, because that is the way in which we have already understood how we should conduct ourselves. This much is a way of dealing with our everyday world, and is not something that we can escape. However, a problem arises when we become overly compliant and think of this as the *only* way to deal with matters as they present themselves in situations. When we do so, we compromise ourselves in holding back from disclosing ourselves in our 'ownmost' being. A simple example might arise in our participation in group discussions, where we feel hesitant to offer our view on more contested issues. A certain withholding on our part then ensues. More widely, we fall prey to general ways of living in which we already draw on only one possibility, namely that which complies with the everyday way of dealing with matters. As such, Dasein has levelled down to those possibilities that are endorsed and considered 'normal' in a culture, even though such possibilities are themselves not explicit or foregrounded. In fallenness, Dasein can tend to absorb itself in being with others in a way that indulges in chatter over relatively unimportant things, as well as in matters that aren't 'close to home', in the sense of being easy distractions and novelties that actually present something that is superficial and merely intended to entertain. Heidegger refers to this as a kind of 'lostness', since Dasein is determined by these distracted ways of being. Putting it into Heidegger's own words,

> Proximally and for the most part the Self is lost in the "they". It understands itself in terms of those possibilities of existence which "circulate" in the "average" public way of interpreting Dasein today. These possibilities have mostly been made unrecognisable by ambiguity; yet they are well known to us.
>
> (BT435)

As Heidegger says, '[t]his term [i.e. fallen] does not express any negative evaluation, but is used to signify that Dasein is proximally and for the most part *alongside* the "world" of its concern' (BT220).

So, fallenness is not a morally flawed or devalued condition to which we have succumbed. Nor has it to do with a loss in status of some kind, as if being a 'lower' form of entity or human being. Rather, for Heidegger, we fall away from the possibilities that can be taken up in responding to the question of what it is to be human.

In fallenness, we become so absorbed in everyday activities and interests that ultimately distract us, such that we cut ourselves off from both a concern for the world and also a solicitous caring for other human beings. As we remind ourselves that to be human is being-in-the-world, we see that there is a tension or dissonance insofar as we are furthest from ourselves, existentially speaking, because our everydayness is inauthentic. Were we to grasp our authenticity, both in terms of understanding and in taking hold and committing to it, we could discern which of our possibilities are our own, rather than going along with those that society, or 'people', would validate, appreciate, and celebrate.

Falling is, therefore, a falling away from being authentic Dasein, according to Heidegger. The issue of fallenness and authenticity can be illustrated in the case of Heidegger's own life. He was destined to enter training for the priesthood as a young man, but eventually decided against it, much to his parents' disappointment and possibly even despair. We can speculate on several likely reasons for their reaction: Heidegger was a member of a pious, religious family; second, his father was the sexton of the village church; and third, becoming a priest, from the community's perspective, was considered a prestigious and laudable aspiration and achievement. In the face of this, Heidegger took hold of his possibilities, which eventually led down the path of becoming a philosopher, rather than losing himself in a communal or public way of interpreting himself. Such a decision required a certain resolve to face the situation and circumstance in which he found himself, rather than fleeing back into the 'they', or everyday norms and practices that ostensibly provide safety, direction, and approval. Doing so would have exacted a presumably heavy cost in deflecting himself away from the possibility of becoming authentic Dasein. Later, we will see how being authentic is brought to bear on us in the course of our everyday existence, when considered through the lens of Dasein's death, conscience, and guilt.

Given the previous example of Heidegger's decision to embrace his own possibility rather than one that had been handed down to him, broader reflections lead us to consider the way in which various institutions and their historical practices provide many of us with an understanding of what it is to be human, based on religious, scientific, and philosophical traditions, but which in fact can, and do, distort and mischaracterise our way of being. The underlying pull towards compliance and agreement, most significantly motivated by our being social beings, or beings who are constituted fundamentally by being-with (a term that will be explicated a little later on), means that this becomes ever more difficult to challenge and hold up to questioning and deeper reflection. Discourse itself perpetuates ways of introducing language that purports to make truth claims, when in fact it closes off other ways of thinking. This becomes acutely more difficult if we also remain seduced by the everyday chatter and distractions that take us away from the more important questions and issues that we face when addressing our being. The environment or setting into which we are thrown always entices us to lose or fall away from ourselves. But we also fall into this way of existing because we just take it that this reaches into the essential truth of what it is to exist. In this way, we are what Heidegger calls, 'tranquilised' (BT222), 'for which everything is "in the best of order" and all doors are open' (BT222). Such attempts at tranquilising ourselves is inauthentic, however, as it brings us to fall into an attitude and stance of complacency, and even assume a privileged standpoint with regard to other cultures that then takes it that we understand everything. In reality, Heidegger says, our falling being-in-the-world is alienating, because 'alienation *closes off* from Dasein its authenticity and possibility' (BT222).

As may be apparent by now, falling is not a deviation from some original pure state of being, but rather constitutes our way of being in a communal or collective context. We absorb a way of being that conforms to conventional ways of acting and behaving, rather than needing to design a template for living from scratch.

7.1.4 Care

As well as being a movement between both being thrown and throwing, the structural core of the client's very being is care. This is a crucially important term in Heidegger's thinking, as it is the very basis of Dasein's existence. In each case, being alive and existing (rather than not) is the most central issue for us, over and above everything else. This even underpins those moments and circumstances in which Dasein might contemplate suicide, since the issue of its own existence is the basis upon which it has its termination in view. My existence matters to me; as John Haugeland put it, Dasein 'give[s] a damn' (2013:xviii), which is not the case for tables, chairs, and spoons, for example. For all the client's various expressions of issues and challenges that they bring in the course of therapy sessions, underlying it all is the fact that their existence is at stake for themself. Nothing can shake this off, so to speak, by either deferring it, or somehow transferring it to someone else to take on, but, instead, is something in relation to which the client must take some kind of stand or other. To put it differently, the client 'leans into' the life they have in their own unique way, since life itself 'gets to them'. This is essentially what is meant by care here: it is a structural phenomenon, and not the sense of care provision, health care, caring for another, and so on. The difference here is reflected in Heidegger's pointing to the formal structure of Dasein rather than focusing on any content. When I am with my client, then, I relate to them as a being whose being matters to themself, ontologically speaking, or one whose very way of being and existing is enveloped in the various concrete expressions of mattering. I meet the client as such, rather than as yet one more self-enclosed entity, or 'count noun' (ibid.:9).

Heidegger describes this care structure as a three-fold unity. To repeat, since it is crucially relevant to care, Dasein's being is an issue for it, for as long as it exists. This is in contrast to the table, for example, whose being is not an issue, because its mode of being is not existence. It is important to appreciate this because it helps us to avoid understanding care as inert, static, and thing-like. Dasein is 'beyond' (BT236), or 'ahead' of itself (BT236), insofar as it lives in possibility, and is future-oriented. This is Dasein's 'being-ahead-of-itself' (BT236). Second,

Dasein has been 'delivered over to itself' (BT236), or 'thrown into a world'. This reflects its past-oriented character, since Dasein always already finds itself 'there'. Following Heidegger, to convey its unitary character, we express this in its hyphenated form, 'ahead-of-itself-in-already-being-in-a-world' (BT236). The third element of this unity reflects Dasein 'being-amid' things (my preferred translation) that are of relevance and consideration for it. Care is then 'ahead-of-itself-being-already-in-(the-world) as being-amid' (BT237). Heidegger uses the term 'concern' to convey the way that Dasein is being-amid, though we should read this as a way in which we always weigh up and assess what we need, or what is useful to us in various situations. For example, when I am shopping for food in my supermarket, I approach the fruit section and consider and assess which of the items look appetising to me, how much I should purchase, whether the price is a little steep, and so on. This is not the sense of concern that I might express in my worrying about things that could go wrong, for example, but a certain immersive dealing and reckoning with issues that arise in a situation. Whilst being-amid things is reflected in concern, and being-in-the-world is care, such care is also reflected in being with others, or Dasein-with, as Heidegger puts it (BT237). The form of care that reflects being-with is 'solicitude' (BT237). Heidegger quickly remarks that, since care is a structural phenomenon, it would be wrong to speak of 'caring for myself', since this mischaracterises care, but is also a way of relating to us as objects or things to optimise or manage. In other words, care in this sense is not about taking a certain attitude towards ourselves. Lest some terms are in further need of elaboration, these will be addressed further as we proceed in our account of Dasein's being.

To conclude, care is understandable only in terms of being-in-the-world. Considering this as a unitary phenomenon, Dasein's being is care because it is always already 'worldly' in the first place. To put it another way, care is a formal structure insofar as it is the way that we already stand out, engage, and act in the world. This includes, amongst other things, the ways in which we deal with things, with others, and with ourselves. This, to note in passing, is not incorporated into science because it conflicts with its principles of neutrality, objectivity, and impartiality. Science only operates on the basis that it controls the conditions under which it conducts its enquiries. But the human being cannot be understood in such a controlled environment. As well as this, it is only on the basis of Dasein's care that science is possible, because science itself matters to it, and us.

7.2 The Existentiales

Why identify the existentiales in the first place? Since they are each constitutive – and essentially so – of being Dasein, they bring us to grasp ourselves as the kinds of beings that we are. They also reflect our mode of being that is different to other kinds of being. This allows us to enter into an exploration of the way in which we express any one or other existentiale, and to see that existentiales themselves are not eliminable, or even ignored or disowned. In our being-with, or our disposedness or mood, for example, we deal with the world and others, as well as ourselves, in certain existentiell ways that reflect the existentiales in question. Keeping the existentiales in the forefront of our awareness assists us in presenting a more phenomenologically true account of ourselves, rather than a more abstracted metaphysical picture that distorts our characterisation of the human.

We should also note that there are privative or deficient modes in which an existentiale is existentielly manifest. The sense of 'deficient' here, however, is not to suggest that something is lacking in some way, but only that such modes are derived, or are parasitic upon the existentiale as a constituent of Dasein's being. This will now be the main focus of this section of the chapter, where I address a number of existentiales.

7.2.1 De-severance

De-severance is an existentiale, and reflects Dasein's 'circumspective bringing-close – bringing something close by, in the sense of procuring it, putting it in readiness, having it to hand' (BT139–40). Heidegger also adds, '*In Dasein there lies an essential tendency towards closeness*' (BT140). He says that, in all this, we are attempting to overcome remoteness, just as a baby might put something into its mouth. This, we might add, is only grasped in its existential sense. This is not a mathematical exercise in which we calculate or measure distances in order to then gauge how far or near something happens to be to us. Rather, we are in a dynamic relation to things and other people, and we often orient ourselves so that we can deal with the world in a 'hands-on' kind of way. We are absorbed in a circumspective concern in our situation and immediate environment, and we bring what is remote into nearness, which is de-severance.

7.2.2 Directionality

Directionality, an existentiale, reflects the way in which we are always directed or oriented towards those things and situations in the world that engage our attention, that preoccupy us or are relevant to our tasks and projects. Being in the therapy room has its own directionality insofar as I relate to my environment by being faced in a certain direction and setting myself down in my chair that faces another across from me. The project of engaging in therapeutic exploration with a client is made possible, in part, by orienting myself towards things in my environment, both spatially and temporally. This environment is both local – in this room – and also regional: the area or part of Europe in which this session takes place. More generally, directionality is a way in which Dasein orients understandingly towards things.

7.2.3 Being-in

Being-in, itself an existentiale, is constituted by three 'equiprimordial' elements, which are *also* existentiales: disposedness, understanding, and discourse. These complement the tripartite structure of facticity, existentiality, and fallenness.

Facticity refers to the fact that we have a particular constitution bestowed on us, as well as context, which is not of our choosing, but rather something into which we have been thrown. It is from our facticity that we project ourselves in becoming who we are. Existentiality reflects the fact that we live out our being-in-the-world rather than having a certain template or blueprint foisted onto us. In other words, our existence is not pre-determined in some way, such that we are marionettes being moved in determinate ways by a being or force that controls us. Fallenness is the way in which we are, at bottom, inauthentic, living according to everyday norms and falling into patterns and ready-made ways of acting and thinking.

7.2.4 Disposedness, Understanding, and Discourse

Heidegger uses these three terms differently to their usual meanings in everyday language. Moreover, the term 'mood' is the ontic – or concrete – sense of the term that Heidegger introduces, which is 'disposedness'. I will elaborate on this in the next section. Heidegger here is extending his phenomenological description of our being-in-the-world, which is reflected in the fact that we always already find ourselves in a certain disposition, mood, or a general 'atmosphere' in which we live; that we already have a practical understanding or grasp in going about our way 'in' the world; and that discourse is a particularly fundamental feature of our being. Richardson attempts to make this more accessible to us by naming them 'feeling', 'grasping', and 'wording' (2012:112), though I think that expressing them in this way poses the danger of overlooking or misapprehending the particularly important senses that Heidegger intends by his choice of words. It is, after all, in the very nature of the terms that he introduces that can tend to dislodge us from a certain familiarity with language, so that we experience our own disruptions and existential 'breakdowns' as we read him.

7.2.5 Disposedness and Mood

In Dasein's thrownness, it 'always already' finds itself being one way or another. Such 'finding' is reflected in the German term that Heidegger introduces, *Befindlichkeit*, which has been variously translated as 'findingness', 'attunement', and 'affectedness'. However, the most literal rendition that I have encountered is Haugeland's 'sofindingness' (2000:52), which is admittedly clunky even if it might convey well what Heidegger is trying to capture phenomenologically. Heidegger's articulation of this feature of Dasein is a focus on its ontological character. I will use the term 'disposedness', mainly because it can be more easily associated with talk about one's disposition. Think of the example of someone who lives a life of resignation: it colours the world in a certain way for them, such that everything that they encounter is flat in its meaning. Or consider someone who displays an open and welcoming demeanour in situations, and a readiness to participate. Both are caught in a certain way of being attuned to the world: one shows a resigned disposition, and the other a more receptive atmosphere in which they encounter things and other people as 'enlivening' to them. The overall sense of this existentiale, then, is its background sense of being disposed in one way or another, ontologically speaking.

Having introduced the ontological term, disposedness, Heidegger adds that our way of finding ourselves in disposedness is reflected in its ontic manifestation as mood. In other words, in our everyday dealings with others and the world, we fall into pervasive moods that might also be expressed in terms of particular feelings or more enduring emotions that reflect how we are already oriented in the world. Heidegger insists on talk about moods, rather than feelings and emotions, because his project sets out to overturn our traditional picture of subjective experiences set over against external objects. Feelings are therefore subjective and internal to us. Heidegger wants to reach a more fundamental description of how we find ourselves attuned in certain ways, such that they reflect our being-in-the-world:

A mood assails us. It comes neither from 'outside' nor from the 'inside', but arises out of being-in-the-world, as a way of such being.

Then:

The mood has already disclosed, in every case, being-in-the-world as a whole, and makes it possible first of all to direct oneself towards something. Having a mood is not related to the psychical in the first instance, and is not itself an inner condition which then reaches forth in an enigmatical way and puts its mark on things and persons.

(BT176)

The mood, then, is not in me, but rather, I am in a mood. It is a kind of comportment, as Dreyfus observes (1991:172).

Each mood or feeling can be understood in terms of its own phenomenological structure. From an everyday perspective, we grasp moods in ways that reflect the understanding that is already embedded in our social, moral, and cultural norms and practices. Certain moods that are reflected in our being in a situation can convey an inauthentic fleeing, rather than facing up to ourselves. Others, such as anxiety and boredom, are authentic or fundamental moods, for Heidegger. I will further elaborate on this in order to clarify this distinction.

7.2.5.1 Inauthentic and Authentic Moods

7.2.5.1.1 FEAR AS AN INAUTHENTIC MOOD

In *Being and Time* (BT179–182), Heidegger provides a first introduction to the phenomenological experience of fear. It is a deeply insightful, though brief and dense, account of this mood, which he distinguishes from alarm, dread, and terror. We might add the phenomenon of trauma to this list too. In his analysis, we witness his inimitable way of undertaking a deeply phenomenological investigation of fear, which, he says, bears three relevant elements: (a) that which is threatening when we fear, (b) the attitude of fearing, and (c) what it is we are afraid for.

(a) Heidegger points to several aspects that further describe the 'fearsome' that preoccupies us, that is, what makes it fearsome. First, it is detrimental in some way. Second, this detrimentality has a definite character, rather than being something opaque and indiscernible. Third, we grasp the location and source of this detrimentality, but at the same time, we encounter something strange and unsettling in what we 'receive' in our experience of it. Fourth, this detrimentality threatens us, though is not something that is within striking distance, as Heidegger puts it, but nevertheless menacingly close. This is what makes it threatening. Heidegger emphasises the tense character of that which is threatening in terms of its being close, or coming closer, and the uncertainty as to whether it will finally reach us or not, either by staying where it is or moving away. This deep uncertainty is what underlies and fuels the fear. We can imagine here being in the physical presence of a lion, and the way that this experience is captured through this phenomenological description. The lion can cause great harm to us; in that sense, its presence is detrimental to us. Its threatening character is amplified by the uncertainty and ambiguity of its spatial relation to us: it is close – too close for comfort, we might say – but our worry is: is it coming closer, or can it simply do so in any moment? Such a phenomenological account also includes an awareness of the possibility that the lion could just turn around and walk away, or run past us, instead of getting nearer.

(b) In the attitude of fear, being disposed to be 'mattering' beings is what then allows fear to manifest. We are always already disposed in a certain way of being attuned to mattering in the first place, since this is what fundamentally constitutes us. In other words, it is not the case that we encounter something as fearful, and then mattering follows. Rather, it is the other way around.

(c) We are afraid for ourselves, as Dasein. This is because Dasein's being is an issue for it, structured as it is by care. It is only on the basis of Dasein always being 'there' that fear is possible. In fact, fear itself reveals this mode of being that is being-there.

Heidegger continues his phenomenological description of fearing, noting that Dasein's being-in-the-world reflects other existentiales that relate most directly to the client's situation or circumstance. Those that he mentions include concern, being-amid, being-with, and being-in. In a therapeutic setting, the therapist listens, intuits, and explores with the client which of the possible existentiales are more pertinent to, and resonant with, the client's experience. In addition, a phenomenological exploration that takes place in the therapeutic dialogue allows for those elements of the experience to emerge in such a way that enables a distinction to be made between fear, alarm, dread, terror, and trauma, as well as, for example, 'timidity, shyness, misgiving, becoming startled' (BT182).

Later in *Being and Time*, as he takes us through a hermeneutic movement from the everyday sense of Dasein, to its existential-ontological character, Heidegger attends to the temporality of fear. Fear is reflected in a falling or inauthentic character, which does not by any means invalidate it as a mood, but only emphasises the way in which it is privative, or deficient, because of the way that it orients itself in relation to temporality. The temporal basis of fear will be explored in some detail in section 7.3.

7.2.5.1.2 ANXIETY AS A FUNDAMENTAL AND AUTHENTIC MOOD

Immediately following on from his account of fear, Heidegger focuses on anxiety. In his treatment of anxiety in Division I, however, we receive only a partial account of the phenomenology of this mood. Heidegger adds that it is a fundamental mood because it individualises us and illuminates the truth of our being-in-the-world. If we return to our way of existing in the everyday world, we are a self that is absorbed in activities and projects that we treat in a routine-like way. These are all familiar ways of spending our time. However, this way of living in the everyday is inauthentic, and is reflected in the way that we relate to ourselves as an Anyone-self, or some-one. That is, we never really pause for reflection or consideration to really understand what being a self actually means. Were we to do so, it would likely come from a settled place of comfort and ease. It would simply be a way of articulating who we are out of our pre-ontological understanding of how we cope in everyday life. For Heidegger, it is not from a normal course of events that we can come to understand ourselves, but in situations where a disruption, disturbance, or breakdown occurs. This is a breakdown in our world, or of being-in-the-world. The breakdown is a collapse of the way in which the world itself has usually manifested itself prior to the breakdown. The situation that manifests as a breakdown can be anything from the sudden ending of our career due to unforeseen circumstances, the termination of a partnership or marriage, adultery, a serious threat to our life, or other but relatively less significant experience. Our world falls through or asunder at such times, and we are exposed to an anxiety that overcomes us. Previously, we had felt 'at home' in the world; it was a smooth, predictable way of living that was marked by convenience and a sense of being able to deal with matters. Now we experience a 'nothing', or groundlessness, as we have nothing to 'hold onto', so to speak. No possibilities are apparent or visible to us in order to experience a way of coping.

The anxiety itself brings us to the realisation that we are beings who are 'in' a world, given that the breakdown illuminates moments or situations in which we are worldless, or 'out' of a world. Being worldless confronts us with ourselves, or what it is to be Dasein. Typically, when a career unexpectedly ends, we feel lost, not-at-home. We have lost the role or identity that gave us meaning when in our work-world. What we come to appreciate from this situation, therefore, is that, to be in the world means to have ongoing projects that give us a certain identity. We build skills, talents, and abilities around this role or identity such that we continually express possibilities for ourselves. That very world undergoing a collapse lights up the very being of a world in the first place, and the accompanying anxiety forces us to face the fact that our being-in-the-world is vulnerable to such collapse. It ultimately places the responsibility on us to face the question of how we choose to exist. This is because the world is contingent on our choosing to sustain it in its meaning and intelligibility, and not something necessary and invulnerable to collapse. In the light of the anxiety, we now realise that we can choose either to be inauthentic as an Anyone-self, by finding our way back into the everyday world, or we can own up to ourselves that our life is in our hands as an authentic self. Dasein now doesn't 'forget' itself, as it does in fear, because it takes hold of a definite possibility for itself. It is in this sense, then, that anxiety individualises Dasein.

7.2.6 Understanding

Understanding, as Heidegger introduces the term, is not the meaning that we commonly tend to attribute to it in everyday conversation. We usually talk about understanding something in a cognitive sense, when we grapple with the facts, engage in further reflection, and then eventually come to an understanding about something or other. For Heidegger, I grasp the possibilities of myself in a situation that reflects my existence. To use my supermarket example again, I enter the store, and move through various aisles in order to reach the gluten-free section. Once I have filled my basket with what I consider to be sufficient food for the next few days, I move to the checkout area, and wait in the queue. All this requires a futural, or forward-oriented engagement that enables me to project my possibilities. My shopping follows its own course, based on certain tasks and goals I pursue by taking action; another person takes their time, ponders over the items and looks for certain goods that I might find irrelevant to my shopping experience.

Understanding, therefore, reflects our grasp of the world, and our knowing how to go about it in the course of our being immersed in activities. Understanding is practical, but it is also pre-ontological, to reintroduce this term. That is, it is a primordial understanding and one that is only vague rather than explicit. If, for example, I open a door, I already understand, in this sense, that there is a floor that I walk over once I enter. In a similar way, I have a pre-ontological understanding of not having the capacity to fly, so I don't have projects and goals before me that involve jumping over buildings, for instance.

Understanding involves our ability to achieve tasks and engage in projects that are directed towards an end. This is all captured in the term 'for-the-sake-of-which'. But this understanding must also include a comprehension of what books are for, for example, if I am attempting to clarify or enquire further on some aspect of my goal to study Heidegger's work. So, I understand the possibilities of the book in its being ready-to-hand for a purpose or end that I have in view, namely studying. As well as this, I disclose myself in this understanding, since it is the way in which the meaning and significance of my being-in-the-world is revealed to me. I understand the significance of books, and how they fit into my world as a student, book reader or user. In that sense, this discloses me in my being a book user, and as someone for whom books matter. In what follows, I address other features associated with understanding , such as interpretation, articulation, and assertion, though Heidegger does not explicitly name these as existentiales. However, he does consider another feature of understanding, namely, meaning, to be an existentiale. The immediate focus is to now look at possibility, potentiality-for-being, and projection, which are all features of understanding, though only the first and last of these are named by Heidegger as existentiales.

7.2.7 Possibility

Possibility is an existentiale, and is an important aspect of our kind of being. As Heidegger says, 'Dasein is in every case what it can be, and in the way in which it is its possibility' (BT183). We make choices as to which possibilities we realise, or make actual. This is how we become who we are, instead of already being pre-formed in terms of a fixed and pre-determined nature. The possibilities out of which we realise ourselves are not unlimited, but constrained by our thrownness and our disposedness. These possibilities, however, are our *own*, even though we rarely recognise them as such. This is what characterises us as Dasein, which is the 'possibility of being-free *for* its ownmost potentiality-for-being' (BT183).

In summary, we project ourselves out of the choices we make from those possibilities that are available to us. In that sense, we *are* possibility, because our kind of being – existence – is one where we constantly choose which of those possibilities that are available to us to bring to their realisation, or actualisation. Polt summarises this succinctly (though with some slight modifications on my part):

> [I] am responsible for my own life. At every moment, I am following one possibility rather than a host of others... As I go on living, I build an identity. I become myself... In this way, it matters to me who I am... [I] determine [my] own existence.
>
> (1999:34)

Being human is not captured by defining ourselves in terms of actualities, such as we might do if we claim that who we are is something rooted in terms of past events, for example. Rather, who we are is established in terms of our possibilities. I am a therapist not because I am defined by the past, and particular actualities that have been embedded temporally over time, but rather by the way that I engage with my current possibilities of being a therapist. I am always transcending, or going beyond, actualities and projecting forward into possibilities. I am therefore a therapist insofar as this is an ongoing possibility for me. It is only when I stop being a therapist that it is an actuality. Perhaps it might be helpful to add here the difference between ontic and ontological possibility. Ontic possibility is reflected in my choosing to eat a salad for lunch, as opposed to chilli con carne. Ontological possibility is reflected in my *being* possibility.

7.2.8 Potentiality-for-being

This term has been translated in different ways, including, 'ability-to-be'. It reflects our way of being towards our possibilities. Rather than claiming ourselves as pure facticity, i.e., the impossibility of being otherwise than our thrown character, we have the potentiality, or ability, to be other possibilities. Prior to becoming a therapist, for example, I worked in the chemical industry for a number of years, which at the time I experienced as the only possibility for me to be. In this sense, my potentiality-for-being means that I am not simply one possibility. Potentiality-for-being is a central feature of our being, in that it reflects the fact that, as Dasein, we can pursue many different possibilities. However, our tendency is to avoid acknowledging this, or finding ways to deflect this truth from ourselves. Such potentiality-for-being is not unlimited, since I cannot be a host of ways to be that were possible in the past (such as a Centurion, or Gladiator), but are now impossible for me given the current cultural background into which I have been thrown.

7.2.9 Projection

Projection is an existentiale. We are always dealing with possibilities, and this is reflected in my projecting those possibilities that I want to bring into an actuality. To capture the sense of this, we can think of our *being* projective beings, unlike tables and chairs. I use the chair as a possible means to meet certain ends that I have in view, such as moving it into the dining area in order to accommodate another guest in my home. In the same instant, however, it is I as Dasein who projects my possibilities onto the chair, insofar as I am the *kind of being* who actualises possibilities onto it. By contrast, things and other non-Dasein entities are not constituted in this way. The possible error that we fall into is to think of this as something that we do, rather than *being* projective, which is what we are as we engage with possibilities. Being projective is future-oriented, but what it is that we actually project on is our *present* potentiality-for-being, not our future being.

We should also not confuse the two possible ways in which we use the word 'project' here. One is a verb – I project onto my possibilities – and the other is a noun, and refers to an overarching goal, proposal, or programme that usually extends over a protracted period of time. When we engage in the latter, it is the particular way in which we do so that comes to define who we are. In fact, Heidegger, in keeping with a consistent phenomenological thoroughness, clarifies the distinction, when he says,

> Projecting has nothing to do with comporting oneself towards a plan that has been thought out, and in accordance with which Dasein arranges its being. On the contrary, any Dasein has, as Dasein, already projected itself; and as long as it is, it is projecting. As long as it is, Dasein always has understood itself and always will understand itself in terms of possibilities.
>
> (BT185)

Projects or tasks determine the way that we relate to things and objects that we use in order to act for the sake of these projects. But it isn't only the projects' ends that are relevant here, but also the way in which the activities and actions that are reaching towards these ends disclose who we are as we perform those actions. On a more general level, how I live my life is itself based on the way I engage in my projects.

7.2.10 Interpretation

Interpretation is not explicitly identified by Heidegger as an existentiale, but simply the 'development of the understanding', as he puts it (BT188). In that sense, we can take it as a feature of understanding itself, as are articulation and assertion, which are covered in the next sub-sections. The easiest way to grasp what Heidegger means by this term is by way of an example. I am standing in an orderly queue in a supermarket. I have an understanding of what it is to queue, and I follow the norms for queuing accordingly. However, this understanding is implicit, and is in the background of my awareness as I go about finding my place in the queue. In the next instant, I notice that someone is trying to merge into the queue near the front. I am alerted to this scenario, and my very way of assessing the event is interpretation. I make explicit what was previously implicit in my understanding of a queue, such that my making it explicit is to interpret. In effect, interpretation illuminates what was inconspicuous in my way of being absorbed in being in a queue. It focuses on the matter at hand because an interruption or question or concern of some kind has now surfaced. Interpretation extends or elaborates understanding. Once such interpretation has been sufficiently or adequately expressed, or met its purpose, it withdraws again, such that understanding returns to its customary way of dealing with situations. Referring this to my example, once the queue returns to its orderly character, interpretation no longer requires making explicit the understanding of queueing.

7.2.11 Articulation

Articulation is the very elaboration of the interpretation, or the structure of being in a queue. For example, to articulate being in a queue is to bring out its ordering character, the temporal commitment to wait until it is one's turn to pay for items, the forward progressive movement as one nears the front of the line, its moral dimension based on mutual cooperation, and so forth. It is a form of further spelling out what has been already implicitly understood.

7.2.12 Assertion

Articulation can be made through making assertions, that is, speaking, even though articulation also includes the spelling out without speaking. In more Heideggerian terms, articulation without speaking is a 'saying'. Making assertions range from an utterance to a whole narrative, all of which articulate an interpretation. We should note here that making assertions are just one possible aspect of language, rather than the generally accepted, but misleading, sense in which language is usually described or defined in this way. Language is much more than making assertions, on Heidegger's picture, because assertions are particularly grounded in articulation, articulation is underpinned by interpretation, and interpretation is, in turn, founded upon understanding.

What should be apparent to us by this stage is that, in our grasping that interpretation narrows or focuses us in on what concerns us, assertion is a continuation of this focusing in that it then flattens or levels this concern to something that we then utter or speak, but in a more decontextualised way. To be sure, making assertions is a way of being-in-the-world, but it covers up the way in which various involvements and references to other aspects of the situation and tasks at hand are present. For example, to assert that 'This person is pushing into the queue' already constricts, reduces, and excludes much of our understanding of the world of shopping. This is an important point when we consider this in relation to the client's reflections and utterances in the therapeutic session. Heidegger's overall account of language, then, reflects a richer phenomenological picture than our usual way of thinking of language as communication or merely as assertion.

7.2.13 Meaning

Meaning is an existentiale. I understand the meaning of the queue when I grasp its possibilities for me. The meaning here is reflected in the queue providing me with various goods that then enable me to feed myself and provide me with various other pleasures and necessities once I arrive home. I grasp the meaning of the queue, in other words, when I understand how it fits in with the overarching project that I am pursuing at the time, namely sustenance and home comforts. The queue means something to me, in this sense.

Meaning is part of understanding since it makes the world graspable for us. As part of understanding, then, it is an aspect of projection, which is a disclosure both of the thing or phenomenon that we project upon, be it a queue or a cup or book, and also ourselves as Dasein.

7.2.14 Discourse

Discourse is the overarching term that Heidegger uses to cover all forms of 'articulation of the world in its significance' (Braver, 2014: 59). However, he makes a distinction between discourse and language. Language is the way in which discourse gets expressed (BT204). There are other ways in which we disclose ourselves through discourse and in being with others. Richardson uses the term 'talk', in its widest sense, to capture the way in which we are beings who are 'saying' something in our every movement, activity, task, or project, when we draw on signs, or show concern in various ways, for example. His view is that discourse is our capacity to mean out of our engagement in our social practices (2012:115). We might also find some sense of this meaning in the statement, 'Oh, that says a lot about him', in which the 'saying' of another person is simply the way in which they disclose themselves in their being in a social world, but that hasn't been explicitly asserted through speech. However, it seems true to say that discourse is perhaps what drew Heidegger to poets, because words, assertions, and statements only capture phenomena to a certain degree. Discourse includes language, but can go beyond it insofar as it reveals the intelligibility of being-in-the-world. If we take the case of poetry, it discloses being human in a way that goes 'beyond words', as we are inclined to say. We only have to consider poems such as Naomi Shihab Nye's 'Kindness', for example, to appreciate the way in which it leaves its reader with a sense of our own life being felt deeply when it is received with gratitude by us (Nye, 1995). But this is only possible if we immerse ourselves in the poem as discourse rather than in its mere words.

Since discourse usually manifests itself in language, we tend to think that we articulate ourselves through one tense or another at any particular time. For example, when I tell my friend that I will be going to the theatre this evening, I take it that I express myself in the futural tense. However, this use and expression of tenses is only possible on the basis that language is simultaneously open to the three temporal ecstases all at once. In my utterance that I will be going to the theatre, I also invoke the other tenses, because I express my current position at the same time, which is also reflected in a particular mood into which I am thrown (pastness), be it one of excitement or reluctance or uncertainty. Any discourse therefore unites all the ecstases in what it expresses in words and language. This means that discourse unites understanding, disposedness, and falling, given that we, as Dasein, are projection, thrownness, and fallenness.

7.2.15 Worldhood

'World' here simply refers to a context or horizon of significance, or meaning, where actions, projects, and practices are relevant to that context, rather than being some kind of global container in which we are placed or positioned. We are always dealing with the world and its environment, typically coping, being immersed, and getting around in ways that preoccupy us with others, things, and the numerous aspects of life that confront us as we go about our daily business. This never stops, even when we are at rest and repose, or withdrawn from the worldly affairs that usually absorb us. The world still 'worlds', or is worlding (away), since this is fundamentally constitutive of being Dasein. To remind ourselves, a table has no world that constitutes its way of being. We typically speak of the business world, the world of theatre, or the therapy world, which reflects what we mean when our involvement is 'worldly'.

Following Spinosa, Flores, and Dreyfus (1997:17), a world is essentially constituted by three elements:

1. equipment
2. identity, role, or self-interpretation
3. tasks, activities, and projects.

7.2.15.1 Equipment

As already introduced on p. 14, in terms of the ready-to-hand mode of being, I elaborate on this a little more to extend the account of equipment.

Taking a book as an example, we use it to engage in thought as we immerse ourselves in the ideas being presented. The book is 'equipment', and it is enmeshed in an interrelated web of other equipment, such as my extending my understanding of therapeutic practice using various sources in social media, attending therapy conferences on certain topics being presented, discussions with colleagues on approaches to therapy, my drawing on this as a way in which I then approach my way of working as a therapist, and so forth. But I only encounter and engage with the book insofar as it is related to all the other relevant equipment, including those just mentioned, such that it forms an equipmental whole, or totality. This means that there is no 'an equipment', as Heidegger emphasises, because it loses its sense of what it is to be equipment in the first place by isolating one item from others. It is important to see equipment in terms of an integral whole, and not as a collection of items that are independent of each other. Heidegger employs the term 'equipment', because it is used to engage and involve ourselves in activities, tasks, and projects that are meaningful, and matter to us. When engaged, this is reflected in the existentiale, being-in, of which there are three equiprimordial elements: disposedness (ontically, mood), understanding, and discourse. This has already been covered on pp. 55–61, but here, Dasein is oriented in this world such that it engages with certain entities that are relevant and 'light up' that world. If, for example, I brought a hammer in to my room whilst reading, it would fall outside that world in which I am immersed, and surely would not cast any light on the therapeutic process. If I insist that the hammer is relevant, then there is a question over the way in which I am being-in. If someone else insists that I bring in the hammer as relevant to questions about therapy, we might say that this constitutes an existentiell breakdown in being-with, but can also bring about anxiety, which then illuminates a breakdown of another kind. Breakdowns are addressed in some detail later, but also where additional comments are appropriate as we proceed through this book.

The book's being, in our encountering it as such, 'frees' the book, as Heidegger puts it, so that it can be seen as a book for reading. Prior to this, it was on a bookshelf, and merely a thing. Its *being* was brought to view when it was lit up in being appropriated for reading. When encountered and used, it is ready-to-hand, which is the mode of being of the book when being read. Of course, if I were to use the book as a doorstop, it would still be treated as ready-to-hand, but we might say that this is a privative mode of its being a book, since a book is 'most' a book when being used for reading. As ready-to-hand, I also already take the book *as* a book; that is, I understand this entity as a book in order to then bring it into use. The notion of reading is already with me before I go on to apprehend the book I wish to read. For Heidegger, this is because the totality of assignments and references are already set up in a way that brings such a meaningful world to show itself in the first place. The book is appropriate for reading because it has been assigned or referred a purpose so that it is available for reading. We understand, or equate, availability with the ready-to-hand mode of being of the book. Any assignment or reference also reflects involvement in a task or project that is meaningful; involvement, we should keep in mind, is central to readiness-to-hand. What Heidegger means when he says that something has been 'freed' for its being is in its being available – freed – for its involvement in a task or project. The entity now has a use, which it did not have prior to the moment in which it was freed for such use.

The ready-to-hand, then, is the mode of being in which a thing becomes available for its involvement in some meaningful activity that has an ultimate purpose (or for-the-sake-of-which). In all this, Heidegger wants to convey the fact that there is a structure to the ready-to-hand, which is the assignment and reference of an entity that becomes appropriate for its involvement towards fulfilling some project or task. It is a holistic, in other words.

The expression 'ready-to-hand', in the sense of the mode of being of equipment, prompts us to identify its direct reference to embodiment, namely, that of the human hand. But, in light of this, we should also consider again the relevance of the previously mentioned floor over which we walk. Since being ready-to-hand reflects an entity's availability, it is perhaps more appropriate in this instance to speak about the floor being 'ready-to-foot'. In fact, more attention could be given to the way in which the foot becomes significant in relation to other things or entities that are available for our use in other respects. For example, I take a stand, or I am my own ground, or I can feel disoriented when I lose my foothold in the world. If anything, these take on a more significant existential relevance, although being able to act in the world usually depends on taking hold, using and manipulating things towards certain desired ends. In that sense, the hand becomes more relevant in terms of realising one's own meaningful projects than the foot, which is not commonly associated with manipulability.

7.2.15.1.1 INVOLVEMENT

Perhaps it is worth pausing here to introduce the idea of involvement. This has a particularly existential character, since it also relates to the issue of being engaged in, about, or with relevant tasks and projects, but that could, in any moment, fail or collapse. There is no guarantee that the task or project will be carried out to completion, or completed satisfactorily. In that sense, disruptions and breakdowns are possible. However, in the main, Dasein is characterised in its way of being involved. Its involvement in a task or activity means that it requires it to assign or give something or other a role in order that it then becomes a meaningful entity in relation to the task, activity, or project. In this respect, Dasein is involved: it has to do the required assigning, like a pen being assigned for the task of writing the letter. As well as this, Dasein has to be immersed in a project in the first place, so that the entity – a book, or a car for a taxi driver, say – can be assigned to it meaningfully. This meaning can only arise where Dasein and the situation, task, or project are involved. Going back to my example of reading the book, first, I am involved in assigning a meaningful role to the book that I have selected for reading: it is something that I have to do, otherwise any book would suffice. Second, my task of wanting to prepare a presentation at a meeting with colleagues, or the more general project of identifying ways of working with clients who express unease in their being-in-the-world, means that the book now has a place in this project: it is the appropriate book for this, and not some other.

Whilst Heidegger brings out the fact that involvement pertains to ready-to-hand entities in terms of their being, I have endeavoured to highlight the way in which this also relates to Dasein itself. Any exclusive and extended focus on Dasein in its involvement per se in *Being and Time* might well have compromised his overall project, and also presumably have drawn criticism for lapsing into an anthropological, anthropocentric, or too subjectivistic account, rather than a reflection of being-in-the-world. However, Heidegger is attempting to convey the way in which we are absorbed in activities and tasks, rather than standing out and apart from our environment, and then taking this as the focus and starting point of our analysis. In other words, he wants to carry out a fundamental ontology – what it is to be as anything at all – which is completely at odds with a Cartesian account of being as substance. Whilst grasping the importance of this, I think that it is also important here to explicate the role of Dasein in such phenomena as involvement, references, and assignments. Whilst the ready-to-hand is a mode of being, for instance, it also expresses something 'handy', and this reflects the embodied being of Dasein. The ready-to-hand is handy insofar as it is equipment that is assigned for certain purposes. But this all happens in a world in which Dasein is 'doing' the assigning, given the purposes that it has in view. In other words, Dasein's assigning is a 'hands on' engagement with the world, and this means that it relates to things as ready-to-hand when being assigned for involvement in a particular task.

7.2.15.2 Identity, Role, or Self-interpretation

Bringing Dasein into this account reflects the fact that, when we speak of a world, a second inescapable feature necessarily emerges: that of the place of Dasein in the world. A world is constituted by roles and identities, or self-interpretations, without which a world makes no sense. For example, Dasein finds itself in a meaningful role as a therapist, and this is a constitutive factor that both announces and sustains a therapy world. As a therapist, I engage in my work as both ontological possibility for as long as I take on this identity, as well as ontic possibility, in making concrete choices as to how I arrange certain relevant activities during the day, for example.

The roles we appropriate can be lived in a diverse number of ways. For example, I might be absorbed in a project but feel that I am way out of my depth, and so relate to myself in this role or identity as, say, an impostor. Alternatively, I might take this role to reflect exactly who I essentially am, whether as a salesman, or engineer, or therapist. Roles that are taken up require a significant degree of appropriation and commitment to 'be' the person with this identity, otherwise such a role becomes simply performative. This is the case with J, a 24-year-old science graduate who started working in a research laboratory for a large oil company upon graduation. As a student at school, he had no inclination or passion to study science but had simply gone along with the advice that his parents and family members had impressed upon him at the time. He lacked any interest in this, which subsequently showed in his work as a graduate science researcher. When asked what he did for a living, he would prevaricate, hesitant to declare himself as someone who worked in this field. In his spare time, he found an appetite and passion for literature, and decided to take up related degree studies on a part-time basis while working. The course consumed him, igniting a certain enthusiasm for Latin American novels that now overwhelmed him. The sense of being overtaken by something that now came from himself rather than others culminated in advanced studies, and, eventually, a scholarly aptitude for teaching on the subjects that were close to his heart. Eventually, he managed to secure tenure to teach at university level and pursue a path that would have been unimaginable in the earlier part of his life as a scientist.

7.2.15.3 Tasks, Activities, and Projects

The third element of a world involves and includes goals and projects towards which Dasein is directed. We absorb ourselves in meaningful projects through our skills and acquired practices for dealing with things and other people that are relevant to being engaged in those projects. In this way, entities show up in the world in different ways according to their relevance for us and our projects. At times, they show up as tools that we can use to assist us towards achieving our ends, and at other times, they are there for us to observe and assess for whatever purpose in a way that is also relevant to our projects.

In the case of a mode of being that is not constitutive of the world in Heidegger's sense of the term – in contrast to that previously mentioned, namely, Dasein's involvement and the mode of being that is the ready-to-hand – certain situations break down or are encountered in alternative ways. In such cases, Dasein no longer encounters entities in their ready-to-hand mode of being, but instead, in their present-at-handedness. This the mode of being of objects, or entities that have been 'de-worlded'. That is, we attend to the thing by isolating it from its connection to other things. For example, when I am in a therapy session with a client, the clock, the seats, the light in the room, and the closed door are all interrelated into a whole, and are inconspicuous, that is, never come into my awareness as I engage in dialogue. However, should the light start flickering for some reason, I am distracted, and I then 'de-world' the light bulb from the whole, thereby isolating it as I try to determine the nature of the problem that is giving rise to its malfunction. The present-at-hand contrasts itself with the ready-to-hand insofar as it is conspicuous, obtrusive, and obstinate, whilst the ready-to-hand is inconspicuous, unobtrusive, manipulable, withdrawn, and reliable. To emphasise the distinction again between these two modes of being, when absorbed in our world, entities that are relevant to our activities are ready-to-hand, such that we are engaged in what we are doing. By contrast, our relation to present-at-hand objects is in our being disengaged.

7.2.16 The Who that is Being-in-the-world

For Heidegger, the 'who' that is Dasein maintains itself, or persists, in its being-in. In this sense, it is not characterised as an existentiale by Heidegger, but is an important element to understanding existentiales such as being-in and being-in-the-world. This 'who' is the 'I': 'Dasein is an entity which is in each case I myself; its being is in each case mine' (BT150). Heidegger stresses that this 'I' is an indicator of an 'ontologically constitutive state', and that it is also ontic, insofar as it is *this* entity, and not another (BT150). He also recognises the different ways in which we commonly refer to the 'who', as the 'I', the 'subject', and the 'self' (BT150). The 'I' maintains itself, he says, throughout the various changes in its experience and ways of behaving, as it lives its life, such that it has its own self-identity. This seems to me to convey a phenomenological truth about us, in contradistinction to the stance taken by the French post-structuralists, who think that the self can simply be dissolved or cancelled out of our discourse about ourselves. To put it bluntly, we can't 'get away' from ourselves, since we are being-in-the-world. There always has to be an experiencer of the world in order for the world to show up at all. This is what makes it possible to construe the 'I'. Heidegger is not suggesting any content to the 'I', only that it is formal, and also indicative, as he stresses on BT150. This reflects again his approach to enquiry that he names as formal indication. The 'I' simply indicates or picks out the person in question.

Heidegger is emphatic that the 'I' is not to be conflated or confused with a present-at-hand way of thinking of the self. This takes the 'I' as a thing with a particular essence. As such, it misses or ignores the fact that we exist, and live our lives temporally, rather than being static objects that move through space and time as if pawns on a chess set. So, we are neither a thing, nor substantial. This goes to the heart of Heidegger's project, which is to explicate in some detail how we exist, rather than occupy space and time as mere objects. In the course of everyday living, we deal with situations, things, and others, such that our self temporally 'endures', from a dynamic perspective. However, in our ready-to-hand encountering things in the world, we already see how others, or other 'I's are implicated in what we are dealing with at any particular time. For example, the shoes that I wear already conveys the fact that at least one other person in the world has made this footwear. Heidegger is trying to show how we assume an encased 'I' that then reaches out to a world of others, when in fact, we always *already* encounter a world with other selves.

7.2.17 Others

My focus on others is relevant insofar as it relates to the existentiale, being-with, and in particular, being-with-Dasein, or Dasein-with. From a phenomenological point of view, in my everyday world my immediate tendency is to never actively distinguish myself from others, unless a situation alerts itself in some way as challenging or unsettling for me. The underlying experience that I have of others is based on the sense that we are all like each other: '[others] are rather those from whom…one does *not* distinguish oneself – those among whom one is too' (BT154). That is, I share my being-in-the-world with others who are like me, insofar as they, too, are being-in-the-world.

7.2.18 Being-with

Being-with is an existentiale that is reflected in a kind of being that is always involved in the world and with other Dasein whose being is being-with. To reiterate, Dasein is constituted such that being-in-the-world is a with-world that is with-others, and not an isolated being from which it then reaches out into the world and relates to the world and others. The existentiale conveys something particular about our kind of being that is starkly contrasted with things. Heidegger puts this well in the following passage:

> When others are encountered, it is not the case that one's own subject is *proximally* present-at-hand and that the rest of the subjects, which are likewise occurents [that is, also present-at-hand], get discriminated beforehand and then apprehended; nor are they encountered by a primary act of looking at oneself in such a way that the opposite pole of a distinction first gets ascertained. They are encountered from out of the *world*, in which concernfully circumspective Dasein essentially dwells.
>
> (BT155)

Here Heidegger is articulating Dasein-with as a more specific kind of being-with. To state differently what has already been said, others are encountered neither as present-at-hand objects, nor subjectively, as if we start from our sense of ourselves and then reach out to others outside us. This is not the way that 'concernfully circumspective Dasein essentially dwells', because it takes an approach that both ignores the world, and also assumes a reflective, Cartesian position that does not access everydayness itself. Since we are in the same world, and are like each other, we dwell and engage with each other concernfully in a 'primordial soup', so to speak.

Being-with is central to therapeutic discourse, both in its relevance to the client's way of relating to others, but also in terms of the relation between therapist and client. This has been generally acknowledged in many therapeutic orientations, particularly those approaches that place relatedness, relationality, or relation at the centre of their theory. However, such therapeutic approaches tend to miss the existential sense of being-with, since they remain in a subject-object-oriented Cartesian way of thinking, and so 'do' the relation rather than see it as a mode of being that necessarily withdraws, so to speak. Existentielly, therapists might talk about the relationship that they have with clients, but should be wary of even inadvertently eliding this with a technical or technological or technique-oriented understanding of this feature of being.

7.2.19 The One[2]

The existentiale that Heidegger describes as the One, the They, or Anyone, as various translations of the original German, *das Man*, is the basic way in which we are inculcated and socialised into everyday norms, conventions, customs, and socio-cultural practices to which we generally adhere and conform, without even really being aware of the degree of conformity that we disclose in this way of being. A certain accustomed way of thinking and doing things becomes perceived as the only possible way to do things and to exist, i.e., according to norms, and to be defined by them. In other words, there is a kind of background standard that operates in terms of 'how everyone does this or that', or 'this is how one does this', that this is the 'done way' to go about whatever tasks, activities, or projects we pursue, but more generally, in the very way in which we live in the everyday world. The 'all', or 'one' that is intimated here, is an 'everyone' that exerts an anonymous pull over each of us, much like a magnetic attraction, without our being able to point explicitly to any actual collection of human beings as the central source for this. The sense of this 'one', or 'everyone', has no specific size attached to it, though it suggests a certain mass that impacts on us such as to comply with its injunctions. As such, it has no specificity, given that there are no members that we can point to who are assembled in the mass or group. In this sense, it is abstract, and presents itself as a kind of image in which we then take our place. Such injunctions might include not talking loudly in a library, joining an orderly queue for a taxi, eating in a certain way when in company with others, or even following certain conventional lifestyles.

The everyone, and its injunctions, constrains or modifies our behaviours in certain ways to the extent that it dictates the way that we exist, or identify ourselves as selves. We speak, dress, eat, and express ourselves on the basis of what is becoming for a person of our age, or profession, or membership of a social or family group to be broadly deemed acceptable. In short, we find ourselves in a homogenised cultural whole. This homogenisation shows itself in two ways: first, we are levelled, and second, we are immersed in averageness. Other terms that characterise this existentiale are publicness, distantiality, the One-self (or Anyone-self), lostness, and accommodation (BT166). In all this, should we lose sight of its primordiality, Heidegger says that the One 'belongs to Dasein's positive constitution' (BT167). In summary, we see Heidegger yet again conducting a thoroughgoing phenomenological description that brings out the finer aspects and nuances of this existentiale.

7.2.19.1 Levelling

Levelling is related to everydayness. It also links to averageness. Since we, first and foremost, encounter difference and diversity in the world, our tendency is to configure all difference into the 'same'. One possible understanding of this is that it creates a stability, and a commonality that reins in chaos and uncertainty. However, at the same time, it artificially marks out categories, much like the *Diagnostic and Statistical Manual of Mental Disorders, Fifth Edition* (DSM-5) and the *Tenth Revision of the International Statistical Classification of Diseases and Related Health Problems* (ICD-10) classifications that operate in the medical and psychiatric professions, and which can then be used to assign a person to such categories or classifications. Whilst wholly different in many respects to its use in medical and psychiatric applications, something akin to this also occurs in the domains of social, cultural, and economic life. For example, we might commonly gather various details about someone being a middle manager from an upper middle-class background, a university graduate, extrovert, sociable, intelligent, and ambitious, that tends to already encourage a certain assumed understanding of the person. In levelling, we can also record the ways in which we introduce certain qualifications, when we 'level down', or 'level off', by simplifying or even devaluing others in some way, so as to feel that we are firmly and securely enmeshed in our everyday world.

7.2.19.2 Averageness

Averageness is a way in which our membership of the group or community is firmly rooted in its values, i.e., what it takes to be good or bad, right or wrong, and the norms that it imposes. It also suggests a compromise of sorts, since certain behaviours have to be reined in and balanced out, or diluted, in order to fit in with what then becomes the 'average' way to be. This can feel satisfying, of course, but there may also be times where this becomes frustrating and can even escalate to a sense of resentment, or a feeling of anonymity. In such cases, the possibility of breakdown situations can emerge, and might also be central to clients' presenting issues that reach across many aspects and domains of their lives.

7.2.19.3 Distantiality

Distantiality, as covered in BT164, is a way in which we relate to others by being aware that we can deviate, or fall away from, a sense of belonging to the group or norm that binds and grips us. This can be exemplified in situations where we express a particular opinion at a general meeting, or in a student group, which might be met with a stony silence or disagreement. In this sense, our discomfort and sensitivity to any such deviation reflects our determination to avoid a disruption or breakdown of our place or membership in the group, with the feeling of being thwarted in our ability to conform to the norms that dictate the way to be in the world. Taking the German term that Heidegger uses here, it reflects a lack in constancy, because we fall into the dictates of these norms and therefore move in accordance with the edicts, fashions, media pronouncements, and comments made by those considered to be authorities in their fields. Our stance can therefore even alter from one day to the next, as we attempt to 'keep up' with these norms, rather than maintaining our *own* stance that confers on us a certain constancy. This distinction between a lack of constancy and constancy overlaps with the two ways of being Dasein, namely being inauthentic and authentic.

7.2.19.4 Publicness

Heidegger says that publicness is 'the specific disclosedness of the 'they' (BT210), One, or 'everyone'. In our being-in-the-world, we are absorbed in certain cultural and social norms that are public in character, or in public 'view'. In more concrete terms, we already grasp the idea of being an engineer, an academic, or having a career, because these all make sense to us in our everyday affairs and our reckoning with the world. We already take for granted that these roles and ways of engagement are commonly understood by us all, such that we never pause for reflection or questioning about the way in which these phenomena are constituted worlds that are shaped and cultivated through conventions and practices, and are established by common or public agreement. Where our world becomes disturbed or breaks down, we gain a deeper sense of insight that we live, in effect, according to a constructed set of rules and norms, and that they are prone to change over time, rather than being necessary, sacrosanct, and inviolable. Under those circumstances in which we realise that they can be challenged and questioned, we throw off the 'conditioning' that has immersed us in this public sense of the One, thereby acknowledging the world *as* world, in its more temporally fragile and vulnerable character:

> If Dasein discovers the world in its own way and brings it close, if it discloses to itself its own authentic being, then this discovery of the 'world' and this disclosure of Dasein are always accomplished as a clearing-away of concealments and obscurities, as a breaking up of the disguises with which Dasein bars its own way.
>
> (BT167)

Previously, in our absorbed immersion in everydayness, the world is taken as constant, enduring, and unchangeable, such that it is taken for granted. In such absorption, in Heidegger's terms, we are in the inauthentic mode of being Dasein, whilst the 'retrieval' of the world is reflected in authentic Dasein. What is clear from this is that public notions of, say, race, gender, politics, or education obscure our own understanding of ourselves and other human beings, since we can only 'see' ourselves and others through the public lens through which we grasp these notions. In other words, I see myself as white, heterosexual, and Caucasian only because these terms and ways of relating to myself are already and everywhere pervasive in the public arena.

Inauthentic Dasein, in being absorbed in the publicness of the One, is 'disburdened' (BT165). It is both disburdened *by* the One, and disburdened *of* its being. Its being, in other words, is taken over by the One, such that Dasein is alleviated from having to reckon with its agency. As Heidegger says, on BT165,

> the One...deprives the particular Dasein of its answerability ... [such that the One] can be answerable for everything most easily, because it is not someone who needs to vouch for anything. It 'was' always the 'they' who did it, and yet it can be said that it has been 'no one'.

In effect, we surrender to the publicness of the One our responsibility for who we are, so that we become 'anyone' rather than 'my own' (self). At the same time, the publicness of the One, as everyone, is pervasive, and so to speak, 'invisible': to think that we can take hold of it is to mischaracterise it, since it is also reflected in a certain pervasive mood in which we live. As we lose ourselves in the world, then, we absorb ourselves in publicness. We become the roles that we take on in our existence, as well as behaving in accordance with what is deemed acceptable, or 'normal', by the world in which we are immersed.

7.2.20 The One-self, They-self, or Anyone-self[3]

Our predominant way of being-in-the-world is the self that is absorbed in the average everyday activities and projects with which it is preoccupied. The particular form of the self that Heidegger names in this case is the One-self, They-self, or Anyone-self, as opposed to a my-self. This is reflected in the Anyone-self's inauthentic way of being, whilst being authentic is reflected in owning myself. Inauthenticity and authenticity will be given further attention as we proceed.

The One-self is not somehow deficient, or 'less' than the authentic owned self; rather, both are ways of being-in-the-world, and do not admit of degrees or hierarchies. This is because being-in-the-world is an existentiale, a constitutive feature of Dasein, as is the One, which, among many other existentiales, is precisely what it is to be human. What is distinctive about authenticity, however, is that it is, as Heidegger says, an existentiell modification of the One. In other words, it is not *itself* an existentiale. So, being an Anyone-self is how we happen to exist for most, or almost all, of the time. We are not cast into the world as authentic beings, who then somehow lose this in publicness. Rather, it is in publicness that we exist from the outset.

What is also distinctive about the Anyone-self is that, since its existence is dictated by everyday norms and practices, it conducts itself in a way that allows such norms and practices to determine or define who it is in and through its behaviours, acts, thoughts, ways of seeing the world, and so on. In other words, it deflects and defers the responsibility for its existence by taking up possibilities of its own, and instead draws on those possibilities that are readily available and already determined through the One.

This self that conforms, and understands itself through everyday norms and practices becomes opaque to itself, or obscures what it is to be Dasein. To take just one example of such obscurity, it distances itself from its own mortality. The obscurity is brought about through the One's dictates that one's death is an event in the far-off future, and that it is considered morbid and strange to dwell on it in the present. Doing so would invite anything from consternation to admonishment that this is not, in some way or other, helpful or 'normal'. Where it is commonly spoken about, it is expressed as a 'passing away', 'gone to sleep', or 'having left us'.

A simple example might illustrate the ways in which norms have a profound impact on who we are. Growing up as part of a Southern European family in London, UK, M moved into secondary education from the age of 11 onwards, and experienced an increasing sense of having one foot in two worlds, or living in two very different cultures and ways of behaving. One was the world of being with English friends, both inside and outside school, and the other was the very different world of the family and the wider circle of the community with which the family engaged. Over time, M felt a certain pull towards belonging in one world during the day, with more nuanced ways of behaving, and a particular other pull towards being quite different when at home with the family, relations, and the wider circle of others in the community. Differences were also expressed in a certain comportment, including various mannerisms and ways of temporalising the world. One was relatively well-ordered and disciplined, whilst the other was spontaneous and relaxed in relation to structuring time and being with others. In this sense, M's way of being was inevitably submerged in the norms, customs, and cultural expressions embedded in each world, but one in which marked differences evoked tensions when both worlds occasionally collided.

7.2.21 Solicitude

Solicitude is an existentiale, and is our way of being with others. It expresses itself in two extreme ways, for Heidegger, and this leaves space for therapists to elaborate and expand on this in much more nuanced directions than we find in *Being and Time*. At one extreme, we can 'leap in' for others (BT158). In doing so, we take over the other's issues and challenges that they face, by stepping in and providing a resolution for them, rather than making way for them to attend to matters for themselves. The therapist's leaping in here does raise the question of whether such a solicitous way of being-with might at times be appropriate, though emphatically not intended to be controlling. This really turns on the therapist's being authentic in the encounter, which means adopting a discerning stance towards the unique moment or situation, and not relying on formulaic and abstract rules. Where the client has been 'thrown out of his own position' (BT158), so that they only take over at the point where the therapist has already provided a resolution, this can mean both that the relation between them is one of the client being 'dominated and dependent', as Heidegger puts it, but also one where the client has escaped the moments of uncertainty, anxiety, and 'owning' that can reflect being in such a situation. On the other hand, the therapist can 'leap ahead' of the client (BT158), such that the client is 'in a place' to authentically care, as they contend with the issues before them. The therapist in this case is not so much engaged in the 'what', or content of the client's issues – although this forms an important aspect of the therapeutic work – but rather in the client's existence. Being authentic, both on the part of therapist and the client, to be sure, is reflected in the idea of Dasein as being-a-whole, or understanding Dasein's existence as a whole. This is a point that will hopefully become clearer in what follows. Leaping ahead, then, as Heidegger puts it, 'helps the other to become transparent to himself *in* his care and to become *free for* it' (BT159).

Solicitude covers a variety of ways in which we can be with others as modes of care, that include love, friendship, liking, being sympathetic, hostile, disliking, hating, indifferent, and negligent, amongst others. All these are possible because Dasein is, structurally speaking, care. Three terms that are also particularly important for Heidegger, and for us as therapists, because they shape solicitude in various ways, are 'circumspection', 'considerateness', and 'forbearance' (BT159). Circumspection is an attitude that is tied to concern, which itself is a way of being with entities, or things. For example, when I open my laptop and begin writing this by tapping on my keyboard letters, I am 'circum'-navigating my way around under a spectral 'sight', or having in view, in virtue of a caring orientation, the things that I am dealing with. Again, just to press the point home once more, this is not something that can also be said about the laptop's mode of being, because its being is not reflected in a care structure. Rather, its modes of being are either that of ready-to-hand or present-at-hand. In short, the laptop cannot show circumspective concern towards me.

Considerateness, by contrast, is a set of (ontic) attitudes towards others, rather than things, that can extend from caring deeply about certain others to being indifferent towards them. Indifference here, however, is a mode of considerateness, even if deficient, since it still matters to us that we orient ourselves in this way towards certain others. Typically, then, we might say that we are considerate in our being with certain others, or consider them as we go about our business. This is implicit, we should add, rather than being brought before our explicit awareness. Likewise, forbearance is reflected in the way in which I can show a certain courtesy, patience, or tolerance towards others, or else convey a measure of discourtesy, impatience, or intolerance towards them. Again, the distinction between two human beings sitting together in a therapy room, on the one hand, and two chairs positioned opposite each other, on the other, is a stark one, since the chairs are neither tolerant nor discourteous to one another. Human beings contrastingly, in one way or another, are marked by some mode of solicitude towards others, including that of indifference, because our existential structure is care. Care is reflected in the idea that our being is an issue for us, that it matters to us.

Heidegger is not attempting here to present a moral philosophy or code based on ways of being-with and solicitude that is expressed in terms of moral injunctions. Rather, he is merely providing a phenomenological description of aspects of being-in-the-world, namely in relation to things and to others. Whilst we focus on this existentiale, it should be emphasised that other existentiales bear on, and intermesh with, these aspects in important ways, especially the One, or the way in which we participate in a shared set of background practices as well as common concerns and purposes.

7.2.21.1 A Note on Empathy

Given that Heidegger provides an account of solicitude that is Dasein's being-with others, he also makes clear that this is not what some might describe as empathy. Other phenomenologists, such as Husserl, Scheler, and Stein had already explored this phenomenon, so Heidegger's own comments can be taken as a form of response. We can also assume his critique of empathy to be a form of challenge to Carl Rogers' conception of the term. On BT162, Heidegger articulates the problem directly: 'This phenomenon, which is none too happily designated as "*empathy*", is then supposed…to provide the first ontological bridge from one's own subject, which is given proximally as alone, to the other subject, which is proximally quite closed off.'

The issue, then, is that empathy, as described, is a concept that is already nestled within a Cartesian, subject-object framework, which then inevitably distorts our human way of being. As Dreyfus has emphasised (1991:150), the problem is based on the supposition that we are minds that can then '[understand] the "psychic life of others"' (BT161). This in turn means that empathy is not a fundamental term, as is supposed: '"Empathy" does not first constitute being-with; only on the basis of being-with does "empathy" become possible: it gets its motivation from the unsociability of the dominant modes of being-with' (BT162)

On my reading of this passage, empathy has been introduced as a concept in order to account for the way in which those deficient or privative modes of solicitude arise, such as intolerance, indifference, hostility, contempt, enmity, or neglect, which Heidegger does not see as reflecting a lack or flaw, but only as being derivative, or 'borrowed' variants, that are parasitic upon considerateness or forbearance, for example. In each and every case, considerateness and forbearance are prevalent, given that, as Dasein, we are being-with, and care, which means that mattering is central to our existence. Heidegger says on BT161 that these deficient or privative modes of solicitude are the predominant way in which they become manifest in our relations with others. On a Cartesian picture, however, this presents as a difficulty or obstacle in understanding what is going on in the 'minds of others', as well as our own. On this basis, a distance, resistance, or recalcitrance then aggravates the ability to 'come close to others' (BT161). The Cartesian approach then tries to overcome this by introducing the idea of empathy as a way to make transparent, and draw near, or bring close, the other's conscious experience. Heidegger's critique, as we see, is that Cartesian thinking gets things the wrong way round: empathy does not constitute being-with, but rather, it is only on the basis of being-with that empathy is a viable term at all. The issue, in other words, is that metaphysics is placed or prioritised above or over ontology. To remind ourselves once more, Cartesian metaphysics invokes the idea of substance dualism, namely, a mind and body, which it takes to be the basic foundation for all knowledge. Heidegger's critique is that this misses and also presupposes there being a world in the first place, and that we are, first and foremost, being-in-the-world.

Descartes, as is clear, was unable to recognise or bring into his account Heidegger's existentiales, given his philosophical approach, because he did not have a sense of the ontological background that is the basis for understanding our way of being. The Cartesian approach problematises and exacerbates the challenge of coming to such an understanding, because it obviates and occludes an ability to bring into clear sight a phenomenological understanding of disruptions, disturbances, breakdowns, and world-collapses. This has obvious implications for most therapeutic approaches, but also very serious consequences more generally for those other regions of enquiry, such as psychology, psychiatry, and counselling psychology.

7.2.22 Being-towards-death

Heidegger takes us through a detailed yet concise phenomenological analysis of what he calls 'being-towards-death'. Death itself cannot be subjected to a phenomenological examination, because it is not something that we actually experience. Being-towards-death is something that we *do* experience, however, because it is one of being-towards-an-end of possibilities. Heidegger is concerned to bring out the way in which our being mortal means something to us while we still exist. We live in the light of the meaning that we give to the ending of our being Dasein. We exist towards an end, or the end of our existing, rather than being-at-an-end, which is to think of ourselves as mere things.

He makes a number of distinctions that are related to the ways in which we talk about this phenomenon, starting with the everyday sense that understands it as an event, and one that only happens to others. We commonly talk about others dying, but, as has already been described, we do so in indirect ways. In this sense, we engage with death in a third-personal and detached way, such that we immunise ourselves from its impact. Heidegger also notes that all entities perish, including Dasein; but, he says, 'it does not simply perish' (BT291). Dasein can also demise (BT291), which is, we might say, its 'existential death'. Demise is reflected in the experience of Dasein's being between dying and death, when we move from existing to simply living out our time as a human being. For example, demise is the period of time in which we witness a close relative or friend quietly moving between times of being awake and also in deep sleep, over a period of several days, before finally reaching the state of death. Demise is a situation in which Dasein releases itself from existence and simply awaits death. It is a part of death, in a sense, though 'comes before' death in its actuality.

Heidegger, to summarise, is pursuing an ontological rather than ontic analysis of death. In so doing, he is looking to uncover the way in which death has a meaning for our kind of being, which is existence. Death, for us, is the ending of possibilities. This is not the same as the ending of life, because that is based on a purely biological approach, and excludes existence from the picture.

Death is the end of possibilities, and it impends as a constant possibility of further impossibility. An existential focus on death is reflected in the idea that we are constituted in such a way that we exist in a 'towards' relation to the limits of our possibilities. In the case of death, we have one 'towards' relation that sees it as an actuality that will happen 'someday'. Another 'towards' relation is that we see it as the ever-present moment of the possibility of the end of further possibilities. In other words, we can have different 'towards' relations to those limits of our possibilities. Which relation we ultimately choose will either be authentic or inauthentic. For example, if I live in a relation to death as something which has no meaning for me until it arrives, then I can be said to hold an inauthentic stance. Authentically, on the other hand, I relate to death as having meaning for me *while* I exist.

Heidegger introduces three features of death on BT294: '[D]eath reveals itself as that *possibility which is one's ownmost, which is non-relational, and which is not to be outstripped.*' In death being our 'ownmost', he says that my death is my own, or mine alone. I am the only one who dies my death. Second, in being non-relational, our relation to the One and its everyday norms and practices for how we should think, act, and behave, fall away and become irrelevant. For example, public norms and practices discourage us from thinking or talking about death, but we recognise that this way of being is no longer relevant to us, because we now lose a sense of interest in conforming to this kind of superficiality. Lastly, facing death is to realise that we cannot get around and beyond death, as if we can somehow leave it behind. This leaves us with the fact that we live by the ever-present possibility of an impending end of possibilities. At this point of the analysis, we have arrived at the idea of being-towards-death: we live an existence of our own in which death is always a possibility at every moment.

Death is always impending for as long as we exist. We tend to think of something 'impending' that has a temporary nature to it, such as the impending hearing that will deliver its result on my application to join a professional body. Since it is *constantly* impending, death is an issue for us, in our being-in-the-world, unlike any other possibility. It is non-relational, but its only relation is towards ourselves; that is, our mineness. I stand before myself as a possibility of being in the face of my being-towards-death. The issue is now my whole being-in-the-world, and not one of my conforming to social norms and falling into a way of being that is aligned with the dictates of the One. My existence is now an issue in a different way, given my being-towards-death. I might prioritise my projects in a different way in the light of this, since my sense and understanding of the temporal is now different to my being immersed in an everyday mode of existence.

Being-towards-death is itself a feature or element of Dasein's thrownness. We are thrown into the world, being the way that we are, and into the background circumstances in which we find ourselves. Our mode of being, existence, is one that means that we are dying from the moment that we are thrown. Being-towards-death is therefore central to being-in-the-world. This is brought out most vividly when we grasp ourselves in our finitude, through the hermeneutic turn from everydayness to our being-a-whole. Such finitude, or limit, is expressed in a variety of ways, whether physically, logically, psychologically, socially, temporally, or historically. To reintroduce my previously-used example, I cannot jump over houses, nor can I escape my being temporal, given the kind of being that I am.

7.2.22.1 Authentic and Average Everyday Being-towards-death

Our way of relating to being-towards-death in the everyday mode of existence is to distract ourselves through the ways that we talk about it. In being immersed in the One's norms and edicts for who we should be, we conceal, evade, and engage in idle chatter, as Heidegger puts it. In such a way of existing, we deflect from our responsibility for being Dasein, thereby keeping anxiety at bay, and avoiding the risk of being ourselves. We pass this responsibility on to the One and its norms and practices, reassured by its apparent control and guidance over how to be. We tend to overlook the fact that this is a kind of authoritarian stifling of any expression of ourselves, by tranquilising us from risk, uncertainty, and anxiety. However, having a different relation to everyday norms opens us to the very experiences that make us feel more alive, and free. On a rather different tack, various authoritarian regimes in the world today enact a form of the One in relation to their citizens, exploiting and manipulating the human tendency to follow norms by creating general narratives that heavily discourage citizens from falling outside them. However, they fail to see that as Dasein, there is a possibility for them to undergo an experience of a call to take a stand, and to throw off such artificial constraints that distort the kinds of beings that they are. In effect, such regimes attempt to suppress and erase the possibility of authenticity by instating or reinstating the sense of norms as the highest value, and of conformity as the only way to exist. Those who take a stand, and are ready to be anxious, face their existence – which includes facing their death as a constant possibility – not indifferently, as they would if they remained caught in the One, but by ceasing to distance themselves from their existence as their own.

In cases where Dasein exists, rather than merely living and surviving its daily existence, it does not avoid its finitude. It faces death, which means that it faces impossibility (of further possibility) as a possibility. To fail to understand our finitude is to fail to understand ourselves, in terms of our being (Dasein). Such authentic being-towards-death, or authentic facing death as a constant possibility, is not something abstract or theoretical. Rather, it is a practical orientation towards our existence, because it engages with what matters to us.

Heidegger spells out two ways in which we think of death in terms of possibility. One way is to *await* death, which throws us out of possibility, since it is a passive form of avoidance, and is an inauthentic way of relating to death as possibility. On the other hand, *anticipating* death is to face its truth as the end of possibilities. This means that we cease telling ourselves that it is a future actuality in the 'someday' that is far off into the future. In the authentic relation to death, it is in each moment a possibility.

In anticipating death, we project ourselves onto possibilities that we appropriate as genuinely ours, rather than letting ourselves be determined by what the One has already decided for us in advance as to which possibilities we are to follow. We therefore decide to reject the everyday understanding of death and to instead take it as an issue that relates uniquely to us rather than as a far-off event. The One is now no longer of concern to us in this regard, because we grasp the way that it occludes the truth about death. As we turn to ourselves and away from the One, we become individualised, since the issue of death cannot be deflected away any longer. In this regard, we are called to be authentic, which is to own our existence as a whole. Existence as a whole is to see ourselves in terms of both being thrown (or born), and, moreover, being thrown as mortal. In being authentic, we are now our *own* basis or ground, since there is no longer a commanding force or source that can step in and guide or direct us on how to exist.

Heidegger, as has already been mentioned, introduces the idea of 'anticipation', which is a key term in the understanding of authenticity, as we will see. In the anticipation of death, we understand ourselves as finite, such that we live in the face of this. Heidegger's way of putting this is that we are being-towards-the-end, which we both understand and also *live* this understanding in every present moment.

Heidegger also says that facing such an end to possibilities, and now seeing our-selves as possibility as we live out our lives, frees us to be who we are becoming. In authentically anticipating my death, any previous guide or template for living has now been shattered, because we are no longer beholden to living according to certain customs and practices. We may previously have lived according to a certain expectation or norm that follows stereotypical patterns. But now we are free to take up possibilities that are meaningful to us.

Abandoning our Anyone-self can send us into a kind of loss and disorienta-tion, as it intimates a death of our past self that we no longer hold as being true of ourselves. But, at the same time, this changes the way that we choose those possibilities that we really want rather than the possibilities that we ought to want. This does not mean that we abandon all norms, such as our culinary practices, or the many practical necessities that we rely on in order to live with others. Rather, we recognise that social practices, when left unquestioned or followed blindly, can suffocate and stifle our way of being, and it is this aspect that is recast as we become individualised.

To recapitulate once again, but with added hermeneutic perspective, being Dasein means to be possibility, which becomes highly relevant to anticipation. In the anticipation of death, it is not so much that we are denuded of veils or disguises that then simply fall away to reveal *who* we really are. This is not how Heidegger characterises our kind of being, i.e., that being authentic means to uncover the 'real self'. This would be to assume that the self is actual, or substantial, and is therefore something that we can discover. Rather, our misunderstanding of what it is to be Dasein is exposed to us, such that it reveals *how* we are in our being. As Heidegger writes, on BT308, 'Anticipation discloses to existence that its uttermost possibil-ity lies in giving itself up, and thus it shatters all one's tenaciousness to whatever existence one has reached.'

Death is a certainty that is my 'ownmost', that is, it pertains to mineness. In this, possibility is disclosed. We commonly tend to think that awareness of my death shuts me down insofar as this weighs on or burdens me, and that, in the light of this, I simply wait to die. But this is an inauthentic denial of death, because it does not face the truth and certainty of our Dasein. It is as if we yearn to make of ourselves an exception, and to be who we are not. When we disclose possibility in the face of our death, we *liberate* ourselves in how we choose to exist. It is our death that brings us to become aware that we *are* possibility – that is what it is to be Dasein – and that our possibilities are limited, rather than open-ended, or endless. At the point of death, what expires is possibility, not actuality, as we are generally accustomed to believe.

Heidegger offers us a summary of authentic being-towards-death:

> *[A]nticipation reveals to Dasein its lostness in the Anyone-self, and brings its face to face with the possibility of being itself, primarily unsupported by con-cernful solicitude, but of being itself, rather, in an impassioned* freedom towards death – *a freedom which has been released from the illusions of the 'One', and which is factical, certain of itself, and anxious.*

(BT311)

Here, Heidegger is saying that if we avoid our tendency to distract ourselves from the reality of our existence as Dasein, namely, as possibility, we free ourselves from the One and open ourselves to the possibility of becoming a self that grounds itself in possibilities that it has freely chosen for itself. I can, for example, decide to abandon my conventional lifestyle and wander the world, living a more nomadic lifestyle. I decide to do so authentically in the light of my anticipating my death as my very own, and as a constant possibility in each and every moment. This frees me to consider how I want to live, as the conventional approach numbs me in relation to possibility and the fact that I can actually choose who to be. Heidegger is only identifying this as an ontological possibility and not drawing on actual instances that will confirm this.

7.2.22.2 Conscience

To build on his view of authentic being-towards-death, Heidegger introduces the idea of our having a conscience, but in terms of an 'attestation', i.e., a way of giving evidence, for authenticity. In other words, he recognises that, in being introduced to authentic being-towards-death, he now needs to provide a phenomenology of *how* we can *become* authentic. For this, Heidegger identifies the way in which our conscience 'calls' or beckons us to face up to our existence.

Conscience, in the way that Heidegger initially introduces the term, is not meant in its specific and concrete everyday or moral sense, although he does want to draw upon this meaning as an initial basis for developing his account. We commonly think of conscience as a feeling that overtakes us when we are in certain situations or with others, and that draws on a sense of duty or responsibility to act morally. Here, Heidegger attends to the 'call of conscience', which speaks silently to us, and only us, in a way that strips us away from any silent call of the norms and conventions of the One. Ultimately, conscience relates to care, because we are mattering-oriented beings in virtue of being Dasein and being-in-the-world. Care, we recall, is the unifying structure of being-in-the-world, or to simplify it some-what, fundamentally futurally oriented out of a past that is present.

Heidegger says that conscience 'discloses' (BT314). Disclosedness here is rein-troduced, since it reminds us that this is 'a basic state of that entity which we ourselves are' (BT314). But in this case, and at no point in his investigation, is Heidegger offering any content, namely, as to *what* conscience discloses. Rather, as in this case, his whole project is to provide a formal account of Dasein, which means that all his terms are formal indications. In fact, psychotherapy works with concrete instances of Heidegger's formal account that provides such indications.

The appeal that the call of conscience makes, says Heidegger, is a certain kind of hearing that is 'wanting to have a conscience' (BT314). That is, a certain mood or disposition takes hold in being receptive to this call. As well as this, Heidegger remarks that, in wanting to have a conscience, we are 'choosing to choose' (BT314). This poses a difficulty, given that Heidegger's whole philosophical approach is non-Cartesian. Descartes, recall, characterises us as the thinking thing that is directing its own will towards achieving epistemic certainty. In willing, it is the Cartesian 'I' that is choosing. By contrast, Heidegger is trying to stay as close as possible to the phe-nomenological experience of 'wanting to have a conscience', which then raises the question of how choosing fits into this account. A further tension in this is revealed in the light of his characterisation of Dasein, and with his project as a whole. Perhaps we can understand 'choosing to choose' in the following Heideggerian way. It is our letting ourselves act on what is already gripping us in some way. So, it is more a response to the circumstances or situation, which we take to be of a unique kind, such that it elicits or calls on us, first, to choose, and that, second, we *choose* this choosing by dint of recognising that this choosing is something that befalls us and no one else. In other words, I am choosing, and, furthermore, I choose this as a way to be, rather than choosing to follow traditionally established ways to respond to the situation. But choosing itself is always a sense of being drawn to then act on – that is, choose – what is already taking hold of us in some way. Our choosing to choose, Heidegger adds, is what he calls 'resoluteness'. He means by this a befalling on ourselves, and no other source or guide, to make a decision in response to the unique situation.

For clients who present with certain issues reflected in the way in which they are living their lives inauthentically, the therapist can act as a form of conscience. This is not meant in an explicit sense. Rather, the therapist finds ways to challenge the client, say, in taking actions or pursuing alternative possibilities, all the while supporting the client to take a stand and be resolute where certain difficult situa-tions arise. Such support is provided on the background of the relationship, rather than explicitly and in a direct or directive way. The aim is for the client to become attuned to a moment or experience of conscience over their responsibility for their lives and the choices that they make. There is also the sense that finitude, as this might become more apparent to the client as therapy proceeds, means that they are not so much endeavouring to discover an inner core in themselves that defines them from the moment that they are born, or that there are ultimate truths about which values to pursue in their lives, but rather that they are responsible for inventing themselves and what they commit to through the possibilities that are open to them. They throw off any tendency or temptation to hide or deceive themselves, but instead see themselves as solely responsible for who they are and how they live their lives. The therapist aims to provide a form of 'invisible presence', not taking on the responsibility for the client's choices and decisions, but simply, in a non-interventionist way, offering the client a space to become increasingly aware of the distinction between an inauthentic and authentic existence. The awareness of the contingency of life, and the realisation of finitude – one example is the death of a world, be it a significant relationship, or a project that has given one a sense of identity, leaving one possibly devastated – can shake us into a sense of appreciation that time has elapsed, and that we have a limited time in which to engage in projects or worlds that are meaningful to us. In such moments, we grasp not a meaning in life, as such, but a nullity that Dasein faces and that opens it to possibilities.

7.2.22.3 Existential Guilt

The existential form of conscience that Heidegger articulates is the insight or realisation that living according to the One, as an Anyone-self, is not the only way to exist. Existential conscience, rather than being a certain experience of discomfort over the feeling that one has done something wrong or committed a grave omission of a certain act, has to do with care, that Dasein's being matters to it, and that it experiences a certain call to own up to its existence as a whole. This call is a form of discourse, since it says something to us. But what does it say? That we are guilty. Again, this is not the everyday sense of moral culpability, but an existential guilt. Guilt in this existential sense means that Dasein cannot bring all its possibilities into actuality, since something is always either shut off, or not completed, or simply left out. Existential guilt is one form of 'not', or 'nullity' as Heidegger names it. We encounter nullity in our lives because we are finite and our worlds themselves are finite. That is, we sustain our worlds, e.g., the world of being a therapist, or an engineer, or scientist, in making them intelligible to ourselves, but that intelligibility or sense can, and does, eventually collapse. Our discourse itself reveals the nullity that pervades our existence, as with the expressions 'is not there' or 'not being'. There are three nullities that Heidegger recognises in relation to Dasein: the nullity of death, the nullity of guilt, and the nullity of possibility. Heidegger puts this in terms of projection and thrownness. First is the nullity of projection, which is the way that we are limited in being able to bring about the kind of future we want to have. The second nullity is that we are limited to only being able to project out of our past. That is, we are unable to go back and make the past into something else, or a different past, in order to make a future that we want. Third, we are limited by the possibilities that are available to us and cannot magically introduce more possibilities than those that are available to us. To employ a past example once again, I cannot be a Roman Centurion and join campaigns to conquer other parts of the world, since that possibility is just not there for me.

The tension that lies in Dasein being both projection, or that we lunge into futurity and our projects, and thrownness, i.e., that we are always thrown into a mood that colours the way we are involved in our projects, is captured in BT330: '[Dasein] never comes back behind its thrownness in such a way that it might first release this "that-it-is-and-has-to-be" from its *being-its-self* and lead it into the "there"'. That is, we are never able to create or design our own 'origin' or basis from the outset, so that we tweak and adjust how we want to project ourselves futurally into the kinds of beings we want to become. Rather, we are thrown into our basis. The possible tension is reflected in projection's trying to pursue tasks, projects, and activities that create a strain against who we are projecting *from*, i.e., from the self that we already are. Think of the newly promoted person who has no previous experience in their role. It is a major promotion, and is an exciting new development in the person's career. They attend meetings, lead groups, and discuss strategies with key managers and executives. After a short time, the stress that emerges for this person is reflected in a certain way of facing the challenges of negotiating and managing major projects, with the accompanying feeling of being stretched to acquire new skills in order to cope with situations and difficulties, but at the same time, finding themselves as they are in their thrownness. John Richardson articulates this tension well: 'We will always find or feel ourselves as something different than we are making ourselves to be. We understand ourselves to be projecting *from* a self we also are, which is discrepant...from the who we aspire to be' (2012:156).

We are both absorbed in our projects and the striving that this entails, and also finding ourselves in our feelings, moods, and dispositions that reflect our thrownness. As Richardson comments,

> [W]e feel how we're doing, all the time we are doing. Often the latter serves the former: we keep track of how we're doing at what we're trying to do. But the more we pass over into this reflective view on ourselves...the more discrepancy opens up between this and our projective aspiration. So moods are often experienced as hindrances to our effort.
>
> (2012:157)

My tendency is to experience my mood as hindering me from being able to undertake or bring about my projects. For example, if I am writing a book, and it seems to not be going well, then I attribute this to my feelings, moods, and emotions – my thrownness – as holding me back from my project, which appears not to be the problem or issue in this case. But Heidegger is taking our projection, that is, who I am trying to become or be, as being the 'problem', because it is in conflict with thrownness, since it imposes a certain constraint or limit on that projection.

Back to Richardson again:

> The problem is the way my projective meanings for things always need to share with meanings coming from the past – meaning thrown into things from behind

me. So the 'call of conscience' is not really directed against our trespasses; it's a reminder of that insuperable limit.

(ibid.:157)

As Heidegger reminds us: 'Dasein need not first load a "guilt" upon itself through its failures or omissions; it must only *be* "guilty" *authentically* – "guilty" in the way in which it is' (BT333).

Being-guilty, as Heidegger puts it, is the way that we are all the time. By contrast, everyday or moral guilt varies according to the situation in which we find ourselves, and is something that we experience through our assessment of ourselves in relation to the One. However, as thrown projection, we are never certain that the choices we have made about which possibilities to pursue are most appropriate or optimal, because we can never go back in time and take a different path in order to check if that might have been a better option to pursue than the one we actually followed. This leaves us with the sense that there are endless possibilities that are now 'not', or nullified, and that we must live with, so to speak. For some, this might be expressed in terms of regret, and for others, it might be a degree of acceptance that these are the inevitable circumstances in which we find ourselves. In both thrownness and projection, then, we are faced with a nullity, because our thrownness brings about a 'what I cannot do', and our projection reflects a 'what I have not done.' This 'not' is precisely our being-guilty, as Heidegger introduces the term, which is neither negotiable nor avoidable.

Being a thrown projection, and the tension between thrownness and projection, manifests all-too-familiarly in our daily lives, and presents itself as an issue that clients commonly bring to therapy sessions. To give an example of this, imagine client G asking for some help from a friend, because he wants a quick and temporary way of storing a number of books that he can access whenever he needs to, whilst in the process of moving home. His friend is reticent and doesn't offer any help on this. G is surprised and angry at his friend's reaction and feels frustrated that help isn't forthcoming. He asks his friend about this to try to get to the underlying reason for his friend's behaviour but is met with stony silence. G is enraged because his project has been thwarted, and this mood of anger reflects this. But G is also experiencing limits, both in his projection and his thrownness, insofar as his thrownness into this situation (of currently having nowhere to store his books) and how G already is, illuminates a 'not' that appears as a limit on what he wants, namely, to store books with his friend. He also experiences a limit on his task, or projection, since he cannot do all that he has planned to do. The tension arises in his thrownness (a limit on what he wants) limiting his projection (not able to do all that he has wanted to do), rather than the incompleted task (projection) being a limit on what he wants (thrownness).

By way of final comments on existential guilt, being-guilty is both structural and also a mood, since it is a way that we find ourselves in our existence. Insofar as it is structural, Dasein is 'being-a-basis' (BT330) or being its own 'ground'. The Western philosophical tradition has transitioned through different understandings of what the essence of this basis is: substance, for example, or being God's creation, to name two. For Heidegger, Dasein has no basis other than being its *own* basis. In concrete terms, then, we are responsible for our situation and how we respond and act in the face of it. The One is our attempt to 'externalise' this basis in order to avoid the responsibility and anxiety that we face when we live in terms of being-a-basis. Another way in which we avoid responsibility is when we claim that our facticity is preventing us from being our authentic selves. For example, a client might insist that they never had the opportunity to study over the course of their life; they never had time, since situations and circumstances never allowed for this. However, we might see in their attitude or mood an intimation of the closing of possibility, such that even in their current circumstances there are reasons and excuses that they present for not being able to pursue this as a project.

7.2.22.4 Resoluteness

Who am I called to be in the face of my existential guilt, and in my being in a situation? As authentic Dasein, I am called to embrace resoluteness. That is, I accept my own responsibility for my existence as a whole – which means my being-towards-death and being-guilty, along with (existential) anxiety – and project myself into the situation with a discernment and openness to what the situation itself reveals or demands. Alternatively, I can be irresolute, or lack resoluteness, by engaging with the situation in an accustomed, habitual way. This reflects an ambiguity or inconstancy in my stance on things, as I am carried along and influenced by the gust of the latest opinions or fashionable positions on matters, one might say. In resoluteness, I own myself insofar as I understand what is possible for me in a situation and choose to resolve the situation with myself as the ground of the decision that I make. For example, say that I have been made redundant, or laid off, dismissed by my employer. I feel dismayed, disoriented, upset even. I am floored by the unexpectedness of this predicament in which I now find myself, and feel 'in limbo', numbed into a sense of meaninglessness. But, perhaps with time, in my resoluteness, I recognise that there are possible ways to be in the situation. I can choose to wallow in this and rail against the world for its intrinsic injustice. I might alternatively choose to tell myself something about these circumstances in a way that is basically at odds with what actually happened. Or I can simply accept that this event happened. In the last case, I recognise those possibilities that the situation now presents for me, and I make a decision that resolves upon the situation in the light of its limit or nullity. The option of continuing to work for my former employer has now been nullified, shut off, but other possibilities are presently open to me. In such resoluteness, I disclose the situation in its truth, rather than in seeing it opaquely and obliquely, through the lens of the One, or in not being my own self. The One, in this case, might be a world in which my norms and ultimate guides for living are drawn from a diversity of possible influences, including religion, a spiritual group, a human potential community, or the more generally pervasive everyday social and cultural practices in which I live.

In our inauthenticity, we do not truly disclose the situation, because we conceal it through taking a conventional attitude towards it. In doing so, we simply fail to acknowledge possibilities, which means that we deflect from taking responsibility for the uniqueness of the situation. In authenticity, conscience calls us to respond to the possibilities in the situation, limited as they are. Authentic resoluteness discloses the situation, which means that we thrust ourselves in its midst, rather than first recognising the situation and then reacting to it in the way that we do. In effect, we can say that being inauthentic in the situation is to 'hold back' from acting in a way that reflects our being that is care. When inauthentic, we are prone to wait for the optimal set of circumstances in which only certain preferred possibilities show up or are to our liking. That means that we might well hold back from engaging with what is there in the situation, because those possibilities that we want to see present are not there. The tendency or general pattern that then develops is to live in a way that reflects this waiting. In resoluteness, however, we acknowledge that we are thrown into the situation where only certain possibilities are available to us, rather than those that we wish and hope for, and we thereby disclose the situation for what it is. Heidegger describes such disclosedness in terms of Dasein being 'in the truth' (BT343). He relates this to authenticity, when he says, 'In resoluteness we have now arrived at that truth of Dasein which is most primordial because it is *authentic*' (BT343).

To summarise what has been covered so far, then, Dasein, in being-in-the-world, can experience its conscience as calling it to be-guilty. This is an existential guilt, not the everyday guilt that we commonly understand in terms of having done something wrong or fallen short in some way. Being-guilty is being responsible, which is to own ourselves. This, as we have established, is what being authentic means. Disowning ourselves, by contrast, is to defer this responsibility to 'them', or what our public norms and practices say about the way that we should be, think, and act. As such, we are not our own self, but an Anyone-self. By acting responsibly in the situation that it discloses, Dasein is resolute. In this resoluteness, since authentic Dasein is being its own basis, and is no longer caught in the One's 'basis' or grounding within norms, commandments, and prescriptions for how to be, it is anxious. In this anxiety, Dasein experiences its uncanniness, or not-at-home-ness, because it has become dis-placed from the familiarity and homeliness of the One. Being responsible means accepting this anxiety, which itself discloses something important about Dasein's being-in-the-world, that is, its thrown projection.

7.2.22.5 Authenticity as Anticipatory Resoluteness

Anticipatory resoluteness, as Heidegger introduces the term (BT349), is Dasein's authenticity. It is not a composition, nor a synthesis, since this is to misapprehend its being-a-whole, as is also true for being-there and being-in-the-world (BT353). However, Heidegger covers the two features of anticipatory resoluteness by attending to each in turn, so that he can then go on to articulate it in its wholeness. In short, both anticipation and resoluteness reflect Dasein's finitude. Anticipation is a facing forwards, or futurally, in being mortal. Resoluteness, however, is facing 'backwards', to thrownness, which is also a finitude, given its nullity. To put it otherwise, Dasein is both the possibility of impossibility and not being the basis of its own thrownness, but also a nullifier, negator, or closer of alternative possibilities that had previously been available to it. This finitude is anxiety-provoking as we become aware of this, and the decision to be authentic or inauthentic hinges on whether we are ready to accept and be in this anxiety or not. If we reject or flee from it, the most that we have experienced is the temporarily unsettled moment that brings us face-to-face with our very existence being at stake; but should we choose to stay with it, we accept that this anxiety is a continuous background mood in which we live in our authenticity. Such anxiety is not a paralysing or disabling disposition, but a certain alertness, we might say, to the situations and circumstances in which we find ourselves.

It is only when we grasp and face our finitude, and the various 'nots' that constitute our kind of being as existence, that we are able to authentically reckon with choices and possibilities. We recognise that we can only project ourselves onto possibilities that are themselves limited, whether this be in terms of quantity or time. In the mode of inauthenticity, however, we face only those possibilities that are closest and most convenient to us. Resoluteness means to accept our existential guilt, which is not occasional and changeable, but marked by its 'constancy', to use Heidegger's term. In this unwavering and certain constancy, we face our potentiality-for-being, or ability-to-be, which is a future-oriented being-towards-the-end (BT353). This is authentic being-towards-death, which is anticipation. When thinking of resoluteness, we should keep in mind that it is not something static, such that it becomes fixed into place. Rather, I can also decide not to be resolute at any moment. This means that I must repeat the choice to be resolute at all times, if I commit to resoluteness. It is, in other words, a practice.

To cover familiar ground again, the 'not' or nullity of Dasein relates to the nullity of our thrownness. We 'inherit' our circumstances (place of birth, time, and culture in which we are born, to one particular family, and so on) over which we have no control and so cannot choose. Were we able to choose, we would be the 'basis' for this choosing rather than being a 'null basis'. As well as this nullity of thrownness, we have to choose who to be in the face of a second nullity, which is our authentic being-towards-death, or anticipation.

In the light of this, we can provide a richer account of authenticity. Being authentic means that I choose myself out of the possibilities that the situation and circumstances present, and in so doing, individualise myself. To not individualise is to remain wedded to the One and its edicts and prescribed rules for living. In being authentic, I face my thrownness, which is to accept both being-guilty and being-towards-death, because I have been thrown into these inescapable features of being Dasein. I do this, even though I experience existential anxiety, and no longer see a return to the One as an option to tranquilise myself from it. Anxiety, Heidegger emphasises, is particularly important, because it is a fundamental mood, which is to say that it illuminates what it means to be Dasein. It also brings to light the nullities that have already been mentioned.

7.3 Being Temporal and Spatial

7.3.1 *Spatiality*

Heidegger characterises spatiality in human, and not mathematical or geometrical, terms. Rather than referring to our position in terms of Cartesian coordinates, we are always in a place; that is, in a situation or environment in which things and others show up in meaningful ways. Things and others are near or far, and this is meaningful insofar as they are relevant or useful to our projects, tasks, and activities. Such closeness and distance are not conveyed in measurable and quantifiable terms, since this would be a basic misunderstanding of what it is to be Dasein. Research studies that endeavour to conduct their enquiries on various elements of the therapeutic process, for example, adopt an abstract approach towards the human being from the outset. This then distorts the enquiry at all points along the study, including aspects of a methodological approach that follows a process of registering numerically the frequency with which themes arise in the data or transcripts collected.

To convey the sense in which Dasein's spatiality is related to proximity and distance, a concrete example might be of some help here. I frequently travel on the London underground to work. On occasion, I find myself on a packed train, and so find myself standing physically close to the person next to me, but am existentially far from them, since I have no existing relationship to them, nor an interest in initiating this. They bear no relevance to me, given the ongoing projects that preoccupy me in my life. Extending Heidegger's account of spatiality a little more, were I to accidentally bump into the neighbouring person and then proceed to share a joke about losing my balance, we might describe this as a moment of existential closeness that emerges as we exchange a few sentiments and cultivate ways of relating to each other. Spatiality, then, is not static, from an existential perspective, but dynamic in character. The human space between us is not fixed and immovable, but fluid and constantly reshaped. It is only when we are pressed to specify the dimensions of the space in which we find ourselves that we lose the sense of human spatiality.

Existential or human spatiality is related to the existentiale, directionality, insofar as we are oriented towards or face the world. We are not a neutral, Archimedean point, much like Husserl's transcendental ego, nor do we understand ourselves in terms of Cartesian coordinates, i.e., occupying a three-dimensional position in space as length, breadth, and depth. Such directionality means that our orientatedness, and the accompanying relevance of what we encounter, is in terms of 'up', 'down', 'below, 'above', 'close', 'far', 'smothering', 'stuffy', 'ordered', 'convenient', 'accessible', 'left', and 'right', and much more. These are all ways in which being-in-the-world has spatial relevance. Insofar as we find ourselves in situations, our spatial orientation is our own. Where we experience a publicly sanctioned way to sit, stand, hold oneself, and generally relate to things around us, as we might find on an excessively formal occasion when attending a dinner party, we are, strictly speaking, being inauthentic in relation to our space. This is because we defer to *das*

Man, the One or everyone, to inform and dictate to us as to how we position ourselves, rather than how we are placed, or even dwell.

When we are involved in something that relates to certain tasks or projects, relevant equipment is assigned to complete the task or fulfil the project to our satisfaction. In such cases, equipment is put into a relationship with things and others, such
that it comes spatially closer to us than various other items. This is a way in which
Dasein, as being-in-the-world, experiences its situation existentially, relating to
equipment as reliable and 'handleable'. Where something that we deem appropriate for use as equipment is remote, we bring it into closeness through de-severance.
But we should note that remoteness is the basic way in which we encounter things
and others in the world. They are not in our 'field of view', or our horizon, as
we might put it, which is to say that we are not aware of them. Remoteness only
becomes recognised by Dasein when closeness overcomes it through de-severance
(BT139). It does this through its concern. This means that those things that are
relevant to my concern are closer to me than irrelevant things that are geographi-
cally nearer. This is all intended to underline the fact that Dasein's spatiality is
meaningful, and derives from being-in-the-world. That is, Dasein is involved, and
engaged, rather than being positioned, which suggests a Cartesian understanding of
spatiality. As involved and engaged, Dasein's being-in-the-world is characterised
in terms of concern and familiarity, and familiarity is made possible through over-
coming remoteness by de-severance. Bringing the remote close is something that
we do all of the time, since it is a basic feature of Dasein's existence.

7.3.2 Temporality

This section on temporality is detailed. As well as providing an explication of
Heidegger's phenomenology of temporality, it also draws on many of the ideas and
insights that have previously been presented in his work. The purpose of entering
into this level of detail is to convey the deeper understanding of temporality that is
commonly missed in our customary grasp of time. As will also become apparent,
the various phenomena presented throughout this part of the book are all integrated
into Dasein and its being-in-the-world. For this reason, terms are reintroduced at
various points, where appropriate.

7.3.2.1 Bringing in Temporality in Being and TIme

Dasein in its everydayness is reflected in its going about its activities and dealing
with the world, constituted as it is of others and things. Heidegger develops this
account of the pragmatic concerns of everyday living in the first part of *Being and
Time*, otherwise organised structurally and designated as Division I of this work. In
this first part of the book, he presents Dasein, or the human being, in an extensive
description of its being-in-the-world as if living in successive moments of time.
Heidegger's account at this point in his presentation describes Dasein in its existentiality, fallenness, and facticity. However, these elements or aspects are constituted

as a unity, rather than somehow being independent of each other. This unity, or structure, is what Heidegger calls 'care'.

In then moving on to Division II, Heidegger focuses on Dasein *as* a whole, but not in terms of the whole and complete picture of Dasein. He treats Dasein as a whole by bringing first death and then guilt into his account, such that Dasein is the living out in its existence that itself is bound by limits. Having presented Dasein in terms of its existentiality, facticity, and fallenness, he now develops his account of care with the whole in view. His prior account in Division I was purely descriptive, simply laying out these features insofar as they constitute Dasein's care, and nothing more. In that account, care was characterised in terms of a tripartite structure: being ahead-of-itself-being-already-in-(the-world) as being-amid. Now taking Dasein as a whole, care is fleshed out in in its *temporal* sense.

7.3.2.2 Care and Temporality

Care is a structure, and can be explored ontologically. In ontic enquiry, by contrast, it is explored in terms of the way that it manifests in our everyday dealings in the world. For example, I care about my work with clients, as I do about my family and their well-being. But the sense of care that makes it intelligible in the first place is not to approach it as something static, or substantial. Rather, its intelligibility, or meaning, is temporality. This now reflects a hermeneutic turn, or movement[4], that introduces a deeper understanding of care. Temporality is the meaning of care, which is to say that it is the basis of care's fundamental unity. Temporality is what allows us to integrate past, present, and future – the tripartite structure of care already mentioned – into our existence. Care is constituted by existentiality (the future being-ahead-of-itself), facticity (the past already-being-in), and falling (the present being-amid), and temporality is what allows us to hold the past, present, and future together such that care is possible. Care reflects the fact that others, things, and situations all fundamentally matter to us, because it is through them that we realise our possibilities and who we are when immersed in our worlds. We unite past, present, and future in existing as care, that is, as the kind of being that, informed by the past, chooses present possibilities that are projected towards a future. Uniting them is only possible on the basis of temporality. This has now brought us to the title of the book, but read through an authentic lens: that being *is* time.

A particularly important reminder to add here is the distinction between an inauthentic and authentic understanding of the past, present, and future. Temporality is the term that Heidegger uses to refer to the human sense of time, although I will frequently use both terms interchangeably. Temporality reflects the way in which we live such that we integrate or unite past, present, and future. We can do so either inauthentically or authentically. The way in which we each live are our own ways of being in the past, present, and future in its unity. This, of course, bears therapeutic relevance, as we work with clients. Temporally, Dasein prioritises its future-directedness, but this happens only on the basis of, or out of, its past. The past is not a static sense of historical events that we lived through, but the more existential sense of having-been, as Heidegger puts it. In other words, we live our past in a continual way insofar as we bring it into situations in the present. So, in brief, as temporal beings, we go forwards through drawing on what has already been into the present. Temporality, then, constitutes or is what is essential to being Dasein. It is not a Newtonian or scientific conception of time. That is, time is not external to us, such that we are in time, as common-sense thinking has led us to believe. Time exists because we are temporal, rather than our temporality conforming to objective time.

We are temporalising beings, insofar as we temporalise temporality. In other words, we temporalise as we live our lives in the past, present, and future. This unity is a form of horizon or frame that unifies and holds our lives together. Animals are in time but aren't temporalising beings: they don't plan their days and set out their schedules for the coming week, for example. We shouldn't think of the past, present, and future as a linear timeline, such that one point in time comes after another. Instead, we see them as equi-present in our experience. When I am driving, for example, I direct myself towards what is coming as I approach my destination, but this is already informed by how I have been driving, and brings me into the present moment as I negotiate my position in the appropriate lane for my journey. None of these stand out separately from each other in my experience. Heidegger calls the past, present, and future the three ecstases that express our temporalising. By this term, he intends the way in which each 'stands out' from the unity in its own way, but nevertheless remains in the unity. My hand, for example, stands out from the rest of the body in its ability to do various things, such as point, handle, touch, hit, and so on, but it is not something that is independent of the body. The ecstases of past, present, and future simply draw us towards different temporal horizons.

Heidegger is claiming that clock time, dating, and considering time as something external all cover over, or conceal, authentic temporality, temporality in its truth, so to speak. We have become accustomed to think of time as something to measure, or use as a resource – 'time is money', for example – and as a succession of moments, rather than time as humanly lived, or existential. We live temporally through the unity of past, present, and future, such that this allows us to express ourselves in a meaningful way. So, as a therapist, I see clients on a regular basis, teach to a set schedule over the course of a semester, study when I have some free time, and attend conferences past and present, such that my identity is reflected in these events and situations that all fall into the lived unity of past, present, and future.

To emphasise the distinction of our ways of relating to time, time-keeping is a feature of being-in-the-world, and reflects our involvement in tasks, activities and projects. In this sense, time-keeping is task-oriented, as well as being public, because it is a shared world in which our projects take place. This publicly oriented way in which such projects take place within a temporal context is then grounded in clock time. Every minute is the same as the next, in terms of their equal valence, which is what Heidegger means when he says that time is levelled off. Everyday time-keeping becomes reduced to atomised moments of time. In such a case, who we are as Dasein moves towards an obscured, inauthentic mode of being temporal human beings, because we settle for this as a simple matter of how things are taken to be.

Public time, as clock time, is a levelling off, as already mentioned. What this means is that, in its inauthenticity, Dasein 'awaits', as a kind of withholding, or holding back, in a certain kind of levelling down of the temporal, rather than anticipating the precious, unique character of the temporal that runs ahead. In so doing, Dasein loses itself in this ordering of temporality, rather than owning itself authentically. Heidegger puts this all in the following way:

> [t]he irresoluteness of inauthentic existence temporalises itself in the mode of a making-present which does not await but forgets. He who is irresolute understands himself in terms of those very closest events and be-fallings which he encounters in such a making-present and which thrust themselves upon him in varying ways. Busily losing *himself* in the object of his concern, he *loses his time* in it too.
>
> (BT463)

One important element to add here in relation to authentic temporalising is Dasein in its possibility. Possibility is itself an existentiale which has already been discussed, but is now given a hermeneutic analysis in the light of a temporal turn. Since we are possibility, we are open to the future, and we realise, or actualise, certain (ontic) possibilities. Such possibilities that we decide to act upon and actualise are reflected in who we become. A young school student has good science grades, for example, and now faces the possibilities before them: whether to pursue university studies to become a medical doctor, a dentist, or a scientist. They must choose from these possibilities, and as they do so, they terminate those possibilities that they will not pursue in order to actualise their final choice. In making this decision, they are committed to a movement towards who they are becoming through the realisation of the one chosen possibility. As authentic Dasein, the student also recognises that they live finitely, and that they have only the horizon of their own life to make something of themself. It is not an endless conveyer belt of temporality that they assume here, but one of living under the temporal limitation of being-in-the-world. This reflects the further fact that they also exist concretely rather than abstractly.

7.3.2.3 Everyday Temporality

From the point of view of everydayness, those features of disclosedness – understanding, mood, fallenness, and discourse – all constitute an integral unity rather than being separate. In other words, they are intertwined, and consideration of one simultaneously invokes and includes the others. Understanding, such as having a grasp of how to get about on the London underground, always has its background mood or disposition. For example, I might carry a certain wariness when descending into the depths of a station, and standing in an aluminium steel projectile that hurtles through dark tunnels. Or I am disposed to enjoy the speed at which I can be carried along and reach one end of London in a matter of minutes. Heidegger says that the features of disclosedness are all integrated in temporality, as is care. In terms of understanding, then, I am futurally oriented, because I grasp being Dasein in terms of my possibilities. In terms of care, this is my being-ahead-of-myself. At the same time, I am thrown into a disposition, or mood, which is the way that I already bring myself into the experience, or situation. I colour the world with a certain hue, tone, or tint, such that things show up as obstructive, cluttered, threatening, or exciting and rich in various ways. With this, my fallenness is reflected in the way that I am engaged in the present, either walking along platforms that allows space for others to walk by, or wanting to stand closer to the platform edge because I'm interested in reading the billboards on the walls of the platform. As well as this, I articulate my being through the way in which my possible gestures, acknowledgements, and exchanges with others as I move through the station all reflect my being in a discourse with them.

7.3.2.4 Everyday Temporality of Understanding

When we exist in our usual everyday mode of understanding, we passively submit to being shaped and determined by our situation and circumstances, such that our understanding is compromised in some way. In an authentic mode of understanding, however, we take charge of our own possibilities by projecting into potential futures that haven't yet been actualised. Inauthentic, everyday projection is drawing on the past (which we can think of in terms of customs, and established norms and practices), to project what is already actual. In this sense, everyday temporalising of the future is really to await an inauthentic future.

Awaiting (BT386) is an inauthentic way of projecting ourselves onto those possibilities that will achieve our projects and tasks. It is a passive mode of being, and simply awaits or expects the future without our letting ourselves come to the fore in our individuality. For example, L says that she will visit South America when she retires and has time to enjoy things more. Her attitude, or mood, we might say, is one of delaying or postponing being herself to an awaiting 'one day' in the future, which is a future possibility. In an authentic mode of being, by contrast, L sees her trip as a present possibility that she is responsible for creating in the immediate present. Authentic temporality is the mode of being in which we understand ourselves in relation to our existence as human beings. We take over our possibilities and anticipate (BT387) the future by projecting ourselves in a way that chooses ourselves in our existence. This also means that we relate to ourselves as being-a-whole, that is, a unity that lives according to limits, or the nullities of being-guilty and being-towards-death, between which we are stretched in our existing.

Temporalising, then, is reflected in both inauthentic and authentic modes of existence. Authentic temporalising is to anticipate the future in the present, whilst inauthentic temporalising is to await the future in a way that we might say, rather paradoxically, 'lacks' a future, because that so-called future is already determined by 'how things have already been all along'.

As well as the everyday mode of understanding, a similar exploration can be made in the everyday mode of falling, which reflects a temporalising in the present. When inauthentically being in the present, we are what Heidegger calls 'making present' (BT388). We are simply amid or amongst our possibilities and not actively understanding them such that we engage with or act on them. In authentic being in the present, we take the present as a 'moment of vision' (BT387), which is to see our possibilities as actual and as, in a sense, new to us, rather than old, or predictable and familiar. We see clearly that these possibilities are *our* possibilities, and not those that have been handed down to us. This means that we experience the situation as one in which we are responsible for making our individual choices. This requires a resolution on our part, as here we establish the basis for projecting into the future.

The two ways in which we temporalise in terms of the past is forgetting (BT388) and repetition (BT388). Forgetting is our inauthentic way of disowning the past aspect of our existence as Dasein. In effect, we keep at bay the fact that our past constitutes who we are, as if we only live according to who we are today. We can liken this, for instance, to someone leaving behind their culture and background in which they were raised, moving to another country, and then reinventing themselves such that who they are on the basis of that past has been effectively erased. By contrast, repetition is to own our past through the present choices that we make, such that we project into the future who it is we are becoming. In this way, we repeat ourselves throughout the numerous changes that we go through over the course of our lives. In our existence, we are continually becoming who we are, but in a way that grounds itself in how we have been, that is, always already are. Our past is always with us, or *is* us, in our existing. In authentically owning our past, we embrace who we have become in the present moment of vision. Repeating the past, then, as we become, is repetition.

7.3.2.5 Everyday Temporality of Mood

For Heidegger, moods are attunements that are based in past experiences. He returns to the mood of fear, which he had previously explored in the context of its everyday manifestation. Now he engages in the temporality of fear. It is presented here in order to reveal the way in which we can understand a mood, or feeling, in terms of its structure, as well as temporal character. Typically, we tend to think of fear, as we do with other moods, as that which is threatening, or about to happen, futurally speaking. In that sense, it points to the present or future, rather than reflecting a temporal 'pastness'. Heidegger characterises fear as past-oriented, however, which is reflected in an inauthentic temporalising. We can perhaps begin to see what Heidegger means here when we consider the way in which we are already taken by a mood, or disposed towards situations. It isn't something that is under our control, but rather reflects how things matter to us all the time. This, as has been mentioned already, has its origin in care. Events always already show up as inviting, joyful, annoying, unsavoury, crass, numbing, or threatening, for example. That is, we find ourselves, in our thrownness, or past-orientation, immersed in certain moods that grip us.

The temporality of fear is a 'forgetting which awaits and makes present' (BT392). Heidegger elaborates on what he means by this when he says that it is an inauthentic temporalising. Fear freezes us in the moment, such that we are bewildered in a 'forgetting'. Think of the way in which we become disoriented and lose our sense of coping when gripped by the fearful moment. We are thrown off-track, and lose our way, as our experience 'jumps around'. This is 'forgetting', which is the way in which I forget myself by not coming back, or bringing myself back to myself. If I take hold of myself, I find myself by 'reminding' myself of who I am in my finite being. In fear, I cling to those possibilities of self-preservation and evasion, as Heidegger puts it, that I have already identified in advance that will save me, which is a passive 'awaiting' rather than an active anticipation, which means taking up a *definite* possibility (BT392) that takes hold of the situation. The future and the past are sacrificed for the present, where I simply address my concern to survive. However, what falls away in this present is the issue of *how*, or the way, I exist, which is addressed by including the past and future. Focusing on the present in this reactive way is what Heidegger means by 'making present'.

Perhaps an example, although extremely vivid and graphic, will illustrate this more clearly. Michael Cimino's film, *The Deer Hunter*, presents a harrowing scene in which two characters, Mike and Nick, are soldiers who have been imprisoned in a bamboo and wire cage on a river by their captors. They are brought to a small area in which they are both seated opposite each other at a table that is directly outside the cage. They are then forced to play Russian roulette. This is a daring game in which a bullet is loaded into one of the six chambers of a gun, with the remaining five chambers left empty. The cylinder with the six chambers is then spun at random, so that no one knows whether or not the bullet has aligned with the firing pin. The gun is now picked up and the end of the barrel is pointed at the person's own temple. The trigger is finally pulled, with either the obviously catastrophic result of death or the survival of the individual. Prior to beginning, however, the captors place bets on the outcome of this 'game'. As this unfolds, Nick is paralysed in fear and is breaking down, insisting that he doesn't want to go through with this. Mike takes the situation in hand and understands that they must play the 'game', because it offers them a way out of their predicament. All that Nick can see is the immediate moment, which he makes present. He surrenders to it in an awaiting passivity. He also forgets himself, holding the present as the only temporal dimension that is relevant. Mike, on the other hand, makes a proposal to his captors that will make the game more exciting for them, but at the same time harbours a secret, though definite possibility for a resolution that will offer them their own escape. He anticipates the futural in this respect, whilst repeating who he has been – a marksman, warrior, as someone resourceful, combative, and so on – which brings him into a moment of vision, namely, seeing clearly who he is in the present as he engages in the game. In other words, he makes a resolute choice in the face of feeling the danger and threat of the situation. This means that he makes a choice that doesn't deflect away from his being-mortal and being-guilty. He is all-too-aware that death is a real possibility at any moment. But being-guilty means that he makes a decision that is not one that he can delegate to anyone else, and so he is his *own* basis for his decision that is made out of certain choices. Drawing on Heidegger's descriptions here, Mike is anxious, because he understands that his world is vulnerable to the possibility of collapse, and in a variety of possible ways, at any moment. The temporal mood of anxiety, as reflected in Mike, is a repetition that anticipates in a moment of vision. The temporal mood of fear that Nick undergoes, by contrast, is a forgetting that awaits and makes present.

Whilst fear is reactive in the face of a specific threat, anxiety is an authentic mood that illuminates our being thrown into the world. It is in this anxiety that we experience the world in its 'uncanniness', or 'unhomely' character. Typically, when we are anxious, it is as if, in that moment, the world has lost its anchor, or is untethered. That is, projects and tasks, our identity or roles that relate to the world, as well as equipment, all lose their previous familiarity, relevance, or place. Heidegger puts all this in the following way:

> Anxiety discloses an insignificance of the world; and this insignificance reveals the nullity of that with which one can concern oneself – or, in other words, the impossibility of projecting oneself upon a potentiality-for-being which belongs to existence and which is founded primarily upon one's objects of concern. The revealing of this impossibility, however, signifies that one is letting the possibility of an authentic potentiality-for-being be lit up. What is the temporal meaning of this revealing? Anxiety is anxious about naked Dasein as something that has been thrown into uncanniness. It brings one back to the pure 'that-it-is' of one's ownmost individualised thrownness.
>
> (BT393–4)

The general upshot of this is that, given that worlds can break down, there is no ultimate answer that captures once and for all the definitive essence of how to live our lives. All we have are the decisions that we make based on the possibilities available to us at any particular time. Those available possibilities are limited by our thrownness.

7.3.2.6 Everyday Temporality of Falling

Fallenness is inauthentic insofar as we are absorbed, dispersed, or 'diluted' in the world with others. Typically, in this absorption, we engage in idle talk, curiosity, and ambiguity, or a levelled down, trivial, and distracted way in which we are being in our being-in-the-world. In fallenness, the existential meaning is in the present (BT397). That is, as opposed to understanding, which temporalises the future, and disposedness (or its ontic correlate, mood) that temporalises the past, falling temporalises the present. Rather than explicate all three ways in which we temporalise inauthentically in our fallenness, Heidegger devotes special attention only to curiosity. In curiosity, we busy ourselves, keep moving from one thing to another, by having a 'craving for the new', as Heidegger puts it (BT397). We do this only because it is novel and piques and absorbs us in the present for its own sake, not because it is relevant to our projects and tasks. Once we encounter the thing or entity in question, it is quickly passed over, or simply forgotten, because the next object or entity now consumes us. In this, our interest towards things is superficial, just a way to preoccupy ourselves in the moment. As with the inauthentic temporality of mood, but also in inauthentic understanding, the temporality of falling is a forgetting which awaits and makes present. In its making present, it 'entangles itself in itself, so that the distracted not-tarrying becomes *never-dwelling-any-where*' (BT398). 'Tarrying' here is a kind of dealing with things in an involved way. In curiosity, however, we are 'everywhere and nowhere' in our being-there, rather than in the authentic, non-distracted present of the moment of vision.

Whilst falling is an inauthentic way of being-there, it is the fundamental way in which Dasein is constituted in its being-in-the-world, alongside understanding and disposedness. It is simply what it is to be human: we 'fall' into societal and cultural norms and practices from the very outset of our existence, and in our basic or primordial way of being. It is only when we become aware of this way of being that we question the extent to which we have become blind conformists, and that this is the only way to be. To summarise the last few points about curiosity and falling, it is best captured by referring to Heidegger once again, when he writes,

> Dasein gets dragged along in thrownness; that is to say, as something which has been thrown into the world, it loses itself in the 'world' in its factical submission to that with which it is to concern itself. The present, which makes up the existential meaning of 'getting taken along', never arrives at any other ecstatical horizon of its own accord, unless it gets brought back from its lostness by a resolution, so that both the current Situation (sic) and therewith the primordial 'limit-Situation' of being-towards-death, will be disclosed as a moment of vision which has been held on to.
>
> (BT400)[5]

7.3.2.7 Everyday Temporality of Discourse

Having covered the temporalities of understanding, disposedness, and falling, we are reminded that they are correlated with projection, thrownness, and fallenness. Heidegger lastly, but very briefly, addresses the temporality of discourse, which unites these other elements of being-there. All that Heidegger offers in this regard is that '[d]iscourse *in itself* is temporal since all talking about…is grounded in the ecstatical unity of temporality' (BT400). Obviously enough, given that we are temporal, our discoursing is grounded in temporality. However, in its everyday-ness, discourse has the tendency to fall into chatter, curiosity, and ambiguity, as has already been mentioned.

7.3.2.8 Different Understandings of Time and Temporality

Heidegger distinguishes between different kinds of temporality in the course of his analyses. He wants to provide as full a picture as he can of the ways in which time is understood. But he is particularly interested in articulating Dasein's authentic mode of temporality, which is relevant to the realm of therapy.

7.3.2.8.1 WORLD-TIME

The particular temporality of everydayness in which Dasein is absorbed in activi-ties and projects explored earlier is what Heidegger calls 'world-time' (BT467), which is 'the time which makes itself public in the temporalising of temporality' (ibid.). This is our usual experience of time, which is the way in which we reckon or deal with time in the course of our everyday existence. Typically, we absorb ourselves in getting certain things done according to our daily work schedules and responsibilities. He also refers to 'within-time-ness' (BT382), which is simply the way in which we encounter non-Dasein entities, such as tools and instruments. This is the sense of time in which the ready-to-hand and present-at-hand modes of being show up.

7.3.2.8.2 ORDINARY CONCEPTION OF TIME

The 'ordinary traditional conception of time' (BT382) is effectively 'clock time', or time as we observe it and render it in explicit ways. In this regard, Heidegger discusses the way in which lived time has been 'given a distinctive *public charac-ter*' (BT468), as a way of enhancing time-reckoning through measuring time. He adds that 'when we look at the clock and regulate ourselves *according to the time*, we are essentially *saying "now"*' (BT469). This 'now' way of interpreting time has become so normalised into our everyday existence that we never question its inau-thenticity. It is inauthentic because it is a time that makes-present in its 'retentive awaiting'. That is, clock time is a '*present-at-hand multiplicity of "nows"*' which are measurable (BT470). Time, in this way, has passed into 'datability, spanned-ness, publicness, and worldhood' (BT469).

7.3.2.8.3 TEMPORALITY OF DASEIN

Having named these different ways of thinking of time, Heidegger says that they all arise 'from an essential kind of temporalising of primordial temporality' (BT382). This is the ecstatic temporality of Dasein. Ecstatic temporality is the basis for world-time and the ordinary conception of time. It temporalises world-time, which is the way that we experience time as human beings. Think of the way in which two people are watching a Béla Tarr film, for example. One of the viewers feels drained as very little action takes place. Time drags on for her: she continually looks at her watch to see how much time is left for her to endure this. The other viewer is so absorbed in the way in which he is living the scenes in the film, as if he is actually there. He is lost in time, as he is gripped by the various moments and situations that develop. In other words, our experience of time is wholly at odds with clock time; when we're enjoying ourselves, we can't believe how quickly time passes. However, the significance only becomes more apparent to both viewers if they appreciate Tarr's use of the *actual* time of the film – neither accelerated nor slowed down, as is usually the case in 'film time' – which reflects the ecstatic temporality of Dasein.

In summary, then, our usual experience of time is world-time. Once we reflect on, and make explicit, what we are experiencing when absorbed in activities in world-time, this is the ordinary conception of time. However, these senses of time are all possible only on the basis of the ecstatic, or 'ecstatico-horizonal' character of temporality, which is Dasein's temporality (BT472). It is horizonal in the sense of the past, present, and future horizons in which temporality is already grasped, but ecstatic in the way in which Dasein 'reaches out' towards one or other horizon in its situatedness, or 'there'. This is authentic temporality, out of which inauthentic temporality arises (Wrathall, 2021:760).

7.3.3 Dasein as Historical, or Historising

Everyday existence is characteristically marked by the way in which we live in habitual and conventional ways, such that this way of living perpetuates itself over time. Heidegger introduces the idea of our existence being stretched across time:

> [i]n living unto its days Dasein *stretches* itself *along* 'temporally' in the sequence of those days...The 'it's all one and the same', the accustomed, the 'like yesterday, so today and tomorrow', and the 'for the most part' – these are not to be grasped without recourse to this 'temporal' stretching-along of Dasein.
> (BT423)

The sense of our lives being 'stretched' intimates the way a life extends temporally over a horizon of a past, present, and future. We commonly refer to this as a life that exists from its birth to death. We should not think of this in terms of specific moments in time. Rather, we understand this as both being thrown and a projection, a simultaneous movement of 'thrown throwing', or thrown throwing off thrownness, as has been discussed earlier. We are in a constant temporalising, or moving temporally, rather than statically positioned on a timeline that then has the future before us and a past that looks backwards. This refers back to Dasein, which is an openness, or 'there', that is both stretched along in its thrownness, and stretches along in its projection (BT427). Heidegger calls this 'stretched stretching', 'historising' (ibid.). It is a living historicality of Dasein, in other words, and not a history, in the traditional sense of the term. History is something present-at-hand, and ontic, whereas historicality is existential and ontological.

There are two ways of historising for Dasein: inauthentically and authentically. Inauthentically, we lose ourselves in a conventional way that a lived narrative develops. To put it rather simplistically with an example, we might pursue a path of education, become a professional, raise a family, build a career, and have a comfortable retirement. All along, we have succeeded according to what our societal norms have presented and endorsed as to how a 'good' life should be led, as in the case of the central character, Ilyich, in Tolstoy's *The Death of Ivan Ilych* (1886/1971). We might feel contented with ourselves, unless we review those moments in our lives when we held a passion or another possibility for how we might have lived a meaningful and compelling existence. Authentic historising, by contrast, is to live with a resoluteness, which means that we face up to the responsibility for living in the face of our finitude. That is, we decide on a course of action, and we show a commitment or 'constancy' in pursuing a path that we alone have chosen. Becoming a painter, deciding to live abroad, or trying our hand at becoming a filmmaker offer no guarantee of a familiar or safe path, but the experience and narrativising of ourselves in the course of making such a commitment is to come into our own, or our authentic being. We historise authentically in the sense that we are being the authors of our own lives.

To take ourselves as historising beings is an important element of therapeutic work with clients, which I will address further in Part IV. This means attending to a narrative that clients illuminate in terms of their understanding of themselves.

Notes

1 Drawing on Braver, 2014:86.
2 I use the terms One, They, Anyone, and Everyone interchangeably at different points in the text. I do so in order to make the reader aware that various other authors will have their own preferred translations, and that they can all be taken as possible translations of the German, '*das Man*'.
3 I use all of these terms, since I think of them as interchangeable.
4 I introduce these expressions based on my reading of Braver and Richardson's references to the form of hermeneutics that Heidegger introduces in *Being and Time*.
5 The translators have capitalised 'situation' here to reflect the authentic, unique situation, as opposed to the inauthentic, general situation, which is expressed with a small 's'. Other capitalised terms have been replaced to retain consistency in this book.

Part III

Dasein's Challenges

We live in a world in which we face any number of ways of describing situations, whether from challenges, obstacles, and difficulties to problems and crises. This can range from the occasional relatively minor experiences of feeling thrown out of the flow of everyday activities, to the deeper issue of being alive and the challenges that this poses at times. At such deeper levels, we might experience an unease in living in a world that sometimes seems out of joint with being human, as we might encounter in response to the technological demands that press for optimisation and efficiency. In all these circumstances, Heidegger's existentiales reflect the way in which we express and embody existentiell ways of being, i.e., in our own particular way. At times, our existentiell stance can contribute to, or manifest in, a situational breakdown for us, along with a confusion that prevents or obstructs us from seeing that which is ontologically furthest from us rather than what is ontically nearest. That is, since we are ontically absorbed in what presents itself to us in the course of dealing with situations, we at the same time close off to the ontological import of such situations.

III.1 What is a Breakdown? What Constitutes a Breakdown?

In everyday language, we encounter the various ways of speaking of breakdowns, such that they convey different meanings. For example, we speak of a 'mental' break, or the breaking up of the mind. Or we think of a breakdown in terms of a collapse of one's integral self. Alternatively, we might speak of 'emotional breakdowns', in which we fail to feel or do anything, which is reflected in an inability to cope with daily life. All these attempts to grasp the essence of a breakdown rely on a particular set of underlying terms that draw on assumptions that originate from a Cartesian model of the human being. It assumes a breakdown of the mind, which is also reflected in the body's capacity to engage with the world. The general understanding is that one affects the other, but this is a complicated matter, in part, because the dualism that underpins the picture has two distinctly separate kinds of 'substance' that can't be comprehensively brought back into a unified whole.

DOI: 10.4324/9781003342137-10

Breakdowns, understood from an existential perspective, are a central feature of being human. It is *we*, in our concernfully being-amid or alongside hammers and knives, for example, that make use of such items in a way that bestows relevance to them in the context of a particularly meaningful activity. We report on their malfunctioning, being put out of use, and in need of replacing or fixing. In this sense, only we are open to assessing these entities, insofar as we use them, as contributing, or giving rise, to breakdowns. We encounter breakdowns because our being is an issue for us, that we take a stance on our being, and that this stance is expressed in the way in which we are immersed in a world of activities, projects, and tasks that involve a 'handling' of equipment. Although Heidegger only addresses this rather briefly, we look to optimise our way of handling, or using something important and relevant to the task at hand, such as the hammer, or the way in which we teach a class, for example. Optimising in this sense is not a robotic, detached orientation towards the challenge or task at hand, but our coordinating and interacting bodily with the thing, tool, situation, and others in a way that promotes a seamless involvement. However, we should note that breakdowns relate to a world, that the way that the world itself is constituted is central to the possibility of there being a breakdown in the first place. This is captured in our being-in-the-world, such that we are beings whose being involves experiences of breakdowns in (and of) the world.

Chapter 8

Disruptions, Ruptures, Disturbances, Breakdowns, Collapses

8.1 General

Our experience of breakdowns can impact on us in ways that lead us to live according to patterns and strategies that we adopt in order to avoid the possibility of any further such disruptions to our lives. We try to keep to a routine way of life, by infusing a sense of order and predictability, such that an unbroken harmony in our activities becomes an understanding of this as constituting a good life lived. But life itself has a tendency to throw us into situations and circumstances that take us out of such comforting routines and patterns. We face the possibility that we, or others, make and then break agreements, promises, and commitments, even if relatively minor in significance, such as turning up late for a rendezvous, or, in relatively more serious situations, the abrupt ending of a longstanding career. Promises and commitments bring us to shape our lives in various ways, such that we embrace some possibilities and exclude others, for example. Some of these situations will be explored a little later.

Of course, we also start out early in life under the guidance of our parental upbringing, inculcated and educated into certain practices, customs, values, beliefs, and habits, based on appropriate, acceptable, or valued behaviours. This intersects with other elements, such as the parental approach and style, as well as one's own sense of autonomy and freedom, accompanied also by degrees of belonging, love, appreciation, and support. From a cultural perspective, as is the case in the Western world, we are thrown into certain possibilities of living that are already framed by or based on economic, societal, political, and ideological models that reflect our age. Education and schooling promote a certain outlook that values achievement through various forms of assessment, including tests, exams, and evaluations. We quickly learn and adapt to various norms and conventions, to greater or lesser degrees, including the discipline of sitting in school classes, and attending school as an already established way of life for an infant. We are also under the influence of messages and putative norms that present a picture of ourselves as consumers, and, on the whole, reliable and conforming employees in the workplace. Punctuality and conformity are taken as standards into which we are thrown and bring intelligibility to our world. To put it more concisely, we become absorbed

DOI: 10.4324/9781003342137-11

into a certain ordering of time and activity in our lives from an early age, under-pinned by regularity and consistency.

Whilst referring to the phenomenon in terms of a breakdown, we might alterna-tively employ the language of disturbance, disruption, perturbation, and collapse, according to the severity, depth, and impact of the event in question. Breakdowns can reflect something deeply significant that is happening in our lives, on the one hand, but equally refer to simple accidents, or minor breaks in the flow of daily existence, on the other. Rather than assuming a wholly mechanistic approach to breakdowns, that is, from a substance-oriented perspective, we are in need of a more coherent understanding of being human based on the way in which break-downs constitute our existence.

8.2 Breakdowns in our Current Understanding of Being

In our usual way of going about our daily affairs, we typically cope in situations that draw on various technological tools that we use, for the most part, transpar-ently. A familiar example is one of going to the local supermarket and paying for items at the self-check-out: I place my credit card over the electronic reader, and a short beep acknowledges that the transaction has been successfully completed. I pass through the exit without an alarm sounding, confirming that all my purchases have been approved in terms of payment. But there is a deeper sense of the way in which we live according to an ordered and optimised way of maximising the effi-ciency of tasks, projects, and preoccupations to their fullest. This way of being is what has been translated as 'enframing'. Heidegger means by this the way in which we already encounter everything in terms of a resource to be ordered, or positioned in some way, so that it is ready to be used, manipulated, and consumed. In relat-ing to things, others, and ourselves, according to this understanding, we encounter something as possessing a certain value only insofar as it acts as a means to meet ultimate ends. We even see ourselves as resources to be ordered and optimised. So much of this is commonly encountered in the corporate world, where we find such conceptual models as just-in-time delivery, manufacturing resource planning, as well as performance reviews. The impact this has in the workplace is to forge an understanding of ourselves within a cybernetic field in which everything is con-trolled and manipulated in order to maximise and optimise outcomes and results. Heidegger considers this way of treating everything as a resource that is ordered and optimised a technological understanding of being.

If this way of understanding our world is considered in the context of a thera-peutic setting, it raises questions about being-in-the-world. A young man attends therapy sessions, for example, because he finds his work challenging and over-whelming. He assumes that therapy provides a rapid and efficient way to remedy or solve the issue. However, since the world already shows up as enframed, includ-ing himself, his expectations are already moulded and shaped in advance. Facing the issue by helping the client to reach a technological solution to his concerns would just be a way of perpetuating his understanding by confirming and endorsing a view of the world that is grounded in efficiency, order, and manipulability. In other words, in trying to solve certain issues that we encounter in this technological understanding, we can easily lapse into a technological form of thinking, by approaching the issue as one that demands a solution. By contrast, for Heidegger, a more human response is reflected in being open to a gestalt switch, or a different way of attuning ourselves to what we face, through a deeper re-orientation to things as a whole. This might well involve prolonged exploration, thus offering the possibility of phenomenological insights. That is to say, the therapist invites the client to participate, through reflection and dialogue, in a hermeneutic or interpretative process that opens them to a deeper understanding of their being-in-the-world.

One possible manifestation of a breakdown situation therefore emerges in the client's realisation that they have previously submerged or submitted themself to a technological understanding, such that it has perpetuated an inauthentic way of living. It has covered over the fact that they have secluded themself in a relatively comforting but ultimately unsatisfying existence. From a Heideggerian perspective, an alternative possible response to this technological understanding is for the client to release themself into such machinations, or, as he puts it, enter into a free relation to it – expressed as a 'letting be' – but at the same time, not feeling overwhelmed by it. The client continues in their use of technological gadgetry and ways of engaging with the world in accordance with efficiency, optimisation, and ordering in various ways, but adopts an attitude or mood that this (technological) world is not the *only* possible world. For example, we typically find ourselves immersed in other worlds that include social and family gatherings, being in the art world as well as in nature, such that they disclose to us a way of being that is not susceptible to a technological understanding. In such cases, however, it is not so much that the 'problem' that might initially be brought to therapy always or predominantly lies with the client, as is usually presented, but that the *world* is configured in a way that presents itself as the *only* possible way to understand what it is to be. When everything is treated as being in need of ever-greater ordering, optimisation, and maximisation, it has the tendency to exclude other possible worlds. Given the fact that we live in a technological age, then, a response to this is to be in a free relation to it.

To take a broader and wider historical perspective, this technological understanding of what it is to be has left us with what can be called a 'nihilistic' outlook. This is an age in which there is no ultimate meaning or giver of meaning that can support our lives and guide us in terms of what is right and wrong, good and bad, or important and trivial. Its beginnings reach as far back as the thinking of Plato and other Greek thinkers. As has been already discussed in Part I, for Plato the experiential realm is lacking in perfection, and is therefore devalued. Those many things that we find in it, such as chairs, tables, cups, are mere renditions of deeper truths. These truths are the perfect Forms or Ideas, where meaning ultimately resides, because Ideas have no flaws or imperfections to them. This leaves us living in a realm of our senses that we effectively relegate in favour of another realm that is not of this world, and which provides us with perfect knowledge of the True, the

Good, and the Beautiful. This division sets up a sense of both leaving behind that which is now deemed meaningless because of its imperfection and illusory status, and also of orientating ourselves towards what is ideal, or holds perfection. As well as presenting this division, we are engaged in a reaching outward and towards the perfect. What is lost in this, however, is the notion of being receptive to what is presented to us. In the times of Homer, Heraclitus, and Parmenides, for example, it was the understanding of situations or events arising, lingering for a while, and finally withdrawing that reflected the way in which we are thrown into situations and a world that is given to us. In Homer's world, people lived according to a certain *medio-passivity*[1] in which they were open and receptive to events, rather than being purely active agents who behaved with intentions in situations. This can be best illustrated by those situations in which we consult a doctor about a bodily pain that we experience. We both surrender to the doctor's questions, as well as their physical touch and tests, but also take an active part in the process in which we provide valuable information about what we experience in our pain or discomfort. The approach taken by phenomenology reflects this understanding by enquiring into what is already given but hidden or covered over, rather than what is not given and in need of a certain excavation through science, for example.

According to Heidegger and others, such as Nietzsche, we live in an age in which no ultimate meaning is given to us. Heidegger, however, distinguishes himself from others in articulating an existential understanding in response to this, rather than a more nihilistic position. For him, we are left to cultivate our own meanings in the very way in which we exist. We do so in a way that draws on those possibilities that are available to us given our background practices, and also in embracing our existence as authentically our own. A technological understanding, by contrast, has effectively severed us from our way of being as Dasein. The existentiale, de-severance, for instance, might be said to have become manifest, existentially, in distorted or compromised ways that endanger Dasein's being-in-the-world, due to the predominant way in which ordering and placing everything is prioritised over and above everything else. In that sense, everything is brought forth such that it is available to us for our ordering, controlling, and optimising.

8.3 Kinds of Breakdown

From a Heideggerian perspective, Dasein incurs several possible kinds of breakdown, based on his account in *Being and Time*:

1 equipment breakdowns
2 world breakdowns
3 world collapse – radical breakdowns
4 temporal breakdowns as time-reckoning.

Heidegger introduces shifts or breakdowns both within each Division of *Being and Time* but also in the very transitions that reflect a hermeneutic turn from Division

I to II. In terms of the fourth form of breakdown mentioned here, I propose that breakdowns are also temporally-based, since the hermeneutic movement that presumably continues after Division II of that work reflects a continuing process of breaking down and uncovering what was previously hidden. In that sense, since *Being and Time* is an unfinished work, and a third Division was originally planned, temporal breakdowns must follow.

8.3.1 Equipment Breakdowns

Equipment breakdowns are best illustrated using an example. Think of the scenario of using an online meeting platform to hold a pre-arranged therapy session with a client. You prepare yourself so that you arrive at your desk in good time, and settle into your chair to operate your laptop computer. You now notice that the time is approaching the agreed moment to enter the online room, and you click on the appropriate link to take you there. You have performed this same operation on numerous other occasions, and so you now go through the motions as you are accustomed to do. As you click on the link, the computer pauses, and a spinning, circular rainbow-coloured cursor then shows on your screen. This means that you now have to wait for the computer to process your wish to be transported to the meeting room with your client. You wait, expecting the wheel to disappear, but it remains firmly in place and unchanged. What's wrong? You don't actually know. And the time has now arrived to begin the session with your client. You fixate on the clock and experience anxiety. You worry about the fact that you will be late. You quickly realise that activating a monitor on the computer will reset the computer to its original state. As you do so, the circular wait cursor disappears, and you now enter the meeting room, feeling somewhat relieved.

Phenomenologically, a descriptive account of what happened might go along the following lines. As you initially settled into your chair, you were in a particularly relaxed and unperturbed mood. Perhaps we might say that you were open to the span of time before you, without reflecting on this in any way. As you began to engage with the computer, the relevant components and images on the screen were all relatively inconspicuous: nothing stood out in any way, but was simply there available for you to use. You treated this equipment as usable in order to meet your ends. This meant that it was reliable – that it functioned precisely and consistently as it did on all previous occasions – and even withdrew from any consideration of it as an actual computer. In Heidegger's language, the computer was inconspicuous, unobtrusive, and manipulable, and you were engaged and involved in this activity of using the computer.

Any equipmental breakdown refers to those aspects of our world that we employ or require in some way or other that are no longer available to us, for some reason. In Heidegger's terms, tools and other relevant entities simply stop functioning in their being familiar to us, and of being ready-to-hand. Equipment, as we said previously, is a totality of those tools, implements, and elements of that world that are used in order for that world to 'world', to sustain itself ongoingly as a world.

For example, in the therapy room, if the door fails to open, or the sofa chairs on which therapist and client sit no longer offer the function for sitting on, such equipment has become 'unwieldy' or unavailable for use, and the therapy hour cannot proceed. However, imagine that this temporary breakdown has been overcome in one way or another. It is certainly equipment that breaks down, for Heidegger, but Dasein *assesses* the breakdown as a disruption and a disturbance of a situation, or else a very minor inconvenience that bears no real impact on Dasein in its focus on the overall task towards which equipment is applied and employed. In this way, it is *Dasein* who addresses and deals with the breakdown in order to resume its original task or project.

8.3.2 World Breakdowns

In Division II of *Being and Time*, Heidegger explores the circumstances in which being-in-the-world breaks down. This has already been given some attention, where Dasein undergoes anxiety and deep disorientation but cannot point to anything specific or concrete that accounts for this. There is literally 'nothing' that can be said to evoke or bring it about, nor can it be somehow remedied and overcome. Take the scenario of a client coming to therapy for the first time and experiencing some trepidation. Understandably, taking the decision to do so intimates a sense of stepping into an unfamiliar world. The client arrives, meets the therapist, but there is a certain anxiety that persists. There is nothing to relate to at this stage that gives them a sense of the familiar, how they are to 'be' in the session, or how therapy might proceed. There are no projects or tasks that the client can engage with or relate to whilst at the same time being present in the room. As yet, they are not-at-home, 'out of place', and in the unfamiliar setting of a therapy session. In this sense, the world is revealed in its insignificance for the client, because the cessation of routines and everyday practices, for whatever reason, brings them face-to-face with themselves as they are, and not as they typically present themself in everydayness. Significance only comes when the client engages in projects, draws on various things that enable that world to sustain itself in its intelligibility, and embraces a role or identity. In anxiety, all this falls away to reveal Dasein's being-in-the-world.

8.3.3 World-collapse – Radical Breakdowns

In this kind of breakdown, imagine a situation where everything just ceases to matter to me in the way that it has up to this point in my life. These are typically what we might call 'moments of crisis', where not just one or two situations or moments break down and leave us disoriented, but where nothing is making any sense at all. These are most familiar to us when we hear about people undergoing a loss of faith, or a religious conversion, or the end of a relationship or marriage. The person, in other words, undergoes a global or general collapse. Their world has fallen apart. This is more severe and disorienting than world breakdowns because it describes a life where a certain intelligibility has been eroded or erased.

It might otherwise be associated with a loss of identity, in which the person's sense of themselves has disappeared. However, this is not to be understood as the loss of a person's mineness. The difference between identity and mineness is that the latter reflects a formal singularity of being this entity and not another. Since it is a permanent structure of Dasein, it means that it is not something that can be 'lost', as such. In the kind of experience being described here as a world-collapse, all of our cares, involvements, and concerns that describe and reflect a meaningful world have been shattered. Life is now described as pointless, because the person has lost the ability to engage in the everyday world, as well as a sense of care about those things that they had previously cared about. It expresses a certain threat to the person as the 'I' that they had experienced prior to this point in time. Life has, we might say, come apart, the person's world has collapsed, and they find themselves in an environment that is foreign and unfamiliar to them. None of the resources that were previously available to them are now on hand, nor are the skills that had allowed them to participate in that world now relevant or meaningful.

The person, in this case, has suffered a radical breakdown in the way in which their ultimate for-the-sake-of-which has collapsed, and which was so central to their relation to themselves as they lived their lives. The death of a parent, for example, can be potentially so disturbing for some because it terminates a bond that has normally been expressed in a myriad number of ways in the temporal realm. It reflects the ways in which so much is at stake in sustaining our identity that, once this is lost, we lose our bearings, or compass.

Much of what I have tried to articulate so far is illustrated in Jonathan Lear's *Radical Hope*, which describes the life of Plenty Coups, the last great Chief of the native American Crow people. He describes the loss of a way of life with the arrival of European American settlers over the course of his own lifetime. However, with regard to the radical changes that he and his people lived through, he discloses to his interviewer:

I have not told you half of what happened when I was young…I can think back and tell you much more of war and horse-stealing. But when the buffalo went away the hearts of my people fell to the ground, and they could not lift them up again. After this nothing happened.

(2006:2)

The last short sentence captures the world-collapse for both Plenty Coups and his people. Their whole understanding of their way of life had been wiped out. The temporalising of temporality was absent, in other words. Lear adds that there is 'no importantly first-person narrative to tell of this period. It is as though there is no longer an I there' (ibid.:3). That is, Plenty Coups himself had lost a way of life, given his role as a chief who led his people. The phrase 'nothing happened' is chilling, as it intimates a void, or nullity.

8.3.4 Temporal Breakdowns as Time-reckoning

For Heidegger, 'temporality is constitutive for Dasein's being,' and 'factical Dasein takes time into its reckoning, without any existential understanding of temporality' (BT456). In our everyday understanding of the world, we reckon with time insofar as we arrange, order, and calculate what we do or do not have time to engage in, or complete certain activities or tasks. This is a basic feature of being human; no other kinds of being, or non-Dasein beings, exist in this way. This is something that we do irrespective of whether clocks or diaries are available for us to organise ourselves and structure time in this way. However, our relation to time in our everyday lives is to treat it in a present-at-hand way, i.e., as objective and public. This is in contrast to time as primordial and existential, which Heidegger calls 'existential temporality'. We can think of the way in which we experience time as we sit in a café, or are immersed in a particular activity. At such times, we cannot be said to be 'clock-watching'. For Heidegger, our everyday treatment of time is to level it off (BT474) so that each second is essentially like the one before or after it, and that time just runs in a recordable way. As such, we have transformed existential temporality into public time (BT464). As public time, Dasein 'does *not* know this "time" *as its own*, but concernfully *utilises* the time which "there is" – the time with which "they" reckon' (BT464).

We understand time in terms of a past, present, and future. These dimensions of time, taken together, are what Heidegger refers to as 'datability' (BT459). This is the everyday temporal categorising of events in terms of 'before', 'during', and 'after'. So, Brexit took place before the Pandemic, but after the 2008 global financial crisis. Datability itself has come into being because we are always concerned in one way or another with things, situations, and events in which we happen to find ourselves, and about which we show concern and care. They matter to us. Datability, as Heidegger presents it here, is not intended to be taken in a statistical or straightforwardly numerical sense, but only as a general way of orienting ourselves in terms of time. In this context, we already have a certain relation to past and future events insofar as they either 'have been' or 'will be' a focus of our concern.

Datability, then, is grounded in temporality. This is not an atomistic sense of time, which is the sense of successive experiential moments that are 'atoms' of time, but rather one that allows for varying time intervals. For example, I say that I don't have time to complete a task, which itself discloses the sense of time as something that endures, and spans across moments. Such spans of time can also vary with respect to the duration of an event. In this sense, 'now' can refer to a press of an ignition switch in my car, or it can refer to our age in which we now live. The 'nows' in question are not merely subjective experiences, such that they are entirely personal, nor 'objectively actual', as Heidegger puts it (BT464). Rather, they are shared with others, such that other people are involved in this datability too. They can dispute or correct my claim that an event took place last year, in insisting that it was more recent. On this basis, Heidegger says that we date according to what Heidegger calls 'environmental events' (BT464). We happen to do this in terms of 'astronomical and calendrical time-reckoning' (BT464).

Time-reckoning is a particularly relevant feature of Dasein, especially in certain cases that clients present in the course of therapy. Imagine the following scenario. H self-identifies as a 31 year-old woman who is in a relationship with her partner of some ten years. She works in a law firm as a solicitor, and has a considerable work-load to manage. She works long hours, and also takes additional work home every evening, much to the annoyance of her partner. At certain times, where a major project requires immediate attention because it demands rapid completion, all the staff, including H, are instructed to come to work over several weekends. This means that longstanding plans that H has previously organised with her partner are now shelved. At such times, she experiences stress and irritation, but says that the job pays very well, that she has been rewarded with promotions to senior positions within the practice, and that she is reluctant to move to another firm. When such projects have been completed, H resumes her work schedule, but has found that colleagues have been able to negotiate their workloads to manageable levels, whilst hers seems to increase. As well as this, H is becoming increasingly frustrated with her partner, who seems to have a more relaxed attitude about their future plans to marry. She is keen to start a family, but he says that he is in no particular rush.

Apart from the many strands of interpretations that this example offers, it is the sense of time-reckoning that is the focus of my attention here. H is being pulled by the demands of those aspects of her life that distend and distort a sense of lived time. But at the same time, she is committed to reckoning with time in a way that matters to her. Time itself becomes shaped by norms that dictate how she needs to be if she is to maintain her world that is held together by her. Only in the course of our therapy sessions does she undergo a temporal breakdown, as she openly challenges her work-world, as well as her personal relationship with her partner. The breakdown is reflected in her recognising that she can no longer sustain this way of living, and that she is committed to pursuing major changes as a result.

Reckoning, in Heidegger's sense, is not purely the dating, or the pragmatic handling of one's time, that has already been addressed, but really discloses the 'existential-ontological necessity in the basic state of Dasein as care. Because it is essential to Dasein that it exists fallingly as something thrown, it interprets its time concernfully by way of time-reckoning' (BT464).

We each cope temporally in our own particular ways. Moreover, it is only because we are thrown in our way of being that there is public time in the first place. That is, it is given, and we have to reckon with it, in one way or another. We cannot remain indifferent or somehow neutral in response to it. In public time, this reckoning threads all the way back to our being as care, that is, that things matter to us. For example, we might express a certain commitment to being punctual. This might be down to a certain attitude about ever being late, whether as a personal principle, or because we hold a certain respect for others and take the agreed meeting time as a promise that one makes towards another person. We might alternatively leave everything until the last minute, and then make desperate attempts to arrive at the agreed time. These are all ways in which we reckon with time. They might also be shaped by our existentiell interpretation of certain other existentiales, such as the One, for example, in which we reckon with time according to behaviours that meaningfully conform to norms. Or we might relate to time in respect of particular moods that habitually grip us and frame the way in which we are already anticipating impending situations as breakdowns, or in other possible ways.

Many kinds of breakdowns can be traced back to the ways in which we engage and interact with others against the backdrop of temporality. Those that come to mind include agreements, promises, trust, and conversations. Each can be investigated in terms of their particular phenomenological structures. However, once we consider them from an existential perspective, we engage with the temporal aspects of the phenomenon, as well as those existentiales that seem most relevant to the enquiry. For example, committing to promises with another person who is not initially known to us takes time, since an underlying mood is required to undergird or provide the basis for believing that any such promises are made with honest intent. As well as this, a promise involves an authentic discourse, such that the promiser is not making a promise lightly, but is someone whose being is at stake in making such a promise. In other words, they recognise that it is a temporal commitment, that their identity is being expressed throughout this time, not just in the momentary act of making the promise. They act with a sense of self as constancy, and treat it as a unique situation, rather than a casual affair. In the more mundane, everyday way of treating a promise, they see it as just a way to deal with the situation, and that their action reflects how one engages in such moments. The existentiale, being-with, also has its place as a key element in making and keeping a promise, as well as being a promiser. In all these aspects of promising, a local world is brought into the clearing, or light, that wasn't previously there.

8.4 A Beckettian Temporal Breakdown

We have various ways of reckoning with temporality. Perhaps a particularly striking and dramatic way in which this can be illustrated is in the Irish playwright Samuel Beckett's play, *Waiting for Godot* (1956). We are invited to immerse ourselves in a temporal experience as the viewer that is simultaneously being played out on stage between the two central characters, Vladimir and Estragon. They are both caught in a mood of hope and expectation of the eventual presence of 'Godot', who never actually arrives. It is a two-act play in which 'nothing happens, twice' as one critic, Vivian Mercer, has put it (1956:29). This itself can be taken in two ways, that 'nothing' is illuminated or made present in the absence of something or other, but also in the sense that there is nothing that supplies us with an ultimate meaning to the day, the situation, or our overall existence. In this hope and expectation, there is a feeling of discomfort and disorientation, which is only filled with yearning and distraction. In other words, there is an existential emptiness and inertia. Waiting for a certain outcome can be a way of living that 'fills' the time that is ahead of us. But both Estragon (Gogo) and Vladimir (Didi) have invested meaning in something that is effectively their life project. It is their ultimate for-the-sake-of-which, since everything apparently turns on this.

The temporal breakdown that we encounter in our own experience of watching the play is that we are left with a self-reflexive awareness of ourselves in the theatre, undergoing the passage of time as we grapple with the play's meaning. As we watch the play, we attempt to discern its structure and meaning, but, certainly on its first viewings, we struggle with this. As a consequence, we conclude that we are perhaps wasting our time, both in trying to understand the play, but also in being a viewer. One possible experience is that we might fail to reckon with the play, and so we consider the possibility of abandoning the project. Our world, and all the elements that constitute it, including ourselves as viewer, the activity of watching, and the stage and seat that we sit on, undergoes its own breakdown.

A breakdown comes with our sensing that we *ourselves* are temporal, and that we attempt to make time 'count' for something. This is the existential insight that such a breakdown might offer the two characters, rather than some kind of truth that is beyond them that will then presumably determine how they are to structure their lives.

Note

1 I take this term from Beatrice Han-Pile; see her 'Ethics of Powerlessness' Research Project (University of Essex).

Chapter 9

Existentiales and Breakdowns

As has already been established, an existentiale is an essential feature that constitutes Dasein, and its way of being. Each existentiale is appropriated and embodied in its own particular way, such that it expresses that existentiale in its own way of existing. This way of manifesting an existentale is what Heidegger calls 'existentiell'. However, we also experience breakdown situations that reflect the existentiell 'style' that is sedimented in our way of being. We manifest an existentiell mode of being that might be privative or derivative, and this might well be considered a kind of breakdown. For example, in the case of the existentiale, being-with, we might be prone to withdraw and seclude ourselves from others, or avoid them in more radical ways, because we harbour a fear of being overtaken by their presence. An instance of this is well-illustrated in the work of R.D. Laing, who presents what he describes as 'ontological insecurity' (1960:38).

For the purposes of extending the account of breakdowns as expressed in the existentiell manifestations of the existentiales, I offer some elaboration on a number of existentiales that could be relevant to any given existential therapeutic analysis.

9.1 Concern

Given that this existentiale reflects the various ways in which we go about our daily business and busy ourselves around the practicalities of what needs to get done, such as shopping, getting our laundry cleaned, or arranging for a home delivery, a more privative or 'deficient' mode in which this might be deemed a disruption or breakdown is when this is neglected or becomes disorganised. A certain disengagement from these everyday practicalities, through a form of avoidance perhaps, or a sense of feeling bored by simple chores, reflects a concern to not be bothered or consumed with any preoccupations. In more extreme cases, this manifests as a profound lack of care. Being aware that various everyday errands are being neglected reflects an existentielly privative mode of the existentiale, concern.

9.2 De-severance

As an existentiale, de-severance reflects Dasein's looking to bring what is remote towards and near it. However, existentielly, it encounters breakdowns insofar as

DOI: 10.4324/9781003342137-12

situations arise in which entities somehow resist or oppose this. Things remain beyond and farther than is reachable, from an existential perspective. Somehow, the world and the entities that Dasein perceives around it seem, and even feel, distant, and perhaps unfamiliar. In this case, entities aren't encountered by Dasein, but are only remote and unavailable. On the other hand, Dasein may even want to enhance or encourage remoteness rather than overcome it, for whatever reason, in which case this is another example of a breakdown of the existentiell mode of de-severance.

9.3 Directionality

Directionality is the existentiale that is very closely associated with de-severance. As Heidegger says, 'every bringing-close has already taken in advance a direction towards a region out of which what is de-severed brings itself close, so that one can come across it with regard to its place' (BT143). A manifestation of a breakdown situation in which Dasein undergoes its existentiell loss of drawing something towards, but is always moving away, or to the left or right of what would be deemed close, is a way in which directionality itself is frustrated because the entities in question cannot be brought into the direction of Dasein. Given that directionality is a centrally important existentiale in relation to Dasein's embodiment, much more could be said about the direction in which we are faced in situations and in our environment generally. It is a significant feature of our experiencing the world, as well as others, if we allow this existentiale a more extended account. To offer but one example of this, something significant is captured in the phrase 'Someone is talking behind my back'. Later on, I will discuss breakdowns in embodiment, though leave its connection to directionality to one side.

9.4 Making Room

Insofar as Dasein is 'in' the world, in the sense of being involved and immersed in its activities and its environment, it deals with things that it employs, and interacts with others insofar as they are relevant to its tasks and projects. Dasein is the kind of being that makes room for certain entities in order that they can be used, and that then enable it to move towards its ultimate goal, or for-the-sake-of-which. As an existentiale, making room is closely tied to the existential space that Dasein requires, whether this even be to sit down and watch a film on a screen, or set an appropriate adjustment for the car seat prior to driving. Breakdown events occur when, for example, a client experiences a work situation in which they have 'no room' to devote part of their day to thinking and reflecting on their approach to teaching, or studying a subject in greater depth so that they might inspire further reflection in their students. Their space is cluttered with meetings and routine tasks that seem pointless and distracting. Their increasingly changing role has brought them to the point of exclaiming that they have no space to breathe. In this existentiell sense, the client has experienced the breakdown of their space and feels that they cannot 'make room' for other priorities.

9.5 Possibility

This existentiale is related closely to other existentiales, such as projection and understanding. Dasein has the possibility of owning itself or not doing so: that is, of being authentic or inauthentic. In terms of ontic possibility, we actualise certain possibilities over others. However, ontological possibility is entirely different. Insofar as I am a partner, a friend, or an engineer, for example, I express this possibility for as long as I am in such roles. Should I experience a collapse in a friendship, the ontological possibility for being a friend in that relationship has now ceased. Possibility might involve a breakdown situation in which I enter a moment of crisis over some event or other, and now experience 'stuckness'. Ontically, I avoid the responsibility of choosing one possibility over others. In the case of ontological possibility, however, I might be ambivalent about continuing in my chosen profession, for example, as I contemplate retirement, and place my ongoing identity into a certain kind of disruption or disorientation.

9.6 Meaning

Meaning is reflected in the way in which something is the particular way that it is, or how it 'maintains itself', as Heidegger puts it (BT370). Meaning is constituted in understanding, and understanding for Dasein is to take up a for-the-sake-of-which that gives it an identity and a world in which it pursues projects that are meaningful to it. In a case of world breakdown, the meaning of being-in-the-world itself is illuminated through anxiety, when that world undergoes a collapse. At such times, we see that we are constituted as beings who are immersed in a world, and this 'seeing' is the meaning. In breakdown cases of meaning, however, we deflect or deviate from seeing this, and defer to some other way of explaining or accounting for it. In other words, we are inauthentic in our way of fleeing from the meaning rather than authentically facing up to it.

9.7 Being-with

Most of the time, we experience our lives working smoothly and transparently. We feel generally confident and immerse ourselves happily in situations with others. In this sense, everyday life flows relatively unnoticed. Then a change occurs in our circumstances. Take the case of an elderly couple who are faced with one partner falling ill, resulting in an inability to engage in various activities that had become habitual. The person who is experiencing illness requires some time to recuperate. In the meantime, the other person in the relationship finds themself challenged by this sudden and unexpected turn of events. It constitutes a form of breakdown for them, even though they are sympathetic to their partner's suffering. They are supportive and understanding and try to disavow their own feelings about the new situation and its unfairness. But they nevertheless face a different person to the one that they had been living with prior to the illness. They admit to themself that they feel disoriented, as they now experience their partner as debilitated, dependent, and incapacitated.

This is a wholly new experience for them. The change is the shift from a prior openness to everyday life, to the unexpected challenge of dealing with this situation that now focuses on illness and impairment. As their partner gradually begins to return to a healthier state, a clear reluctance to return to a formerly active life prior to falling ill now emerges. It seems that a sense of security or comfort through relative inactivity has become the preferred way of life. More to the point, this formerly ill person is dealing with the breakdown from their own experiential point of view. Their partner now becomes irritated by this, since they want to deal with the breakdown differently. In other words, they want their now healthy partner to become more like them, so that they won't feel alone in the broken-down situation.

9.7.1 Others

In what follows, I advert to a sense of 'they' and 'them' that we tend to use in distancing ourselves from others, rather than the sense that Heidegger intends when he talks about the One. The sense that I introduce here is a derived or deficient mode of being with others that is inauthentic and constitutes a form of breakdown. This usually manifests in everyday life where difference and 'othering' are prevalent, in the sense that we treat others on the basis that they lack some particular quality, characteristic, behaviour, social, or economic class or background, or are simply 'strange' to us. To be sure, language has played its own part in creating terms that take hold in a culture and invoke a 'them' who are not like 'us', and that then implies that this 'othered they' ought to be avoided, shunned, or ignored because of such difference. However, in a more positively conceived sense of breakdown, perhaps, we also tend to circumscribe a more select 'they' for ourselves, or those that we welcome and follow – we commonly speak of a circle, or group, or community, in this sense – whether this be family, friends, relatives, or those with whom we are in familiar relations, such as the local coffee shop baristas. A further elaboration of this might extend this account to Heidegger's various other features of Dasein's existence, such as existential space, the One, and worldhood, though this will not be attempted here.

9.7.2 Being-with-others

As humans, we manifest a virtually endless number of ways in which we might express being-with-others. In certain instances, however, privative, derivative, or deficient modes of the existentiale can manifest in our own existentiell way of being. One possibility already mentioned is to either intentionally or incidentally seclude or withdraw ourselves from contact with others. In all cases, we are always shaping and determining the meaning of how we spend our time in a way that always takes others into account, but which is at the same time constantly in the background. That is, this is never explicit and foregrounded, unless certain relations become confusing or concerning. Another derived mode or breakdown case of being-with-others is in the way in which others are treated in either a ready-to-hand or present-at-hand way, rather than being seen in their existence as human beings.

Being-with, as it manifests in our existentiell interpretation of this existentiale in being with others, can be expressed in a manifold number of possible ways. From a therapeutic point of view, the challenge on the part of therapist and client is to enter into a phenomenological exploration that uncovers, or unconceals, what was previously covered over. The unconcealing itself, as it happens in the course of the dialogue, or through the therapist's challenges, is a form of breakdown, not only of what had been concealed, but also of the assumed relationship between the therapist and client. The client's sense of being with the therapist in the breakdown moment is one that is reflected in an existential tension between a sense of trust towards the therapist, on the one hand, and, on the other, the client's mistrust in the therapist's challenges, because they are making the client feel somewhat uncomfortable, anxious, and uncertain.

Phenomenological exploration facilitates a way of opening up and reinterpreting what had seemed a familiar and stabilising stance towards our experiences. However, a familiar challenge reflected in being-with, and one that many human beings face, is the way in which they become embedded, habituated, and sedimented into ways of relating to themselves as the 'victims' of others or particular circumstances. This then becomes a habitualised way of drawing on language that reflects an inauthentic way of being. It 'positions' the person in their relation to the world and others. They encounter or 'await' certain future moments or situations that are similar to those that they have previously found disturbing, with a sense of already interpreting what presents itself to them in such situations. This is typically expressed in a context of being taken over by the other, and in extreme cases, of feeling bullied, criticised, or demeaned. Such a possible manifestation of a breakdown is reflected in being-with-others.

9.8 Solicitude

Solicitude is our way of being with others that conveys a caring-for, caring-about, and caring-towards the other, or others. In breakdown cases, however, the therapist attempts to take over the client's search for meaning, or be tempted to impact on, or even alleviate, the client's unease. We take this as a case of the therapist 'leaping in', or leaping into the client's space, thereby taking over the client's responsibility for finding their own way through the issues that they present. The question then is, for whose sake is the leaping in being enacted? Heidegger, though not making it so apparent as I am attempting here, is presenting a leaping in that is analogous to a Cartesian way of being at the centre of things, rather than recognising that our being-there, the situation, or 'there', leaves us thrown into things and with others, as if we somehow follow on from behind. Rather than anticipating, with a readiness, what the situation brings in its uniqueness, that is, as its being one of a kind, the therapist, in this breakdown case of solicitude, 'makes present' the situation by treating it in a general way. In this sense, they head off the possibility of any anxiety, and tell themself that they are supporting the client in a way that is compatible with their theoretical approach to therapy. Silence in the therapy session is also an important element of solicitude. In cases where the therapist might feel uncomfortable in moments in which this arises, this might reflect a breakdown case of solicitude. For Heidegger, silence is an authentic form of discourse, and in the case of the therapist's silence, it makes way for the client to find *their way* forward. In solicitude, the other is just like us, insofar as their being is an issue for them. In other words, we are solicitous towards them in their 'mineness'. To leap in reflects an attitude of reducing the client to a thing to manipulate, or object to observe, or to settle into an Anyone-like mode of existence.

9.9 Understanding

In understanding, we grasp those possibilities of ourselves in the situation, and project our potentiality, or potentiality-for-being. So, in understanding, we grasp our own capacities to act and engage, such that we can realise certain tasks and projects, or our 'for-the-sake-of-which'. For example, I buy certain groceries in order to prepare a meal, and act in certain ways that are ultimately for the sake of my sustenance and health. In much the same way, I write this book in order to convey a particular therapeutic approach, such that it then hopefully opens further reflection on the meaning of therapy, which is ultimately for the sake of supporting others to further clarify the way in which they are living their lives.

Where we might happen to fail in our understanding, we might commonly think that this is because we lack the necessary background information to cope in certain situations. However, the failure is really a deficient mode of understanding, because we misunderstand our possibilities in relation to the task at hand. If I use the pen inappropriately, for example, I 'break' the possibility that I can project myself when I use it appropriately. I fail to project myself into the task through not understanding the pen's possibilities for me, and so display a certain ignorance, one might say. The breakdown, then, is concerned with my failing to project into possibilities by using equipment appropriately, freeing it up in a way that is consonant with the task at hand.

A more general way in which a breakdown in understanding might manifest itself in one's world might be imagined in the following way. E comes to therapy because he experiences an emptiness in his life. Now 29 years old, he acknowledges that he has been successful, academically speaking, and is well-established in his profession as a lawyer. He is financially secure and does not want for any material comforts or leisurely pursuits. He is wholly committed to his role as a partner in a law practice and works long hours to meet the demands of the job. As well as this, however, he feels that he is caught in a trap that renders his work and, more widely, his life, meaningless and ultimately unfulfilling. As he uncovers more details, he reveals that his father and grandfather had both been lawyers themselves, and that the expectation and assumption in the family was that E would follow suit. He admits that he had been unsure of what to study whilst at school and had increasingly accepted that it was prudent to select subjects that would allow him to study law. He had been all-too-aware of the success and satisfaction that the legal profession had brought to his father and grandfather, which convinced him that this would be a sensible direction to pursue in his own career development.

Understanding, according to Heidegger, is 'equiprimordial', that is, equally fundamental, with the other existentiales, mood, discourse, and fallenness, as is the case in E's way of being. A fuller exploration of E's experience might well address each of these in turn, or at least take them into account. However, E's grasp of who he is in terms of his projects is reflected in a breakdown, or disturbance to his being involved in his work as a lawyer. He no longer finds satisfaction in what he is doing, but feels guilty, and so decides not to disclose this to anyone. He acts as if he is happy with his situation, and at times questions whether he is just being lazy or ungrateful. He feels that he is compromising himself in his tasks and projects, constantly behaving on 'autopilot'. This analysis of a breakdown in understanding might also be further elaborated when considered from a temporal perspective.

9.10 Moods

Our attunement to the world, or dispositional mood that pervades our everyday encounters, affairs, and activities, determines how we deal with situations. If I am in a grateful mood, for example, I might well experience gratitude for everything that I encounter in a situation. I see the world and others with a sense of valuing the very fact *that* they are, rather than *what* I want or expect from them. I see them as an end in themselves, which is to embrace them in their humanity. They are not things to exploit, since they are the same as myself: their being is an issue for them, and they are trying to establish and maintain meaning in their own lives. I am grateful for being privileged in being able to share this world with them, and to experience life in its wholeness, and not simply as a string of separate and unconnected moments in time. In the authentic way of being, gratitude is reflected in a repetition that anticipates in a moment of vision. I embrace the nullities of death and guilt that ground my existence in its wholeness, whilst being resolute in my choices in the face of anxiety. I live with a sense of openness towards situations and experience a freedom in being both the basis of my choices and a freedom that has been 'released from the illusions of the "*they*"' (BT311). In my being receptive to this, I give thanks, or am grateful.

Heidegger makes special mention of fundamental moods, such as anxiety and boredom, but might also include gratitude here. Such moods reflect certain situational breakdowns. However, some moods might be deemed privative, derivative, or deficient, though this does not mean that they are devalued or disregarded in some way. Instead, they disclose our way of being in our thrown situatedness.

To quickly summarise the character of moods, let me set out its main features. First, we are always 'delivered over' to a mood; we always find ourselves in one mood or another, rather than it being a matter of choice (BT174). Second, moods are equiprimordial with understanding: they are integrated into a whole rather than separate. This means that moods have their own understanding of the circumstances in which we find ourselves. This understanding discloses far more than any rational analysis or conceptual thinking can muster (BT173). Moods also disclose the way that I encounter a situation, whether bored, frustrated, fearful, or joyful. The mood illuminates both the situation and my being in the situation. Returning to my earlier example of boredom, let's now imagine that I attend a birthday party and find it tedious and dull. Of course, someone else might experience the same party as entertaining. But this does not invalidate the mood of the party in all its different facets. The other person is simply picking up on other features of the same party. In this sense, it might well become entertaining for me if I am intrigued by other elements that might be taken as quite amusing, for example. It *is* a boring party, we can say, but I can also see it from different angles and perspectives. A mood also reflects the way in which we are always attuned to situations, much like a tuning fork, so to speak. Moods, moreover, disclose the way in which we care. Since our being is an issue for us, and that our existence is at stake, our moods reflect what is significant for us. In being bored whilst at the party, what matters to me is how much I value time, and how meaningful it is when it aligns with my aims and projects. If I am keen to encounter others who are aligned with my interests, and the party frustrates this possibility, then this might account for my being bored by the party. Lastly, moods reflect the way that I am in relation to the 'there' in my being-there, or in the world. In being bored, the mood discloses to me the realisation that I take my temporality too much for granted, and that I need to reconsider which social events are worth attending in the future.

Moods can also colour the way that we live over the course of our whole existence. Consider a case of someone living in a mood of anger that reflects their general outlook on life. F is a 40-year-old man who works in a call centre where he provides advice and assistance for customers who call in with questions and queries[1]. He was raised in a strictly religious family background, with six siblings. His father was a drunk and a bully, and frequently picked on F whenever he was in an inebriated state. No one else dared intervene on such occasions, which meant that F had to face his father's unruly behaviour on his own throughout his childhood. At 16, he escaped the family home after leaving school, and moved from one job to another, earning just enough to pay for his share of the rent for lodgings where he lived with two other people. After a few years, he started a small business as a carpet layer with two friends, but this eventually collapsed because his business partners had, unbeknownst to him, colluded in creaming off most of the company's earnings. Suspicious of this after some time, he eventually uncovered the facts, but could do nothing to claim his rightful share of the profits that had accrued over the course of their collaboration. His sense of anger and injustice escalated further as he tried to hold down other employment but just couldn't settle into any jobs. He now found it extremely difficult to work as an employee. His anger and rage fed on itself, to the point that he fell into drinking and taking recreational drugs. His several long-term romantic relationships became volatile and acrimonious, and he ended up feeling very bitter towards each of his former partners for their 'unreasonable' behaviours. F's overarching mood in which he lives his life, then, highlights important aspects of the way that he has become defined by anger, presumably due to a deep absence or loss of trust in others and the world generally.

9.11 The One, or They

I consider here only one possible manifestation of a breakdown of the One. Take the case of a client who is living with a partner, but under a cloak of complete secrecy, in order to avoid parental rejection and exclusion from his family. As might happen, this situation can run on for many years. A breakdown case of the One in this instance is reflected in the way in which conforming to certain norms becomes stifling to the point that it constrains a person's ability to live their life on their own terms. I am particularly reminded here of the Russian philosopher, Lev Shestov, who, as a young man, moved to Europe with his then partner. They married and raised a family together, whilst his parents were left in complete ignorance of this major development in his life, presumably motivated by his fear that this would be met with their disapproval and outright rejection of him. Such is the possible hold of norms and expectations over us, but more acutely so in certain traditional communities, cultures, and families.

9.12 Embodiment

Although Heidegger does not explicitly say so, being-embodied can be considered an existentiale, such that it is basic to Dasein's way of being. He considers the body to be a more complicated issue and acknowledges this as his reason for not addressing it in *Being and Time*. A difficulty with embodiment is that deeming it an existentiale might miss the possibility that it relates to Dasein's being at an even deeper level. Given our factical backgrounds, however, we comport ourselves in certain ways in the light of our experiences. Without intending to fall into crude oversimplification, someone who has been brought up to 'sit up straight' at all times, whether this be due to the influence of one's parents, for example, or a rigorous, military-like school discipline, say, conveys a certain way of being-embodied that contrasts itself with others who might have undergone very different experiences.

The posture that we take as we enter into unfamiliar experiences, such as giving a presentation to an audience for the very first time, or facing the considerable pressures of a work environment, or encountering difficult and strenuous phases of our relationships with partners, are all examples of the way that one comports oneself in certain situations.

Where one's comportment is deficient, or a private mode of being, one experiences a change in one's embodiment that deviates from being settled or grounded. In other words, this is when the body itself becomes more noticeable in its unease, whether this be a certain heaviness, or numbness, for example, or emptiness. W comes to her therapy session following an experience in a meeting with her boss a few days previously. Unexpectedly, her boss had 'eviscerated her', as W put it, laying out quite directly that W was falling woefully below any acceptable standards and expected quality of her work. It was, she says, all the more shocking, because W felt that she had a relatively relaxed and friendly relationship with the boss, given that they got along well and tended to sit together at lunch breaks. Over the following days and weeks, W felt that her body had shut down: she lost all sense of appetite, her facial expression reflected a drained demeanour, and she experienced herself 'dragging' her body around in a mechanical fashion, rather than W actually 'living' her body. She experienced difficulty in doing the simplest chores, and became more careless as she handled things without due attention or care. Carrying out such simple tasks was laden with immediate self-criticism if she failed to complete a task well. In terms of mood, nothing really mattered, each day was like the next, and no one activity or interest really stood out such that it absorbed her in any way. Even bringing herself to the therapy session was like wading through treacle, she admitted. After some time, however, W had said that she had managed to glean some further details about her boss's unusual behaviour, which altered W's understanding and interpretation of this distressing episode. As she explored this further, her bodily experience eventually resumed its former 'invisibility' and flow-like absorption in the world.

9.13 Being-towards-death

In our inauthentic stance towards our own mortality, we distance ourselves in the ways that we talk about death and dying. This is shaped considerably through the norms and conventional ways in which conversations take place. For example, reflecting on the impact of a friend or parent's death in a social setting might be viewed as unwholesome or inappropriate. Whilst we attempt to discern those forms of behaviour that are deemed to be appropriate for the various situations in which we find ourselves with others, and not just in this example, we nevertheless live in ways that reflect a 'denial of death', as Ernest Becker has put it, that is 'all-consuming…when we look it full in the face' (1973:15).

The ways in which we might experience breakdowns in relation to death, and the existentiale, being-towards-death, are diverse, since each person experiences the issue of their mortality out of their 'mineness', rather than following standardised ways in which death is understood generally.

Note

1 Example adapted from Budd and Rothstein (2000).

Chapter 10

Some Breakdowns in Therapy

10.1 Breakdowns in Promises

Promises are vulnerable to breakdowns, as are the many other ways of engaging with others. However, taking a simple scenario of a promise made and then broken, one possible form of breakdown is the promiser's decision not to honour the promise. A simple promise to meet an acquaintance for an evening meal, for example, and then not showing up at all, warrants a certain apology but also some form of explanation or narrative for this in order for the other to grasp the context in which this event developed. It perhaps takes time for the possibility to come to understand such a breaking of the promise, and might simply be attributable to some kind of equipmental breakdown ('my car broke down, and I forgot to take my phone with me when I left the house, so I couldn't call you to tell you'), or a breakdown in the promiser's world ('I had a sharp chest pain just before I was leaving, and was quickly despatched to hospital for checks to make sure everything was OK').

As therapists, we might occasionally experience breakdowns in promises agreed with clients. This can range from the client being regularly late, or else attempting to cancel a session with very little advance notice. Perhaps this is better understood as a form of breaking an agreement or contract that had been discussed and agreed at the outset of therapy. However, from a phenomenological point of view, this bears further reflection since it discloses something about a client's world. Breaking agreements can disclose a way of being-with, in the form of being with others, which includes their relation to the therapist in this case. One possible way in which this might be understood is the client's general assumption about agreements: that they are sufficiently flexible and malleable to accommodate the client's lateness or late notification. Another possibility is more specific: that 'being late' on one occasion is a minor deviation or violation of the agreed time, such as to be of no consequence for either party. A third possible understanding in this case is that lateness was due to some external cause, such as heavy traffic, or that the trains were running slow, or that a situation or mitigating circumstance arose such that this prevented the client's prompt arrival. The client, as is clear, attempts to throw off any sense of ownership or responsibility for their keeping to promises. The temporality of the breakdown is based on an inauthentic way of forgetting that

DOI: 10.4324/9781003342137-13

awaits and makes present: the client forgets themself in this by failing to address who they 'have been' in their thrownness up to this point, and so forgets their past. In this sense, they fail to 'take hold' of who they are, as themself. They also await the future as they just passively wait for what comes, rather than resolutely anticipating the finitude of being in the therapeutic relationship with the therapist (that it will end at some point, for example, and that they only have a finite time to work together). They also inauthentically make present, insofar as they effectively let things take hold as if they were just meant to be like this. Other existentiales, such as solicitude and possibility, also point to relevant aspects of the client's existence.

Other breakdowns of promises can be understood more in terms of a betrayal, such as an infidelity in a marriage, for example. In such cases, it is the breakdown or collapse of a person's world. A couple come to therapy to address a secret affair that one partner had previously pursued for several months, and which only came to light when this was revealed under certain unexpected circumstances. The breakdown manifests itself in terms of a break of trust, but also in the sense of the betrayed partner's own possible loss of self-trust: how could she ever trust her judgement of others again, she asks herself. From a Heideggerian perspective, the partners' 'couple world' was constituted by those aspects that they shared, such as the living space, the same taste in music, and their attending numerous concerts together; the common use of various items that made their lives mesh so inseparably, such as the car that they both drove at different times; the laptop they used together when calculating their bills and other expenses; the friends and family that related to them as a couple; the plans to buy a house together and have a family; and the identities and roles that had been appropriated in the relationship, affording them a constancy of meaning in their lives. This 'couple world' has now become vulnerable to collapse, and in the process, has thrown each of the partners back to an awareness of the world in terms of the fragility of its sustainability and preservation. As well as this, a breakdown has occurred for each partner, insofar as they become individualised in this change of circumstances. They can no longer rely on a 'ground' that had previously existed in being a couple.

In continuing with therapy sessions, each partner now faces their predicament. Authentically, it is a 'facing up to', rather than an inauthentic 'fleeing from', the process of understanding and interpreting each other's worlds until a point is reached where they are resolute in their decision to either work on their relationship or declare that this is a death of possibilities for both of them. Were they to engage on a path of rebuilding trust in order to make authentic commitments and promises to each other, a phenomenological exploration of the meaning of trust would offer each of the partners an understanding of what is at stake for them.

10.2 Conversational Breakdowns

To return to the previous example of clients experiencing therapy for the first time, there is no precedent for how to engage in conversations on such occasions. Some clients might assume that they will be advised by an expert in the field, or be treated in a similar way to a visit to a medical doctor or specialist who will fix or mend the client's experience of a breach in their everyday existence. Therapeutic conversations, however, in this sense, follow no correct procedure or presumed model for treating issues, but rather pursue a genuine dialogue that is unlike others in the wider sphere of their life outside the therapy room. In this sense, some clients, at least, follow a precarious path over the course of several sessions in establishing a way of familiarising themselves with the process of engaging in dialogue and reflection. This course of engagement includes attempts to articulate feelings and experiences that might well not be so easily or straightforwardly conveyed in language. Over the course of time, however, narratives emerge that perhaps express aspects of the client's existence as a whole, rather than on those more specific details that brought them to initiate therapy in the first instance. This new or different way of articulating and disclosing themselves can be considered as positive conversational breakdowns that emerged as the therapeutic process proceeded.

Conversational breakdowns can also manifest when treating the client effectively as an object, or as present-at-hand, in a way that places them under categories and classifications instead of encountering them as a human being that lives according to a completely different set of descriptors, namely Heidegger's existentiales. Such an approach may also confirm and exacerbate the client's possible sense of alienation from the world in relation to the issues that are being presented in the therapy room.

Other forms of breakdown, ones that reflect a 'positive' experience, occur in dialogues or conversations that are considered significant when the client experiences the therapist as a deep listener. For the client, this stands out in stark contrast to their experiences of being with others in their wider world and sub-worlds, as in the case of their relationships, family situations, work conflicts, and so on, where a more profound experience of listening becomes a relatively uncommon experience. In such cases, the meaning of conversations, we might say, is brought ontologically closer, in contrast to the now more distant ontic sense of a conversation being an exchange of information, or a competitive space to have one's say and to speak. Harlene Anderson captures well some of the points mentioned so far, when she writes,

> The structure of the therapy conversation is spontaneous, determined by moment-to-moment exchanges that zigzag and crisscross. It does not follow a predetermined script such as a structured question guideline or sequenced actions. I cannot know my questions ahead of time; I cannot choose words to produce a specified outcome…I am inside, not outside, the process I am trying to create. Hence, the conversation may appear disorganised to an outside observer or one who has a preconception of what the conversation should look like…A therapist does not control the [dialogue] by moving the conversation in a particular direction of content or outcome, nor is he or she responsible for the direction of change.
>
> (1997:126)

The breakdown points to the hermeneutic turn that moves from everyday conversations to ones in which the client feels free to 'move things around' in what they talk about, so that certain unplanned emphases are now brought out that had never been considered or articulated in their usual way of talking and communicating with others. Accompanying this is the experience of an altered mood or atmosphere in sessions, including a sense of freedom. Other existentiales, such as being-with, solicitude, the One, projection, and possibility undergo their own positive existentiell modifications as the client relates to the session as an authentic space in which they can be who they are. One possible change that might also become apparent to the client in the light of such breakdowns is the opportunity to relate to others differently in their everyday world, and to engage in conversations that are based on choosing to listen and engage differently with others.

Chapter 11

Transitioning Breakdowns

Having identified the very existence of breakdowns, irrespective of their nature, depth, and scope, a question now arises as to how we come to face, engage, and reckon with them. In the main, we tend to find ourselves returning to a certain familiar way of living that has transitioned from the experience of disruptions and breakdowns. We move on from marriage or relationship endings, job losses, bereavements, possible humiliations, and numerous other difficult ruptures in our lives. The question that then becomes one of therapeutic relevance is: how are such transitions from breakdowns to feeling once more at home in the world possible? No formula or theory can aspire to fully capture or reflect the manner in which we live through this movement towards a resumption of a relatively familiar routine in the everydayness of our existence. The temporal element of breakdowns has a significant impact on the experience itself. For example, an unexpected decision that one will be made redundant in one's job might herald a new beginning and opportunity to pursue a long-cherished new venture and direction in one's life. The end of one world opens the possibility of another meaningful world emerging for the client. In this case, the temporal character of the breakdown is one that does not create an abrupt disorientation, but rather a welcome moment that offers a different future relationship to time. But in many cases, the suddenness and unexpectedness of breakdowns throws the person into the sense of worldlessness that becomes difficult to navigate, as might well happen for some in this example.

From a Heideggerian perspective, therapy offers the client an opportunity to reflect on and review the meaning of the breakdown by gradually undergoing a process of 'seeing', or bringing whatever is hidden into the light by making it intelligible, or graspable. In the breakdown situation, understanding, in Heidegger's sense, has been temporarily unable to project possibilities, such that Dasein cannot draw on any actions or activities in order to ground itself in the world. Therapeutic discourse invites a process of looking that is 'guided by considerateness and forbearance' (BT159) rather than through 'deficient and indifferent modes up to the point of *inconsiderateness* or the perfunctoriness for which indifference leads the way' (BT159). The therapist's solicitude, guided, as Heidegger says, by a way of caring that is considerateness and forbearance, gives to the client the time and attentiveness to disclose their moods and feelings, the experiences that they are undergoing,

DOI: 10.4324/9781003342137-14

and the gradual process of interpreting and coming to understand themselves in the light of the breakdown in their world. In other words, the hermeneutic movement that a therapeutic dialogue offers brings about a new understanding for the client over time, whilst also offering a sustained consistency and reliability of the background relationship with the therapist that constitutes the therapy world. In this sense, the client accepts, however reluctantly or unwillingly, that a former world or sub-world has now been closed off and is no longer available to them. In so doing, they 'come back' to their being-in-the-world and the possible projects that now absorb and preoccupy them.

Therapy offers the client the space to articulate and possibly reconfigure who they are in the light of the breakdown, by taking themselves as a whole rather than a being who lives according to successive moments in time, from one day to the next. Transitioning through breakdowns also allows the possibility for clients to become increasingly aware of the second-hand way in which they have been living their lives. Once the distinction between living authentically and inauthentically becomes apparent, the client is confronted with the responsibility of choosing, however much of a difficulty and challenge this might pose for them. Moments in which clients are challenged by therapists to acknowledge the possibilities that are available to them, and the growing realisation that their attitude to life has been to assume that there is an ideal guide or template for how to live, allows the possibility for transformation in their attitude towards themselves and their existence. However, any form of transitioning is a gradual process in most cases, unless clients are already deeply preoccupied with the question of how to live in their truth, and that they acknowledge that their existence is marked by nullities.

Chapter 12

A Cartesian Breakdown: Winnicott

By way of contrast, I now consider a possible understanding of breakdowns from a non-Heideggerian perspective. The psychoanalyst, Donald Winnicott, wrote a paper in the last year of his life entitled *Fear of Breakdown*. It is a short essay that was left unfinished, and reads more like a draft paper that was undergoing further development. It attempts to illuminate breakdowns from a more psychodynamic perspective, but, more specifically, does so from the perspective of the *fear* of breakdown. Underlying this is a conception of the human being for whom the possibility of breakdown can occur in terms of an internal psyche that contends with an external environment. Winnicott draws on his previous work on the maturational process, as well as the facilitating or holding environment. However, whilst we also read Winnicott readily acknowledging the ambiguity of the term 'breakdown', he then goes on to reveal an explicit and theoretically laden psychoanalytic path that he follows towards an understanding of the process that clarifies the dynamic of the fear of breakdown.

In its past, the infant is in an original state of 'absolute dependence' in relation to the mother, such that 'I' and 'not I' has not been differentiated. At such a time, the infant had not moved developmentally through the maturational process, given that their emotional growth would proceed from absolute dependence to relative independence and finally towards independence. In this process, the infant 'undergoes development which can be classified as integrating' (Winnicott, 1974:104). Since the infant remained at a dependency stage, some original anxieties ('primitive agonies', as Winnicott calls them), such as a 'falling for ever' and the 'loss of the sense of real', have not been overcome or dealt with. Such anxieties or agonies would have been overcome or integrated at a later mature stage. Given this, defences, or a 'defence organisation', are developed to mitigate against the possibility of having to experience the underlying primitive agony. This inability to overcome these agonies because of the infant's inability to get beyond the dependency stage is the breakdown, and the client has developed defences against this very fact. However, as the analyst works to address these defences, the client experiences a fear of the breakdown. In first coming to therapy, the client might have presented themself with phobias, for example, which have served them as a form of defence, but as the phobias are analysed, the underlying fear emerges as one of a breakdown of the

DOI: 10.4324/9781003342137-15

establishment of a successful 'defence organisation relative to a primitive agony' (ibid.). The issue, as Winnicott presents it, is that the 'breakdown is the fear of a breakdown that has already been experienced' (ibid.). That is, the breakdown which occurred in infancy could not be experienced at that time, because the infant had not reached a maturational stage in which they could move beyond absolute dependence, and therefore free themself from the breakdown by grasping this as a past experience from the perspective of a present experience. In other words, the client couldn't differentiate themself from the past breakdown in order to get some distance or perspective from it. They are still bound up in the past, but don't have the means, or developmental maturity, to process this in their present experience. It is as if they are in a fog, and can't separate themself from a breakdown, given that 'I'/'not I' has not developed into a separation.

Winnicott concludes that it is the breakdown in the client's past that needs to be 'remembered' in the present. He extends his examples to the fear of death, of emptiness and non-existence. In each case, he says that we experience fear because we haven't 'remembered' having died, as is the case with our emptiness from the past, and indeed, our past state of non-existence. We need, he claims, to experience these in the present, as something that happened to us in the past. These reflections on death, emptiness, and non-existence by Winnicott are unfortunately rather too concise and brief, given that he seemed to be touching on the margins of an existential sensibility. Even so, I think several general comments can be made with regard to Winnicott's paper.

First, considerable metaphysical scaffolding has been erected or constructed in Winnicott's account that it behoves us to question the viability of theory in attempting to explain our human way of being. Even if we were to concede that theory can make an ontic contribution to an understanding of our way of being, we should address and question the foundations upon which it is built. The ontological question of what it is to be human has been effectively ignored in favour of a metaphysical account. As such, this account is presented as holding explanatory power, but this simply avoids the pressing question of being, and the way of being of the entity that is a being 'there'.

It is obvious that so much happens to us in the course of our becoming Dasein, if we are to grasp this in terms of the existentiales that are all essential features of being human. In the course of our upbringing, for example, we are thrown, i.e., disoriented, in a breakdown sense, by what happens to us, but also in the sense of our being thrown into situations that either register and mark us in some way, or else pass us by. It is, however, a rather bold assumption to lay claim to certain explicit and determinate causal paths that explain who we have become. As well as this, any attempted mother–infant link is an overambitious attempt to either define how or where a relationship has contributed to the client's deficient or derivative – breakdown situation – way of expressing the existentiale of, say, being-with, when the permutations of how they become who they *are* are endless, or else to simply see this in very definitive terms of their existentiell way of projecting themselves into the world 'existingly'.

Perhaps a final extended quotation by the psychoanalyst, Thomas Ogden, in response to Winnicott's paper offers a more coherent approach to, and understanding of, breakdowns, by avoiding at least some of the metaphysical language that is both unnecessary and unhelpful:

[W]e all, to differing degrees, have had events in our early lives that involved significant breakdowns in the mother-infant tie to which we have responded with psychotic defence organisations. Each of us is painfully aware that, regardless of how psychologically healthy we may appear to others (and at times to ourselves), there are important ways in which we are not capable of being alive to our experience, whether that be the experience of joy, or the ability to love one or all of our children, or the capacity to be generous to the point of giving up something highly important to us, or the capacity to forgive someone (including ourselves) who has done something that has hurt us profoundly, or to simply feel alive to the world around us and within us. These are but a few of the myriad forms of emotional limitation that derive from having been unable to live the breakdowns that occurred when we were infants and children. Each of these limitations is an aspect of our unlived life, what we have been, and continue to be, unable to experience. We all have our own particular areas of experience that we have been unable to live, and we live in search of those lost experiences, those lost parts of ourselves.

(2014:214–5)

Part IV

Heideggerian Existential Therapy

In what follows, I draw on previous parts and sections in order to consider a therapeutic approach that reflects a Heideggerian perspective, captured most fundamentally by the issue of what it means to be our kind of being. In keeping with much of the approach taken throughout, I revisit topics, themes, and issues already covered, but now extend my thoughts and reflections more to their relevance to therapy.

DOI: 10.4324/9781003342137-16

Chapter 13

Working Phenomenologically

For Heidegger, the fundamental principle of phenomenology is that phenomena are given to us. The expression, as Heidegger presents it, that 'it gives', is in direct contrast to actively identifying objects in a way that we present and represent to ourselves, according to a more traditional approach. What is given, then, is related to facticity.

Let me review and recapitulate on Heidegger's manner of investigating phenomena. He takes a phenomenological approach to enquiry and does so in the service of 'fundamental ontology'. In other words, Heidegger is addressing the question of what it is or means to be, rather than merely describing what something is. The being of a book, in this sense, is a fundamentally different issue to the book's function, purpose, or essence. Since we as Dasein already have an implicit and vague understanding of what it is to be – a pre-ontological understanding – this enables Heidegger to pursue the question of being by investigating and elaborating such an understanding through phenomenological enquiry. So, instead of directly addressing the question of being itself from the outset, he finds an accessible point from which his enquiry can begin.

Heidegger's approach is inimical to any thematically oriented enquiry, which pursues the content of what it is to be Dasein. This is left to the domain of psychology, anthropology, sociology, and the human sciences generally. These subjects are ontic kinds of enquiry, which is in direct contrast to an ontological form of investigation. That is, his focus is more fundamental, given that ontological enquiry asks, 'what makes that possible at all? What is the condition for its possibility?'. Rather than exploring in detail how we live in societies and interact with others, for example, he is elucidating the formal structures that are the basis for such enquiries to be at all possible in the first instance.

In investigating Dasein, Heidegger's starting point is everydayness: how we exist on a day-to-day basis. Throughout Division I of *Being and Time*, Heidegger is mapping out being-in-the-world, which is the unitary structure of Dasein's way of being. Here we see his phenomenological approach most clearly at work, which does not exclude any entities from the enquiry. Neither does it start from consciousness, a term which Heidegger avoids, because it has a purely Cartesian, 'internal' understanding of our way of being and is therefore a wholly misguided starting point for his enquiry.

DOI: 10.4324/9781003342137-17

13.1 Being Phenomenological

How might a more practical application of the phenomenological approach look, and be introduced in therapeutic practice? In what follows, I attempt to show how the phenomenologies of Heidegger and Husserl might be applied in a practical setting, but also endeavour to highlight the ways in which they radically differ. This will then offer a way of showing how this bears on therapeutic work, both specifically and more generally.

Let me start with a simple example of a situation or scenario, which can then be explored through a Husserlian and then Heideggerian phenomenological lens. Imagine that you have just finished a very late shift at your workplace – you are a carer at an animal rescue centre – and are now ready to drive home after an exhausting day at work. You feel relatively relaxed, and your partner has promised to wait up for you on your return, so that you can spend some valuable time together. It's a late cool summer evening, and darkness has descended on everything around you. You take your usual route home, turning onto a dual carriageway, which allows you to drive your car a little faster. As you do so, you notice the open road, with only a few other cars in the very far-off distance. The overhead street lighting casts a yellow yet intense glow over the road and the barriers that follow along the sides of the carriageway. You feel at ease, and even hum along to the music playing on your radio. You enjoy this kind of drive: it's liberating, and poses none of the obstacles or challenges that you experience in the mornings, when you are caught in traffic, and dealing with other drivers who are competing for the same spaces. As you continue on your car journey, something unexpected happens. A brown dog suddenly runs directly across your path. You freeze, slam on the brakes, and try with the greatest effort to steer clear of any contact with the dog. The car almost immediately comes to a halt. You open your car door, leap out, and run round to the front to attend to the dog. You feel mortified, completely disoriented. As you look down, you see that it is a brown paper bag[1].

From a Heideggerian point of view the situation or world is disclosed in its breaking down, as in this instance, and not when we reflect on the world from a more detached standpoint. Phenomenology is an unconcealing of what has been concealed. It brings the phenomenon into plain sight, but because there is usually a 'motivated concealing', any deeper unconcealing might also evoke anxiety. In most cases, however, a phenomenon is usually obscured because we have become accustomed to see the world and entities as our culture and society has presented it, and this means that we assume we already understand our world and its phenomena. In the course of doing phenomenology, however, we bring to light what is concealed. This is how Heidegger characterises truth.

Phenomenological enquiry requires of us that we stay with the phenomenon, rather than lose our focus or attention towards it. This might sound a straightforward task, though in practice, poses its own difficulties and challenges. At times, it may appear that the phenomenon is in view, but, in fact, only seems so. Or the discipline of being phenomenological is itself an arduous undertaking, particularly where a dialogue between therapist and client can potentially deflect away from this, for whatever reason. In some cases, the challenge might also be one of not being clear on what the phenomenon actually is, which might leave the therapist, at least, in a space of uncertainty. At such times, certain interventions might be offered to encourage a more attentive focus on what is being disclosed over the course of the therapeutic dialogue.

13.2 A Husserlian Analysis

For both Husserl and Heidegger, phenomenology is, according to the term itself, the study of the phenomenon. At the same time, they distinguish themselves from each other in terms of the differences in their approaches. For Husserl, since phenomena are presented in or through consciousness, and not in the natural world, the focus is on describing that which appears to the client in their experience of the situation. Phenomena are what we find in conscious experience and not the external objects in our environment, so any talk about or reference to an external world, whilst being real and undeniable, is not the predominant or central focus for the Husserlian therapist. Attending to these phenomena, according to Husserl, requires a 'bracketing' or suspension of the world, so that a phenomenological exploration can unfold. Bringing the external world into the picture assumes a naturalism that Husserl's phenomenology opposes, since he is an anti-naturalist. Naturalism takes it that there are indubitable facts about nature, and that such facts are the foundation for knowledge and explanation. In contrast, Husserlian phenomenology aspires to describe as closely as possible the experience as it is given to consciousness.

How, then, would a Husserlian therapist work with the experience of the driver and the brown paper bag? Imagining that they now come to therapy, they are invited as a client to describe the moments and details of what happened, so that previously unnoticed aspects of the set of events might be revealed. From the point of leaving their workplace, getting in the car, driving along a main thoroughfare, experiencing the impact of something against the car, as well as the moments that followed, these all allow the client to bring themselves towards a clearer and more detailed account of that experience. At some points, the therapist might also suggest some possible aspect of the experience that might have also been present, but that had not yet been revealed by the client. The client might either reject this as simply not pertinent to the event, or else see it as a key element that is essential to that experience. Either way, the therapist has followed an aspect of working phenomenologically, which Husserl calls 'free imaginative variation' (as introduced in *Ideas I*). The narrative description presents a series of moments, each moment being what Husserl names as a 'noema'. The experiencer has also been *perceiving* a string of connected noematic moments, rather than dreaming them, or hallucinating the experience. This overall 'how' of the experience, as a 'perceiving' in this experience, is the 'noetic', according to Husserl. Throughout, the aim has been to set aside any claim about what is *objectively* there, through the use of bracketing, and to stay with the structure of the experience, its feel, texture, and its look. It is only the structure of lived perception, or lived experience, that is of interest here. In staying as close as possible to the client's experience, the therapist contrasts their approach to, say, that of a clinician or medically trained specialist who differentiates between a subjective experience, on the one hand, and what is objectively there, on the other. In such a dualistic approach, then, the client's subjective experience might be assessed, diagnosed, or classified as a 'panic attack', or a neurologically based disturbance, for example, because their subjective experience fails to correspond adequately with objective reality. In other words, it takes a naturalistic approach to the client's experience.

Returning to the client's phenomenological experience, however, they were panic-stricken as they drove into an oncoming running dog, got out of the car, looked down, and saw that it was a paper bag. In Husserlian language, they experienced a series of noemata that culminated in a final noema, or appearance, of a dog, or dog-like look. This set of events in which an object of a certain size moved at rapid speed across the path of a moving car and made contact with it all assumes something important that is not emphasised in the account. The client had a series of noematic experiences that each required **interpretation** *in the act* of experiencing them. This is because we never just look at things, but rather, *construe* them in a certain way. That is, the client underwent a series of appearances that could have been construed in other possible ways. Where a perceptual moment might become ambiguous, or misconstrued, our experience reaches a different noematic sequence. But, even more importantly, a careful phenomenological exploration shows that the world that we experience is marked by certain noematic regularities, or routines. These are, we might emphasise, only regularities, and not facts. Moreover, these regularities are built up in a contingent fashion out of experience, rather than being based on objectivity. We also constantly adjust and correct these sequences as they happen, in order to be able to then construe what is happening in our experience. Having laid out such a phenomenological approach, what hopefully stands out is its emphasis on the way in which our understanding of what it is to be human determines the kind of therapeutic approach that is taken up in the therapy session.

13.3 A Heideggerian Analysis

In contrast to Husserl's starting point of conscious experience, Heidegger starts from the idea of our being-in-the-world. This removes any talk of an internal experience that is then in need of description, but instead, one of finding oneself already involved and immersed in an unfolding situation that leads to cases of breakdown or disturbance in one's everyday way of dealing with situations and our environment. In the case of the client, however, their driving, the car, the steering wheel, and the road ahead were all in the background of their awareness, because they were all being used or appropriated in their ready-to-hand mode of being. In this way of being, they were, in other words, reliable and withdrawn. They formed a 'web' insofar as they were all interrelated into a whole, and all functioning in ways that contributed towards fulfilling the task or goal of arriving home. Were one or other item to malfunction, such as the gearbox, or the windscreen suddenly becoming misty, a minor disturbance might have altered the client's mood, to whatever degree, and brought them to take appropriate action. However, as they continued their journey, they were relaxed, and engaged in the task of driving home. They were also expressing themself as a driver whilst making the homeward bound journey, driving the car skilfully and with a sense of competence in dealing with such matters as road spaces, other drivers, and the possibilities that were open to them in their choice of route.

The suddenness of the impact of the dog-like appearance then presented a disturbance, and this now presents an opportunity to describe phenomenologically what happened. However, the description develops in such a way that stays with the *structure* of the situation as seen from a third-person perspective, but then, as this proceeds, moves hermeneutically to an existential, first-person perspective. In other words, the client personalises the situation and explores the way in which its contingency is reflected in the precariousness of the world, and the realisation that it is vulnerable to falling apart, or breaking down.

If the exploration extends further, deeper existential insights might well ensue. It may be that the driver becomes aware of the finitude of existence – their own – through the perceived unintended death of the dog in question. They also feel guilty. Their guilt in this case is based on having done something morally bad. But the hermeneutic turn in persisting with further phenomenological enquiry might bring them to consider the deeper questions of their own existence. From a moral guilt to an existential understanding of guilt, or being-guilty, they recognise that no one else could take away the responsibility for how they lived, what actions they had taken, and which choices they had pursued over the course of their life. This moment of running into something individualised them: now they stood out apart from the One, the anonymous others amongst whom they could tranquilise themself. This meant that they had to face this alone. Perhaps these become insights for them as they gain more of a comprehension of what being-in-the-world means. They can't make being-guilty vanish somehow, since it is ontological: they are the null basis. They live with this and see that it is something that they must face, and not convince themself that it is something from which they must escape. There are many alternative possible endings that we could envisage in this scenario, but let me add just one here. If the client thought they had hit a dog, and then could see that there was nothing as they got out of the car, they might have concluded that they had indeed committed this act, and that the animal had run off with its injuries. This might have then affected their sense of being-in-the-world more deeply, insofar as they now assessed and interpreted themself in their *being* as a being who is deeply flawed. Their world is crushed, whether temporarily, or more permanently, since in such a scenario they live in a 'derived' or 'privative' mode of being-with and in the One, by perhaps secluding themself from others and avoiding the perceived public glare of living amongst others.

13.4 A Critique of a Husserlian Approach from a Heideggerian Perspective

This now affords us the opportunity to review and draw out some conclusions from this example. Husserl's language of consciousness is Cartesian. As such, it inevitably deforms any account of the human body, and the experience of our own embodiment. In other words, there is no possible way that we can talk about or accurately capture being a body if we start from consciousness. Moreover, Husserl takes a more abstract stance on the human being in thinking of it as a conscious ego, whilst Heidegger understands our kind of existence as being-in-the-world. Finally, Heidegger takes it that being is the most fundamentally important question that presses upon us, rather than questions related to consciousness. The move that Husserl makes that is at odds with Heidegger's approach is that he brackets the world. Given that we are being-in-the-world, this grossly distorts our way of being. This means that Husserl inevitably looks at things differently, in two senses. That is, he takes the world to be something that we look at, rather than noting that we are already actively engaged in the world. Husserl is also thinking according to traditional metaphysical or substantial categories, whilst Heidegger understands the human being in terms of existential 'categories', or existentiales. Husserl elides the substantial with the existential, treating us as things or substances that can be described and captured under the same terms.

Both take a certain stance towards the everyday: Husserl's phenomenology brackets, or maintains a distance from it, whilst Heidegger takes it as the basis for phenomenology to first get under way. Husserl's approach loses a sense of world, or cuts it off, and with it, the human being. By contrast, Heidegger's phenomenological approach starts not with us, or Dasein, or the human being, or a 'conscious ego' first, then moves out from this in the process of exploration. Rather, he recognises the primacy of the situation, and then explores, through a formally indicative process, i.e., hermeneutically, that which manifests itself in that situation. So, rather than my feelings, thoughts, actions radiating out from a centre to the world, Heidegger starts from the everyday and allows a phenomenological 'dance' to emerge between aspects of the situation and Dasein in its own involvement in it.

Perhaps the example provided also illuminates the fact that Husserl cannot really offer a sufficiently coherent phenomenological account of breakdowns. For this, we are better served by the work of the brilliant French phenomenologist, Maurice Merleau-Ponty, who draws significantly on Husserl's phenomenology in order to explore the ambiguities and tensions that emerge in the phenomenon of breakdowns in embodied being.

Note

1 I have adapted this from an example given by John Caputo in a lecture on Husserl.

Chapter 14

Formal Indication as a Therapeutic Approach

In the course of a conversation, the client introduces certain key words that seem worthy of further exploration. For example, something is being expressed as 'unfair', and this invites further elaboration and reflection in order to clarify what strikes the client as true about this particular assessment of their experience. The therapist is usually already somewhat familiar with the meaning of such words, but holds this in abeyance in order to engage in further enquiry. In the main, the therapist holds the therapeutic space for the client to deepen the enquiry by treating the term in its formally indicative presentation. This means that a general, third-personal sense of the phenomenon is employed as the starting point for the process of phenomenological investigation. As the phenomenon is opened and clarified through a rich depth and breadth of description, this invites the possibility of bringing it closer to the client so that its deeper existential import comes to the fore. The manner of enquiry is also accompanied by a background mood, from one of a readiness, and positive engagement fostered by mutual collaboration, towards an incipient discomfort and perhaps eventual anxiety as the phenomenon is now revealed out of what had initially been closed off to awareness. Such uncovering now reveals the existential meaning of the phenomenon for the client. The line of mutual enquiry has proceeded towards an ontological truth about the client's existence, be it related to their being-in-the-world, or the fragility of their world and its vulnerability to collapse. This invites a possibility for the client to open themselves to their lives and live in a way that is meaningful to them in their mineness: in other words, a certain facing up to themselves and the limits of their existence. This contrasts with a way of being absorbed in the One, which takes over the client's responsibility in addressing the question of how to live.

Perhaps to introduce an approach to enquiry that is wholly at odds with formal indication, we should consider the contemplative attitude that is advocated by Heidegger's contemporary, Karl Jaspers. The difficulty with this approach, from a Heideggerian viewpoint, is that it assumes a more traditional understanding of our way of being. As we have noted, since Dasein's being is an issue for it, and its being, at the same time, is understood vaguely or is obscured, this makes it impossible for Dasein to simply disclose its way of being through some kind of theoretical or scientific analysis, since that would treat Dasein as a present-at-hand object.

DOI: 10.4324/9781003342137-18

Pure contemplation never allows us to see the practical, involved, and engaged aspect of Dasein, which is reflected in the fundamental structure of Dasein, namely, care. A similar criticism has been made of the approach taken by Heidegger's colleague, Edmund Husserl, too, who takes up a more contemplative attitude in his own phenomenological approach.

In the light of Heidegger's criticism of Jaspers' approach – that he grasps the human being as an object, or as objectively given, thus placing himself in a detached relation to the person – we can now see what is important about formal indication in this regard. For Heidegger, the *reflexive* element in the investigation, or the acknowledgement of the presence of the enquirer themself, is crucial. This is lacking in Husserl's own approach too, since the element of relating to something or someone is not taken into account. This is because, for Husserl, everything is seen from a theoretical standpoint. We can now understand why Heidegger moved away from Husserl's understanding of phenomenology, which assumes consciousness as the fundamental structural starting point of the human being. We can emphasise the point further by considering the simple example of playing football, or any other team game. We simply can't have a sense of what playing football is like just by studying it from a detached, theoretical standpoint. To do this would be to pursue a study of football without revealing the immersed and absorbed way of losing oneself as one is playing the game. That is what it means to understand football.

From a therapeutic standpoint, when we are with a client, approaching enquiry through formal indication means attending to the 'how' of their experience, which is the structure that gives form to the concrete experience, or content, in which they are immersed. Once we have identified the structure of what they encounter in their concrete experience, we can return to the concretely actualised details of that experience, in order to assess whether the form gives sense to the content. In other words, this step of the formal indication is to indicate where in their own case, as Dasein, there is a certain resonance and access to the structure that has been brought out and made explicit.

There are also several striking points to note about the use of formal indication. For one, Heidegger cannot make sense of such phenomena as guilt, conscience, and death, without subjecting them to this approach. In starting with the everyday understanding, Heidegger claims that this is our most familiar relation to the phenomenon in question, since it is the way in which it already shows up for us in everyday existence. At the same time, however, and as Heidegger goes on to show, this familiar understanding is wholly at odds with its ontological sense, which is existential in character. The only way in which Heidegger can arrive at the existential sense is through formal indication. Moreover, Heidegger also shows that the basis for our everyday understanding of all formal indications, including guilt and death, is a reflection of the reason *why* we flee from and cover up these aspects of ourselves: to avoid the ensuing experience of anxiety.

To consider this differently, imagine that we approach the phenomenon as a concept. This term is reflected in the German sense of the word, which means 'grasping'[1]. In grasping an entity such as Dasein, for example, it is rendered as an object, such that I have it, so to speak, 'in my hand'. In other words, I control it, and can do with it what I will. But for Heidegger, what is essential about Dasein is that it is not an object. Heidegger talks more in terms of something being 'on hand', or 'to hand', which is a wholly different relation. Now we see why Heidegger makes use of formal indication: he is not objectivising what he is directing his investigation towards. Rather, he is noting the phenomenon as it appears or is given to him, and then conducting a phenomenological investigation. The tendency and danger in trying to understand Heidegger's ideas, especially in a therapeutic context, is to turn the existential structures of Dasein, such as being-in-the-world, being-with, and being-in, into definitions. As is by now hopefully apparent, definitions or concepts cannot be provided, precisely because the issue of being Dasein is not amenable to a conceptual approach.

14.1 A Formal Indication of Resentment

In order to illustrate once again a way of introducing formal indication in a therapeutic setting, I look briefly at the mood of resentment[2]. Whether the client introduces this explicitly or not, we nevertheless hear the phenomenon as a formal indication. The enquiry then proceeds by conducting our investigation according to this approach to enquiry. The experience of resentment first requires that one acknowledges that a certain situation or context had transpired that brought this mood into being. Through further exploration, we then identify the sense of injustice and unfairness that this state of affairs has served upon the client. In this unfairness, our analysis now reveals that the world has treated them inappropriately, something that they did not deserve, nor did it seem warranted. As we open the phenomenon further, we draw out other formal aspects of the experience. The exploration notes that the situation imposed significant limits on the client's possibilities and damaged the client's freedom to pursue such possibilities. This further confirms the unfairness and injustice. The next phenomenological revelation is that some other party, be it individual or collective, must be held culpable for this injustice. Here we identify that the attribution of responsibility is a key aspect of the structure of resentment: that someone or something must be held to account, and not the client. As we proceed yet further, the client discloses that there is no action or change that the culpable party can enact or implement in order to compensate or remedy the injustice incurred. Thus far, the exploration has addressed the phenomenon by a pointing to and indicating, and doing so in a formal or structural sense. However, a further observation is an existential tension that the client holds onto, which is reflected in the factical stance that nothing can be done to rectify this *but*, at the same time, that this *should* be rectified in some way. This grounds the client in a self-justifying stance of maintaining a punitive attitude towards the culpable party in question. Whilst this has brought the client to a certain level of clarity and understanding in what they are experiencing, it maintains a third-person stance in the manner of disclosing the phenomenon. Resentment, as characterised here, is an inauthentic mood, since it reflects the passivity and abnegation of responsibility for reckoning with the situation authentically. In being in the moment, and effectively trying to render the situation static so that possibility is excluded from consideration, the client pulls back and awaits in relation to the present moment, which is the situation in its ongoing state of affairs. This has now become a factical event that has effectively set itself in concrete, so to speak.

Should any further development in the formally indicative enquiry proceed, a hermeneutic turn towards an existential orientation would allow the client to reflect on their 'mineness' and the impact of limit, or nullity and finitude, on their way of being. That is, a more existential emphasis attends to what is at stake for the client, in terms of their being. The client expresses anger, for example, and notes that this is an outward expression of the resentment that had been held back through silence. The client's world had been disrupted, which illuminated its significance for them. But rather than opening up to their being-in-the-world and reckoning with the not-at-home-ness of their being, they had embraced the everyday world that was protective of being 'right' and condemning the 'other' who had violated certain standards of behaviour and was injurious towards them. In other words, the stable, static, and immovable experience that resentment afforded the client was much more preferable to the anxiety of opening up, standing out, and possibly even being 'right' *and* 'wrong', in certain respects. The role or identity that this person embodied in that world was 'resentful' insofar as this enabled them to sustain a meaningful way of being, and one that gave them a 'home' or place in which they could seemingly dwell in their rightness.

Bringing out the phenomenon in this way allows for numerous elements that constitute it to be challenged or questioned. In the example of resentment, for instance, appropriate and timely challenges or questions could be made with regard to the abnegation of responsibility, that nothing can be done, that the client's possibilities were somehow quashed or restricted, that the event should not have occurred, that an overall stance of opposition is being held fast and with unyielding rigidity, and that some form of self-righteousness is the apparent reward for their entrenched mood.

Generally, clients identify meanings, experience certain realisations, and gain insights, all of which are more structural or formal in character about the way in which they are living their lives. Someone might, for example, come to a different perspective about themselves in terms of the time that they have on their hands, and their failing to commit themselves to an overarching project that might absorb them in their existence. Whether this be down to the passing of the years, the death of a close friend, or the sense of hanging too tenaciously onto the career that they have established for themselves, it invites a more formally based assessment of who they are becoming as they recognise the wider choices that confront them.

Note

1 From the German, *Begriff, Begreifen.*
2 I draw here on, and develop further, the Newfield Network's analyses of moods.

Chapter 15

Working Hermeneutically

Heidegger's hermeneutics developed out of his early attempts to understand life itself, and in this regard, formal indication was used as the basis for his investigations. In *Being and Time*, however, whilst formal indication was retained as a method of hermeneutic enquiry, understanding became the central and overarching focus of his project, based on a hermeneutics of Dasein. For Heidegger, understanding and interpretation are only possible on the basis of a mood, or disposedness that reveals the world in a certain way and allows it to be grasped or understood. This grasping, as Farin puts it, is always related to '(1) the understanding of world and the entities in it, (2) one's own Dasein, and (3) other Dasein' (2015:117). And as Farin further elaborates, such understanding takes the shape of a back-and-forth movement, which itself only happens on the basis of temporality, which means anticipating future possibilities in light of the recollection of what has become (ibid.:117–8). However, understanding is articulated, or made concrete, through discourse and language. In fact, as Farin says in quoting Heidegger, '[t]o talk is the most fundamental characteristic of human Dasein' and that 'talking-with-one-another is in fact the fundamental way of being together with-one-another-in-the-world' (ibid.:119). In the course of speaking to one another, as therapist and client, a certain atmosphere or mood of disclosing and interpreting the world is shared between them. At the same time, we understand this space to be ultimately for the client, given the therapeutic context in which it is being held open. However, the therapist, in their being with the client, is a 'presence', insofar as interventions are made, but also a form of 'absence', given that the client's deeper reflections in the presence of the therapist are made possible on the basis of the therapist's silent, but active, listening. This clears the way for the client to take a stand on, and stand out, in their being.

In conducting his existential analytic of Dasein, Heidegger brings out the ways in which speaking, or conversation, can be prone to inauthentic modes of discourse, as is seen in cases of gossiping, chattering, and making small talk. Whilst this is a way for Dasein to be in its everydayness, along with its way of being consumed in curiosity and ambiguity, as has been discussed earlier, therapeutic dialogue can provide a space that at the very least tends towards an authentic discourse through conversations. The challenges for engaging in such conversations for both the therapist and

DOI: 10.4324/9781003342137-19

client in sessions are multifarious, though the possibility for this is nevertheless present. In one sense, an authentic hermeneutic approach recognises that the situation, or the duration of the session in which the dialogue takes place, is uniquely one of its own, and is never itself repeatable or replicable. It holds a certain call for both participants to recognise the significance of the moment, which is time-bound, whether this refers to the session itself, or the fact that therapy and the therapeutic relationship can and will end at some point in the future for both. As well as this, the possibilities for both therapist and client to relate in authentic ways – challenging, expressing feelings of frustration or anger, or disclosing one's experience of the other, for example – are always present. Without there being any way of identifying how this will impact on the therapeutic work itself, it is nevertheless significant in further shaping the background understanding that underpins the relationship. This understanding, to remind ourselves, is not meant in the sense of a cognitive grasp of some facts or details, but rather a certain embodied way of being in situations that has enriched the client's manner of coping and dealing with the world, others, and things.

Since understanding and interpretation are pivotal to a hermeneutic enquiry, the client's presented issues within any one session allow for a certain kind of enquiry to emerge. This is based on a close attentiveness both to what the client is saying as well as how this is conveyed. Along with this the therapist is attentive to the possibility that words and speech do not become reified and well-worn expressions that can already be understood without further clarification. In other words, the client's reflections and uses of words themselves are open to being questioned and explored, given that they hold particular meanings that might be at odds with the therapist's way of using them, for example, or that they cover over the phenomenon in its deeper ontological meaning. Feelings, whether they be guilt, shame, or embarrassment, are themselves formal indications, as are most other terms introduced, and so are usually held as provisional linguistic placeholders in the course of a dialogue. They call for a hermeneutic engagement and investigation to uncover their meanings, and in the process, embrace an authentic temporality in which the conversation takes place.

A hermeneutic investigation starts with the idea that a phenomenon is ontically closest to us, yet ontologically furthest. This means that it does not tend to immediately show itself, or even at all. Rather, it lies hidden. The aspect of the phenomenon's hiddenness also belongs to what shows itself, and, to quote Heidegger, 'it belongs to it so essentially as to constitute its meaning and its ground' (BT59).

The hermeneutic process requires a certain patience and forbearance, in terms of being led by the movement of the enquiry, rather than having a particular template to adopt that directs or guides it, in some way. In Heidegger's terms, it amounts to a 'letting go', rather than 'holding onto', which reflects a certain Cartesian self-oriented stance of exerting control or mastery over the entire endeavour in order to arrive at a conclusion or insight. So, the intention of a hermeneutic enquiry is not to engage in a mechanistic or mechanical or formulaic approach, which has the sense of pushing or pressing for something to emerge. Rather, it remains open to whatever comes forth of its own accord, as a free movement.

As clients introduce certain topics, themes, or issues that are then explored in the course of dialogues, but only after some searching and insight perhaps, this eventually culminates in a certain ending of the enquiry, from the client's perspective. In a sense, the client has pursued a hermeneutic path up to a certain point, and, for whatever reason, has now chosen or decided to close this off from any further exploration. We might see this as the end of one hermeneutic process; but this always leaves open the possibility of re-engaging with the same issue at some other time, perhaps even months later. In other words, the client is free to re-engage with the issue but from a different perspective or understanding. It is, in short, a resumption of the hermeneutic process. A client might have a sense that they have resolved the issue of being assertive with their colleagues at work, for example, but with the challenges of new situations and circumstances, they then face other perspectives on the same or similar experience. In this way, we become engaged in a conversation that reflects another level of the hermeneutic spiral.

In terms of the way that hermeneutics might manifest in therapeutic practice, several key points can be made in this regard, and some that also bear repeating. First, it is important to clarify which phenomenon the conversation is focusing on, as at times this might not be so transparent. Once this is clear to both therapist and client, the hermeneutic enquiry is led by the phenomenon and not by any procedure as to how the enquiry should be conducted. At times, there is a real possibility that deviations and digressions detract from continuous attention being given to the phenomenon. In such cases, it is then a matter of following the client and seeing whether this was a form of avoidance for whatever reason, or the client's way of distracting the process of looking more deeply into things generally, or whether another, more compelling detail has emerged that draws the client to disclose more about it. In the course of the exploration, the client's interpretations provide the possibility of a different understanding, based on 'seeing' (as in discerning) perspectives that might not have been previously apparent to them. The hermeneutic process, as has been hopefully conveyed in examples previously given, is based on an ability to pose questions in a way that opens up enquiry, but at the same time maintains the phenomenon in view. The everyday understanding is where we begin the analysis, as it has to start from a relevant situated context. This is an appropriate place to start as this allows for a way to investigate the phenomenon in its accustomed understanding. However, because the phenomenon is covered over or concealed in the everyday understanding, it requires phenomenological probing until an element or detail in what has emerged effects a change, however small, in the way that the phenomenon now appears to us. As we proceed from this point, further phenomenological investigation reaches a more replete understanding that was previously unavailable to us.

As might become apparent in the course of working phenomenologically, or with a persistent focus on description rather than explanatory analysis, any emerging interpretation comes out of a sustained attempt to bring out the descriptive elements to a point where another perspective or meaning is delivered. Such a possibility of seeing differently emerges only where a certain degree of discipline is embraced. The ability to explore the phenomenon, bring out its elements, and then relate what has been uncovered to the concrete circumstances that the client faces is the movement that expresses Heidegger's sense of the hermeneutic.

Insofar as the hermeneutic process reveals to the client something that had not previously been so clear, we can relate this to what Heidegger calls 'transparency' (BT186): 'The sight which is related primarily and on the whole to existence we call "transparency". We choose this term to designate "knowledge of the self"', which Heidegger goes on to say is a 'seizing upon the full disclosedness of being-in-the-world' (BT186–7). This is not a simple reassessment of what has broken down in a particular situation, such as a miscommunication, or a malfunctioning tool, but a paradigmatic transformation in realising how we exist as human beings. This isn't something that we can arrive at in one giant step either. Rousse captures the hermeneutic element that is relevant to this when he writes,

> Transparency is a quality Heidegger attributes to certain interpretations. If an interpretation has transparency, this means the interpreter does not take the pre-suppositions structuring her interpretive point of view for granted, no matter how self-evident they seem; the interpreter actively maintains a readiness to revise or reject the presuppositions initially guiding her interpretation so that new possibilities for understanding can be revealed.
>
> (2021:774)

The 'sight' that Heidegger is referring to is, as mentioned previously, a seeing as understanding, since the world is meaningful to us. That is, we project possibilities onto the world and what we encounter in it only insofar as we understand the world *as* a world of possibilities. As Braver clarifies, '[a]nxious transparency frees us from our usual fusion with our world and routines. This allows us to "see through" all the specifics of our life to its underlying structure' (2014:67) so that it brings 'Dasein face to face with its world as world, and thus bring[s] it face to face with itself as being-in-the-world' (ibid.:67, quoting Heidegger in BT233). In transparency, we see *how* we are in the *way* we are, and how we have been 'hiding' this through our daily routines and everyday practices. Whilst unsettling, this also serves as a significant revelation about our way of existing.

15.1 Heidegger's Anti-dialectic Hermeneutics

To clarify further on the way that Heidegger conducts his enquiries, he is not at any point adopting a dialectic approach. He, in fact, disparages any consideration of a dialectic method of enquiry, as we find in the work of Heidegger's 19th century predecessor, Georg Hegel, for example. In short, for Heidegger, a dialectical enquiry isn't a free movement of thinking, but, rather, a rigid and set process that follows a thesis – antithesis – synthesis pattern in order to conduct an analysis of concepts. Hegel, in adopting this form or style of thinking, runs this dialectic process by way of examining a concept, or thesis, then identifying the concept that is its exact opposite, and finally sublating or transcending the two to arrive at a synthesis that integrates both opposing concepts. The process, as a result, is effectively complete, although the synthesis now qualifies as a newly identified concept that emerges and is analysed under the same dialectic process. Dialectics adheres to the path that it has already set out, formally speaking. It locks us into a certain pre-set movement of thinking that does not allow for something original to come from other orientations or directions. In that sense, it is not strictly free. But dialectics also takes itself to be addressing concepts, which means that it treats entities as present-at-hand, and ontic. In this sense it doesn't really access the phenomenon that lies hidden, such that we pursue a hermeneutic path that reaches towards the existential (Braver, 2014:40).

To give a more concrete example of how a dialectical approach might obviate rather than open enquiry, Jill Drouillard, with reference to Heidegger's *Ontology: The Hermeneutics of Facticity* (2008:35), reports that 'Heidegger accuses dialectics of committing the same error as static juxtapositions' (Drouillard, 2022:163) that reflect fixed understandings of 'man' and 'woman' in relation to sex and gender. Drouillard quotes Heidegger here, who says that, 'It steps into an already constructed context, though there really is no context here…Every category is an existential and *is* this as such, not merely in relation to other categories and on the basis of this relation' (ibid.; Heidegger 2008:35). In Drouillard's article, 'man' has already been set up in a dialectical relation to 'woman', and, moreover, devalues 'woman' as flesh in contrast to 'man' as spirit, according to the Judeo-Christian tradition. It is in this sense that Heidegger wants to open up enquiry and break away from dialectical presuppositions that simply cover over the phenomena that are in need of disclosure.

Chapter 16

Working Existentially

Once we have brought out the phenomenon through a phenomenological explora-tion, we engage in an existential analysis. Braver (2014:60) mentions that whilst phenomenology brings out and describes what goes on in terms of the structure, or the elements that constitute the phenomenon that is related to the everyday situa-tion or set of circumstances, an existential analysis then attends to what has been uncovered and regards it with a sense of suspicion in order to bring out the way that we are *there* in such situations or circumstances. This offers the possibility of illuminating the ways in which the existentiales are expressed in their ontic-existentiell character. For example, and again citing Braver, the One becomes pivotal to our way of being there in everydayness, through chatter, curiosity, and ambiguity. We are always looking for reassurance that we are 'doing well', which connects back to the fact that our being is an issue for us, since we are beings who find ways to avoid or overcome ambiguity. Whilst we gain such a reassurance, we lose ourselves and what is most primordial about our existence. In that sense, we are alienated, without even being aware of this (ibid.:63).

To draw on what has previously been established, an existential approach embraces phenomenology rather than theory, as it makes a concerted attempt to avoid abstraction. Our own concrete way of living, which is an ontic-existentiell interpretation of the existentiales, is itself only interpretable through exploration via description rather than the application and appropriation of theory. Theory places itself on the level of explanation, which holds legitimacy for scientific enquiry directed towards objects, forces, and substances, but not when it attempts to study the existence of human beings. Theory therefore commits an error in directing itself towards human beings, both for its move to abstraction as well as its concep-tion of our kind of being.

16.1 Existentiales

The essential features of Dasein's existence, namely the existentiales, can be iden-tified in the course of the client's reflections and disclosures in the therapy ses-sion. As has already been stressed, it is the client's existentiell way of manifesting an existentiale that is relevant to their way of being-in-the-world. Moreover, the

DOI: 10.4324/9781003342137-20

exploration between therapist and client takes the form of identifying those deriva-tive, deficient, or privative ways in which the existentiell way of enacting the exis-tentiale is evident. Since no one existentiale stands separately and independently from others, any therapeutic enquiry extends to an illumination of a number of existentiales that are relevant to the issue at hand.

16.2 Breakdowns

Existentially oriented enquiry attempts to conduct phenomenological investiga-tions that attend to those situations that the client considers problematic or unset-tling in some way. These have been variously named as disturbances, disruptions, breakdowns, or collapses. As well as illuminating the temporal aspect of the break-down situation, therapeutic enquiry might also address the very way in which the client relates to breakdowns in life generally. Are they to be avoided at all costs? Or do they illuminate something that has been a worry or concern for some time? As has been mentioned, breakdowns offer the possibility of understanding and reviewing the deeper significance of what they disclose about ourselves, rather than being disruptive and unpalatable experiences that we need to extirpate. Being immersed in a career that structures our lives gives us a sense of meaning, purpose, and direction, such that we are making something of our existence; but break-downs offer the possibility to reappraise this, and to review or take stock of what we value in the way that we live. Breakdowns ultimately offer a way in which an inauthentic mode of existing can be exposed, and an authentic alternative be brought into view, such that a choice can be faced in the light of the truth of one's nullity or finitude.

16.3 Inauthentic and Authentic Ways to Be

In its daily existence, Dasein is caught in its 'inconstancy', insofar as it lives according to its own sense of 'keeping up', 'lagging behind', or 'doing better' in relation to the norms, guides, and practices that shape and determine how to act and behave, what to pursue, and generally what to value. In this way, we don't take hold of ourselves and maintain our stance in seizing those possibilities that present themselves in the moment. Since we are only open to those possibilities that the norms and practices dictate to us, we are in a flux-like inconstancy or adaptation to what we see as fixed norms and injunctions to which we then conform.

By contrast, as an authentic self, I relate to myself in my self-constancy by acknowledging that time is not a succession of unconnected atomic moments, but rather the past, present, and future that we constantly live as a unity, and which we articulate in our constantly becoming the person we carry from the past into the present. In other words, we are never solely in the present, which is the sedimented assumption of traditional thinking, but rather, we launch ahead of ourselves futur-ally in a way that can only draw itself on what is already past or ingrained into us, and all coming into the present. The past is already 'embedded' in the future, and both are carried in the present. This is the way temporality reflects the self in its constancy.

16.4 Disclosedness in the Therapeutic Relationship

Having set out in quite some detail how we as Dasein are in our being-in-the-world, we can now relate this to the idea that we are fundamentally disclosive, or an openness. We usually reserve this way of speaking when we describe our sense of being expressive, or of articulating something perhaps previously withheld. However, the term has a more basic meaning in that Dasein is always, at bottom, disclosing its being, whether it happens to utter, do, or express anything or not. This is because, in our being, we are always already there (*Da*), that is, situationally, or contextually, and the there that is our being is always an *issue* for us. It 'gets to us', in other words. In the case of the client, then, they cannot but help disclose themself, because they are fundamentally an openness. At the same time, we also encounter the ontic sense of openness that is expressed in honesty, trustworthiness, and candour in the client. But the ontological sense here underlines the fact of always already being oriented to the world. We might add, along with Heidegger, that this openness is truth itself.

Although the client discloses issues and situations that concern or trouble them, the therapist can never claim to fully know or understand the client. It is the client's existence that is at issue here, and not the therapist's 'knowledge' about their existence. In each individual case, the client's existence is uniquely their own, and in this sense the therapist enters the therapeutic space with this in view. Many therapeutic approaches reveal a regretfully naïve oversight in assuming that their theoretical underpinnings provide them with a certain knowledge and understanding of clients, as if the client's 'mineness' can somehow be 'outstripped', to use a Heideggerian expression. What is central, however, is the therapist's way of being with the client as disclosedness or openness in the ontological sense, since this is what is fundamental to the therapeutic process. The tendency, by contrast, is that other therapeutic approaches focus and remain exclusively at the level of the ontic, since this is tangible and concrete, but overlook any consideration of the ontological. At the same time, the ontological is not itself directly accessible, as if ontic, but only discernible through an ontic manifestation of the ontological. To reiterate the existentiale-existentiell distinction, an existentiell stance towards my mortality is disclosed concretely, perhaps in expressing my deep unease about dying one day, but is reflected ontologically in the existentiale, being-towards-death.

To elaborate a way in which we can gain a further grasp on this, the client as a 'discloser' expresses their own way of being-with, and being disposed or 'enmooded' in a certain way, whilst at the same time disclosing their understanding in relation to the project that brings them to therapy in the first place. Disclosure in the process of discoursing, that is, of 'opening up' to the therapist on the background of their relationship, is at the centre of therapeutic experience. 'Opening up' also bears on the very way in which the client might be 'fleeing from' or 'facing up' to their way of being in therapy.

16.5 Historising

Following Spinosa, Flores, and Dreyfus (1997), we are historising or history-making beings, in the sense that we narrativise our lives in the very act of living. We are immersed in practices that reflect worlds, and a world, as has already been mentioned, has three features: equipment; the various things and entities that we employ in order to engage in and pursue tasks and projects; and a role or identity that we take up in pursuing ends and purposes in that world (ibid.:17). In our way of historising, we open disclosive spaces. When we reflect on the very early contributions of Sigmund Freud, for example, he opened a disclosive space for psychoanalysis and psychotherapy. In that sense, he was disclosing a new world in the act of history-making. However, we are all involved in disclosive activities, be it in the ways that we work as therapists, or as chefs, or lawyers. Spinosa et al. make a distinction between two ways of being disclosers: one is the general everyday kind of disclosive activity which they call 'customary disclosing'. This is the way in which we typically adapt and adjust to changing situations that we face in the course of navigating our way through tasks or activities that are related to our projects. The therapist, for example, makes certain interventions that are appropriate, relevant, and timely in response to what the client is disclosing in a particular moment. The other way of being a discloser is in what Spinosa et al. call, 'historical disclosing' (ibid.:22). Customary disclosing reflects an inauthentic way of being, since it engages in activities that coordinate and maintain a harmonious state of affairs in a given situation. Historical disclosing, however, reflects an authentic way of being a discloser, since it expresses both a sensitivity to certain disharmonies in the discloser's activities, as well as a preparedness to respond to these disharmonies or breakdowns by reshaping the space in which the activities take place. In this way of disclosing, the therapist engages in the disruption that has developed as a result of the client becoming angry and threatening to leave the session, for example. The therapist is open to exploring the basis of the disruption not in order to calm the client, or to follow a textbook approach that they can reliably draw on when facing such situations, but rather to take the situation, and the client's anger, as one of a kind, and not interpret it as a predictable or expected pattern in their behaviour. The therapist is not grabbing for standard or well-worn interventions in this situation, nor a general theory about dealing with angry clients, but rather facing the client's anger and the breakdown that is now manifest in the space between them. The therapist invites the client to stay with the experience, as something important is happening in this instant. The client remains angry, but nevertheless remains in the room with the therapist. Both now explore the breakdown by taking a stance that does not deflect from their contribution to this situation, that both are fallible beings, and that they wish to understand the disharmony that has now manifested in the session. The therapist, for their part, looks to 'take care' of this disruption by inviting a sense of possibility in how this can be addressed. The background mood changes from one of being tense and perhaps adversarial, to one that appropriates the disclosive space by bringing near what was remote and distant. The client comes to recognise that their relationship with the therapist includes the possibility of disharmonies and breakdowns, that the relationship can incorporate and bear such moments, but also that the client can relate to their occasions of anger in a different way. The possibility of anger now potentially becomes less of an issue for the client, and might even influence the way in which they proceed to experience the world in other ways. Both kinds of disclosing are experienced in this scenario, and it should be clear that, analogous to the inauthentic–authentic distinction, customary disclosing and historical disclosing are both elements of being human. That is, neither is subject to some kind of moral assessment or hierarchical superiority or preference of one over the other.

On a more general level, the client becomes a historical discloser insofar as they face disharmonies and, in doing so, historises or makes history in articulating a modified or different way of relating to themself and others. Just as their relationship with the therapist has shaped itself in other possible ways to their earlier experience, they are open to historising in other domains and areas of life. Their mood is one of being receptive rather than stubbornly closing off, or closing down the situation, as was potentially the case with their anger. In contrast, as a customary discloser, the client follows a pattern that avoids disharmonies, seeing them as deviations or disruptions to the comforts of a conventional everyday life, or a generally agreeable way of being with others and living their life.

Chapter 17

Working Existentially with Dreams

From a Heideggerian perspective, dreams disclose the dreamer's being-in-the-world, moods, as well as certain existentiales, according to what is being presented in the dream. A particularly relevant and dominant existentiale that seems to be reflected in many dreams is in relation to the One, or that feature of Dasein's existence that has, in respect of its background concern, a 'constant care as to the way one differs from [others]' (BT163), and which we, for the most part, have hidden from ourselves. Dreams bring this issue to the fore in the scenarios that are being dreamt, as well as the tensions and anxieties that accompany this. That is, the dream illuminates those aspects of everyday living that can fall prey to disruptions, disturbances, and breakdowns of one's conformity to our social practices, as well as the experiences of anxiety and guilt, in the dream, or in dreaming the dream, that reflect this.

However, to bring us back to Dasein once again, in order to grasp the way in which dreams relate to our experience of being alive, my being is an issue for me, and I 'stand out' to myself because my being is uniquely my own. My existence is, in other words, 'mine' and no one else's: it is not substitutable or replaceable. I have to reckon with my existence, make something of it, now that I have been thrown into the world. I make something of myself through my projects, but in doing so I contend with the fact that thrownness and projection are in a certain friction with each other, because, as Richardson puts it, there are structural limits to projection (2012:159). That is, 'guilt shows thrownness that it will always fail to rise to what projection wills' (ibid.).

We also find ourselves in a fundamental not-at-home-ness into which we have been thrown, and this brings us to search for ways to ground ourselves in some way, and cover or conceal this 'not being at home' by settling ourselves in the One. Settling in the One, however, brings its own challenges, unease, and conflicts, because we are confronted with others, who are also trying to do the same, so that misunderstandings, self-interested attitudes, and behaviours that render an 'us' and 'them' exacerbates a distance from others. We also can't accurately gauge how we might be faring in our relations with others, because situations are always bringing new challenges, and the world and others aren't wholly transparent for us in order to 'read off' what is actually going on. We assume an understanding of certain states-of-affairs, and at times, breakdowns, however minimal, disrupt that

DOI: 10.4324/9781003342137-21

settledness such that we worry about the extent to which we are at odds with a certain norm or standard that usually provides us with a sense of coping satisfactorily.

We carry a conscience insofar as we are being-in-the-world, since we are, to varying degrees, sensitive to any deviation from the moral norms that point to purported errors or misdeeds that we have committed, and that pose a threat to a sense of safety in the One. This understanding of conscience is specific and ontic. However, the dream that 'presents' conscience, whilst not overtly on an ontological level, reminds us that existence cannot be approached from a ready-to-hand perspective. That is, we can't assume that following, or manipulatively 'using', any moral law or principle for our purposes and interests automatically reassures us that we are living a 'good life'. We glimpse the fact that moral frameworks are relative to our current practices, since they are ontic, and that they have been handed down to us and presented as if they are woven into the very fabric of nature, that is, unchangeable, rather than contingent and culturally dependent. The dreamer, in this sense, can open themselves to the ontological insight that the dream offers: the concern to do the 'right thing' might have become overly constricting in the way that the dreamer is living, for example, and that their underlying worry is one of feeling accepted and not rejected by others.

Similarly, the inauthentic and authentic distinction only becomes apparent to the dreamer where they sense that their desire and wish to possibly transcend or be more playful in relation to everyday norms and practices can now be rehearsed and played out in the dream. As well as this, such issues as freedom and temporality might also relate to the meaning that the dreamer is disclosing in and through the dream. A dream that has its dreamer attempting to free themselves from a situation or person by physically distancing themselves, for example, whilst experiencing time as a sluggishness, and the difficulty in making time run in a way that enables the dreamer to meet their own needs and goals, is but one of many ways in which such features of being human become relevant.

In the light of the extensive elaboration of Dasein that has already been covered, namely, its being-in-the-world, being-there, and its mode of being that is existence, much can be drawn from this as we undertake an existential approach to dreams. Medard Boss has made important contributions in this area, as has his colleague Gion Condrau, but what remains is a need for a more thoroughgoing exploration of dreams based on those features of Dasein that illuminate the dreamer's concerns and preoccupations. Alice Holzhey-Kunz has made some laudable attempts in this regard, providing a more Heideggerian account of dreams. I am in agreement with her two main claims, namely that dreaming reflects or expresses a 'wrestling with our own being' (Holzhey-Kunz, 2014:128–30), and that moods illuminate what we experience in our dreams (ibid.:126–8). Leaving aside some, at times, highly contentious and disputable Freudian-sounding language in her ontological interpretation of the dream, the key contribution that she makes is captured in her conclusive comments:

[t]he dreamer…is *especially sensitive* to the anxiety-inducing fact of being placed as an individual into the not-at-home of the world and having to lead

his own life and be responsible for it, which is why that primal desire for an at-home in which he can hide is actualised.

(ibid.:130)

As is so obvious to us, the possibility of making dreams intelligible must originate from the fact that it is *Dasein* who is dreaming them in the first place. As far as we know, non-human animals do not reflect on any experiences that can be claimed to be oneiric. This means that Dasein discloses features of its very way of being that are expressed in dreams, which then potentially leaves it to ponder and question the experience in order to make some sense of it. For example, Dasein's disposedness, in its practical and concrete ways of living, means that it always finds itself in a mood. Further, dreaming discloses to Dasein the relevance of the existentiale, meaning. Whilst meaning constitutes Dasein and is manifested in various projects and activities in the course of daily life, it is not so discernible or accessible to us whilst we are preoccupied and distracted in our absorbed way of living. The dream experience, therefore, offers the possibility of disclosing more vividly to the dreamer the meaning of their way of living.

As Dasein attempts to make sense of its dreams, meaning can either come from 'others', whether this be 'dream experts' or other theoreticians on dreaming, in which case this suggests an inauthentic way to relate to one's dreams. Alternatively, the therapist can act as a presence that gives way to the client's attempts to alight upon the meanings that they attribute to their dream. This invites a space in which the client comes into their own, by experiencing themself in terms of living according to their own nullity, or limits: they make of their dreams what they will, and this reflects their being the null basis. In being their own basis, in other words, they take responsibility for their own interpretations, which are finite and vulnerable to possible collapse in the face of other possible meanings. Being authentic in one's interpretation of one's dreams is to embrace the fact that there is no metaphysical standpoint from which to determine *the* meaning of the dream.

In terms of the way in which the therapeutic exploration itself can be understood, hermeneutic interpretation allows for the therapist to stay with the *form* of what the client is expressing in the dream and hold to this as a basis for challenging the client's presentation of its content. Following a process of deeper exploration of the dream, the client might uncover some unsettling truth(s) about their existence in the light of this. At this point, the feeling of anxiety that reflects this unsettledness indicates that an ontological bedrock has been reached. Trying to recall the details of a dream when awake usually becomes challenging, because the now awake dreamer has returned to a predominantly inauthentic way of covering over that which is unsettling for them. However, where they face up to their anxiety whilst in the act of recalling their dream, they offer themself the opportunity to interpret it in a way that is not constrained by an inauthentic stance that they might otherwise take while awake. In interpreting the dream in this way, they embrace the nullity of their existence, rather than selectively recalling its relatively more bland and everyday details, for example.

Final Comments

Having now presented Heidegger's account of our kind of being, namely Dasein, I hope to have introduced a way in which a therapeutic approach can be embraced, or at least considered, based on such an understanding. Since its fundamental starting point is at odds with prevailing therapeutic practices, I am under no illusion that this will seem jarring to many existing practitioners whose extensive body of work with clients over the years has convinced them of the solidity of the foundations upon which their approaches rest. My only intention in such cases is to encourage dialogue and discussion among as diverse a set of practitioners as is possible, rather than a stance that reflects rigid positions, or more commonly, oppositions.

The attempt here has been to approach Heidegger's work afresh, from a therapeutic point of view, in order to offer a more comprehensive account of the richness of his ideas and the possible implications that follow from such an endeavour. Since Heidegger's earlier work, that is, from the earlier part of the 20th century, has addressed those features of human existence that, in turn, allow easier access to its relevance for therapy, this has been the focus of my attention here. In fact, this phase of Heidegger's work conveys more clearly and transparently the real struggle that he faces in pursuing a path of thinking that loosens itself from the Cartesian approach. In this, *Being and Time* reflects this difficulty all too well, given both the style in which it is written as well as the language that inescapably limits him in certain ways. However, notwithstanding this constraint, I believe that the wealth of ideas as well as overall methodological approach that is to be found in that work leaves us with much to further consider. In fact, as I already elaborated in the Introduction to this book, my own journey in reading and attempting to understand Heidegger continues for as long as I contemplate the question of what it means to be human. That is to say, this question endures both because my being is an issue for me, but also because it constitutes my identity as an existential therapist.

Since this book has been based on this earlier period of Heidegger's thinking, this has meant that the rest of his significant output has necessarily been ignored here, save for one or two comments that draw on his later work on the technological mode of being. For those who might be inclined to undertake explorations of Heidegger's ideas and overall approach, I believe that his later philosophy would

DOI: 10.4324/9781003342137-22

offer much food for thought for therapists, since texts that appear much later than *Being and Time* offer different approaches to the question of being human. However, in order to really understand the meaning and significance of this difference, I also think that it is important to ensure some familiarity is acquired with this earlier work. For example, Heidegger talks about such fundamental moods as anxiety and boredom at the earlier stages of his work, whilst in his later thinking, he is more interested in articulating the overarching mood of a time or epoch in which there is a particular understanding of what it is to be as anything at all.

If there is one wish or hope that I harbour at this point, it is that a seed of possibility has been sown in being able to distinguish between a Cartesian and a Heideggerian approach to therapy, even if this is constrained by the entrapments of Cartesian language that continues to prevail in our everyday world. As well as this, I hope to have shown that therapists have not exhausted the possibilities of offering new perspectives in applying Heidegger's thinking to the realm of therapy.

The book has refrained from commenting on Heidegger's place among other thinkers. Perhaps this is an opportune moment to remind ourselves that such philosophers as Maurice Merleau-Ponty, Jean-Paul Sartre, and Jacques Derrida owe an enormous debt and acknowledgement of the influence that Heidegger has made on their own valuable contributions. For example, it is nigh-on impossible to conceive that Merleau-Ponty could have written his major work, *Phenomenology of Perception*, without having already become well-acquainted with Heidegger's prior output. In this regard, any attempt to claim a truly existential approach to therapy cannot afford to overlook Heidegger's work, however unpalatable or objectionable this might be for some. If we do object to Heidegger, then we also need to reflect seriously on our stance with regard to certain other philosophers' contributions, such as Immanuel Kant, David Hume, Georg Hegel, and even Edmund Husserl, just to name a few. In each, we will find disturbing, and in some cases, unquestionably appalling views and beliefs. This, however, cannot disqualify them from remaining great philosophers and thinkers.

Bibliography

Aho, K. (2006). Metontology and the Body-Problem in *Being and Time*. *Auslegung: A Journal of Philosophy*, 28 (1).

Anderson, H. (1997). *Conversation, Language, and Possibilities: A Postmodern Approach to Therapy*. New York: Basic Books.

Aubry, T. and Travis, T. (eds.). (2015). *Rethinking Therapeutic Culture*. London: The University of Chicago Press.

Becker, E. (1973). *The Denial of Death*. New York: Free Press Paperbacks.

Beckett, S. (1956). *Waiting for Godot*. London: Faber and Faber.

Braver, L. (2014). *Heidegger*. Cambridge: Polity Press.

Budd, M. and Rothstein, L. (2000). *You Are What You Say*. New York: Three Rivers Press.

Caputo, J. (2011). www.trippfuller.com. Accessed April 2016.

Cimino, M. (dir.) (1978). *The Deer Hunter*. EMI Films.

Critchley, S. (2002). Enigma Variations: An Interpretation of Heidegger's *Sein und Zeit*. *Ratio*. 15(2): 154–75.

Descartes, R. (1641/2003). D.M. Clarke (trans.). *Meditations and Other Metaphysical Writings*. London: Penguin Books.

Dreyfus, H.L. (1991). *Being-in-the-world: A Commentary on Heidegger's* Being and Time, *Division I*. Cambridge, MA: MIT Press.

Drouillard, J. (2022). Heidegger on Being a Sexed or Gendered Human Being. *Gatherings: The Heidegger Circle Annual*. 12: 162–5.

Elpidorou, A. and Freeman, L. (2019). Is Profound Boredom Boredom? In C. Hadjioannou (ed.). *Heidegger on Affect*. London: Palgrave Macmillan, pp. 177–203.

Erwin E. (1997). *Philosophy and Psychotherapy*. London: Sage.

Farin, I. (2015). Heidegger: Transformation of Hermeneutics. In J. Malpas and H-H. Gander (eds.). *The Routledge Companion to Hermeneutics*. London: Routledge, pp. 107–26.

Foschi, R. and Innamorati. M. (2023). *A Critical History of Psychotherapy, Volume 1: From Ancient Origins to the Mid-20th Century*. London: Routledge.

Furedi, F. (2004). *Therapy Culture: Cultivating Vulnerability in an Uncertain Age*. London: Routledge.

Hadjioannou, C. (ed.) (2019). *Heidegger on Affect*. London: Palgrave Macmillan.

Haugeland, J. (2000). Truth and Finitude: Heidegger's Transcendental Existentialism. In M.A. Wrathall and J. Malpas (eds.) *Heidegger, Authenticity, and Modernity: Essays in Honor of Hubert L. Dreyfus Volume 1*. Cambridge, MA: MIT Press, pp. 43–77.

Haugeland, J. (2013). *Dasein Disclosed: John Haugeland's Heidegger*. J. Rouse (ed.). Cambridge, MA: Harvard University Press.

Heidegger, M. (1927/1962). *Being and Time*. J. Macquarrie & E. Robinson (trans.). Oxford: Blackwell.

Heidegger, M. (1923/2008). *Ontology: The Hermeneutics of Facticity*. J. van Buren (trans.). Bloomington: Indianan University Press.

Hersch, E.L. (2003). *From Philosophy to Psychotherapy: A Phenomenological Model for Psychology, Psychiatry, and Psychoanalysis*. Toronto: University of Toronto Press.

Holzhey-Kunz, A. (2014). *Daseinsanalysis*. S. Leighton (trans.). London: Free Association Books.

Husserl, E. (1913/2012). *Ideas: General Introduction to Pure Phenomenology*, vol.1. D. Moran (trans.). London: Routledge.

Laing, R.D. (1960). *The Divided Self*. Harmondsworth: Penguin.

Lear, J. (2006). *Radical Hope: Ethics in the Face of Cultural Devastation*. London: Harvard University Press.

Malpas, J. and Gander, H-H. (eds.). (2015). *The Routledge Companion to Hermeneutics*. London: Routledge.

Mercer, V. (1956). The Uneventful Event. *Irish Times* (February 18); repr. in *Critical Essays on Samuel Beckett*, ed. L. Butler. Ann Arbor, MI: University of Michigan Scholar Press, 1993.

Morrall, P. (2008). *The Trouble with Therapy: Sociology and Psychotherapy*. Maidenhead: McGraw-Hill Open University Press.

Newfield Network Inc. Course Notes. (2005).

Nye, N.S. (1995). *Words Under the Words: Selected Poems*. Portland: The Eighth Mountain Press.

Ogden, T. (2014). Fear of Breakdown and the Unlived Life. *International Journal of Psychoanalysis*. 95: 205–23.

Polt, R. (1999). *Heidegger: An Introduction*. London: UCL Press.

Purton, C. (2014). *The Trouble with Psychotherapy: Counselling and Common Sense*. London: Palgrave.

Richardson, J. (2012). *Heidegger*. London: Routledge.

Rogers, C.R. (1961). *On Becoming a Person*. Boston: Houghton Mifflin Co.

Rousse, B.S. (2021). Transparency. In M.A. Wrathall (ed.) *The Cambridge Heidegger Lexicon*. Cambridge: Cambridge University Press, pp. 774–6.

Spinosa, C., Flores, F., and Dreyfus, H.L. (1997). *Disclosing New Worlds: Entrepreneurship, Democratic Action, and the Cultivation of Solidarity*. London: MIT Press.

Tolstoy, L. (1886/1971). *The Death of Ivan Ilyich and Other Stories*. L. and A. Maude (trans.). London: London University Press.

van Deurzen, E., Craig, E., Längle, A. Schneider, K.J., Tantam, D., and du Plock, S. (eds.). (2019). *The Wiley World Handbook of Existential Therapy*. Chichester: Wiley Blackwell.

Winnicott, D.W. (1974). Fear of Breakdown. *International Review of Psycho-Analysis*. 1: 103.

Wrathall, M.A. (2021). *The Cambridge Heidegger Lexicon*. Cambridge: Cambridge University Press.

Wrathall, M.A. and Malpas, J. (eds.) (2000). *Heidegger, Authenticity, and Modernity: Essays in Honor of Hubert L. Dreyfus Volume 1*. Cambridge, MA: MIT Press.

Zeig, J.K. (ed.). (1987). *The Evolution of Psychotherapy*. New York: Brunner/Mazel Publishers.

Index